TODAY'S IMMIGRANTS AND REFUGEES

A CHRISTIAN UNDERSTANDING

Office of Pastoral Care of Migrants and Refugees
Bishops' Committee on Migration
National Conference of Catholic Bishops

In its planning document, as approved by the general membership of the National Conference of Catholic Bishops in November 1986, and again in November 1987, the Bishops' Committee on Migration, through the Pastoral Care of Migrants and Refugees division of the Migration and Refugee Services, was authorized to prepare a collection of papers by experts in the field on the theology of immigration. The present work, *Today's Immigrants and Refugees: A Christian Understanding*, was reviewed by Archbishop Theodore E. McCarrick, Chairman of the Bishops' Committee on Migration, and is authorized for publication by the undersigned.

Monsignor Daniel F. Hoye
General Secretary
NCCB/USCC

September 9, 1988

ISBN 1-55586-204-7

Contents

Introduction

Silvano M. Tomasi, cs*

Immigrants are the changing face of the Church in the United States. The Catholic community gathered around the first American bishop, John Carroll of Baltimore (1735-1815), was a collectivity of ethnic groups, mostly English, but also German, French, and Irish. From the time of American independence, the dynamic growth of the Church implied adaptation to its social and political environment and, at the same time, incorporation of newcomers. The arrival of large numbers of Irish and German immigrants, and later on of southern and eastern Europeans, did not bring about only a demographic change in the composition of the Catholic population. Different devotional expressions, cultural attitudes, and organizational methods emerged as a consequence of the addition of the new immigrant groups' talents. The challenge faced by the receiving Catholic community was the integration of diverse gifts, the building of communion in diversity, a process not dissimilar to that of the country itself, whose motto has been: *e pluribus unum.*

1. A New Pastoral Situation

Today, the sustained influx of refugees and immigrants from all over the world challenges anew the pastoral creativity of the Church. The decade of the 1980s is expected to match the number of immigrants who came into the United States in the first ten years of the century. The estimate of more than 8 million newcomers entering the country from 1980 to 1990 speaks of the vitality of American society and of the attraction of its ideals. These immigrants add to the multicolor fabric of America. The diversification comes from the new sources of immigration. The legal immigrants, who number 600,000 annually, do not arrive from countries that were traditionally sending people to settle in the United States. Roughly, close to 50 percent of the recent legal immigrants are from Asia, only 10 percent from Europe, and the rest from Latin America and the Caribbean Islands. Thus, a national debate on the meaning and impact of current immigration has developed in Congress, in the media, and in policy and academic networks. The ambivalence toward welcoming the newcomers and rejecting them as a source of disruption provokes occasional outbursts of anxiety and xenophobia—fear of unknown cultural groups—and the temptation to retrench, if not to close the door to asylum seekers, refugees, and the poor, whose presence may limit our comfort and remind us that we are not alone in an increasingly interdependent world. The Church could not avoid becoming a protagonist in the immigration debate. Most newcomers identify with the Catholic community, and many parishes and diocesan agencies are the first point of contact for them. The phenomenon of migration has become "a sign of the times," and it calls for reflection and understanding.

2. A Theology of Migration

The plight, tragedies, and hopes of immigrants and refugees have always found an echo in the heart of the Church. The contemporary, massive displacement of people because of violence and hunger in various regions of the globe, on the other hand, invites a renewed reading in the light of faith. The Second Vatican Council teaches that "the Church has always had the duty [as an expert in humanity] of scrutinizing the signs of the times and of interpreting them in the light of the gospel" (*Gaudium et Spes*, 4). In this context, a theology of migration is the discernment of God's design in today's migrations and the investigation of their place in the general plan of salvation as disclosed by Revelation. Pastoral agents and the immigrants themselves need a vision to motivate their service and to understand their experience.

In 1987, the Bishops' Committee on Migration of the National Conference of Catholic Bishops sponsored a "Migration Theology Project" to clarify the presuppositions and underlying principles that determine, from the standpoint of Christian faith, the motives, methods, goals, and activity of the Church in the pastoral care of newcomers at a moment of renewed change in its history. A theological approach situates migrations within the social teaching of the Church, where principles of reflection, criteria of judgment, and directives for action assume a moral force capable of resolving difficulties and of creating the right attitudes for mutual acceptance and just cultural, economic, political, and social relationships. The Pope John Paul II's encyclical *On Social Concern* (1987) is a masterful reminder of such possibility. The "Migration Theology Project" was carried out by the Office of Pastoral Care of Migrants and Refugees (PCMR), Migration and Refugee Services of the United States Catholic Conference, which commissioned seven essays on biblical and pastoral topics chosen to bring light to the foundations of the pastoral care of immigrants and displaced persons, as well as to indicate new directions in pastoral service. A grant from the Raskob Foundation for Catholics Activities, matched by the bishop members of the NCCB Committee on Migration, made possible this project, which was coordinated by Fr. Silvano M. Tomasi, cs, and Dr. Anna Webb. It was presented in a successful conference of persons engaged in ministry to migrants, refugees, and people on the move in Washington, D.C. (November 19, 1987). As the first collection of essays attempting a systematic theological and pastoral reflection on a major modern social concern such as migrations, which have complex ecclesiological and ethical implications particularly in the United States, an incentive is provided for further research. At the same time, an immediate contribution is offered for pastoral agents confronted with the striking contrast of affluence and the poverty of the latest newcomers, and with the task of enabling individuals and groups of different cultures and social standing to participate with equal rights, as Pope Paul VI stated:

> [in] a human society in which everyone, regardless of race, religion or nationality can live a truly human life, free from bondage imposed by men and the forces of nature not sufficiently mastered; a society in which *freedom* is not an empty word,

and where Lazarus the poor man can sit at the same table as the rich man" (*On the Development of Peoples*, 47).

For seminary students, men and women religious, and lay persons concerned with the incorporation of the latest immigrants and refugees in the community of faith, the essays presented in this volume are an insightful resource. Other themes, however, require attentive reflection for a comprehensive understanding of the worldwide phenomenon of migrations and of the individual persons caught up in its uprooting and resettling process. An analysis of the New Testament's message of universal love—Jesus' identification with the stranger and the gathering of peoples at Pentecost—is surely an additional, necessary dimension. The rich body of teaching developed by the universal Church and by the bishops of the United States is yet another area open for investigation, as indicated by the NCCB document, *Together, A New People: Pastoral Statement on Migrants and Refugees* (1987, II:4). This collection of essays is a preliminary step, the start of a challenging journey.

3. An Inclusive Review of Pastoral Care

The path chosen by the Church in addressing social concerns is concisely stated in Pope Paul VI's *Instruction on the Pastoral Care of People Who Migrate:* "Man, 'whole and entire, body and soul' is the proper object of the Church's pastoral concern" (1:5). The comprehensive, if still incomplete, approach of the "Migration Theology Project" extends to the biblical message; to the existential experience of migrants and host Church as they meet; to the interplay of faith, culture, and justice. The first two essays, like two sides of a coin, are biblical studies that look at the unique history of Israel in the Old Testament, as a people incorporating strangers and forced into exile. Patrick D. Miller writes on "Israel as a Host to Strangers" and shows the moral obligations linked to the various categories, the special relationship to God embodied in the acceptance of the sojourner, and the surprising possibilities provided by hospitality. The memory of migrant life, the military and political defeats that pushed Israel out of its land, and the purifying role of exile are discussed by Leslie J. Hoppe, OFM. Dolores Liptak, RSM, introduces an overview of the pastoral practices of the Church in the United States in dealing with immigrants over the years, the policy changes adopted with recent ethnic groups, the Church's good record of openness to immigrants, and the option for a pluralistic integration. The essay of Joseph P. Fitzpatrick, SJ, explains the relation of faith to culture as an essential consideration in the pastoral care of immigrants. It complements Liptak's historical review with the contribution of sociological analysis and comments on the unique situation of Spanish-speaking immigrants, who struggle to maintain their language and culture and adjust to a middle-class Catholic Church, following, it appears, the same process of integration as earlier immigrants. On the contemporary American scene, the care of migrants and refugees raises some moral dilemmas when national interests and laws are seen as conflictive with Christian conscience. Drew Christiansen, SJ, offers a context in which to understand the demands of the global ethics of Catholic social teaching when it comes into conflict with the sovereignty of nation-states.

The question of pastoral strategies and of the possibilities of how to minister to new-comers among us is dealt with in the last two essays by Silvano M. Tomasi, cs, and William A. Logar, respectively. In church directives for ministry to immigrants, a great deal of flexibility is evident, which allows a creative adaptation of models for pastoral care accord-ing to the geographical concentration of immigrants, the availability of the immigrants' own clergy, diocesan pastoral policies, and the training and sensitivity of parish staffs. Together, the essays of this volume constitute an articulate and insightful basis for Christian under-standing and outreach to today's immigrants, refugees, and displaced persons. They take us beyond the economic and political causes of contemporary migration movements to see God's plan and the Church's compassionate service. They are an invitation to pursue a theological reflection that, in the suffering and hopes of immigrants and refugees, discovers the unity of the human family, the dignity of every person, and the presence of the Lord, who made himself one with the newcomers when he said, "I was a stranger and you wel-comed me" (Mt. 25:35).

---

*Silvano M. Tomasi, cs, Ph.D., is the Provincial Superior of the Missionaries of St. Charles-Scalabrinians, New York Province, and former Director of the Office of Pastoral Care of Migrants and Refugees, United States Catholic Conference.

Israel as Host to Strangers

Patrick D. Miller, Jr.
Princeton Theological Seminary

The title of C.P. Snow's nine volume magnum opus, Strangers and Brothers, points to a rather fundamental fact of human relationships, that is, that the encounter of one person with another is for the most part either as brother/sister or as stranger. Human beings live with and relate to people as friends, neighbors, kinfolk, those who belong to the family or the community, however narrowly or broadly that may be defined, or they encounter and deal with others as "others," persons who are unknown, with whom no bonds or commitments are shared, no contexts, experiences, or presuppositions are held in common, at least as far as one knows.

The instinctive reaction to each of these categories and to persons who fit within them is quite different. The image of brother or sister and the reality embodied in sisters and brothers, or for that matter in the language and conceptuality of family and community, is a very positive one. Exceptions to that exist, of course, but for most individuals and groups primary relationships, if not indeed primary meaning, depend upon and are built upon a network of persons who in some fashion function as brother/sister (that is, family member) or neighbor (that is, community member), persons with whom one lives, works, plays, or shares interests, values, and commitments.

Reaction to the stranger, whether the actual stranger or the thought of the stranger, is another matter altogether. That category is approached with uncertainty, questions, hesitation, and often alarm. The very term "stranger" is a rather ominous one and the word "alien" tends to create resistance, repugnance, or hostility. The stranger is the outsider who is not known and, precisely because unknown, threatening and certainly without claim upon another in the way that sister and friend have and make claims.

What is clear from the Bible, however, is that the stranger, no less than the sister/brother or neighbor, is a *moral category*, one whose very existence in the midst of a community requires certain modes of response. It is the aim of this paper to explore some of those responses with a view to discerning what direction they suggest for those who claim to find in the story of Israel something of their own story and a way that still is appropriate for the people of God.

Terminology

There are three Hebrew words or roots that provide the primary lexical stock for speaking about strangers, outsiders or foreigners. These are *gûr*, "to sojourn," and *gēr*, "sojourner;" *zûr*, "to be a stranger, to estrange," which occurs almost entirely in the participial form, and *zar*, "strange or stranger," and *nekar* and *nokrî*, "foreign" and "alien."[1] The terms *zar* and *nekar*[2] belong together and are to be distinguished from *ger*, "sojourner," which is the primary term to be discussed in these pages.

1

Zar and *nekar/nokrî* often appear in parallelism or collocation indicating their similarity of meaning (e.g., Isa. 61:5; Obad. 11; Job 19:15; Prov. 5:10; 27:13; Lam. 5:2). They are the terms that most extensively serve to distinguish Israel from other peoples, those who are really outside the community. The term *zar, zarîm* can refer simply to another person, or in a rather technical usage to those who are not of the priestly family, and so are "other." Most often it refers to those who are foreigners who conquer and dominate, who enter and defile holy spaces (Obad. 11; Lam. 5:2; Prov. 5:10; Ps. 109:11; Jer. 51:51). Sometimes these are foreign nations taking over and subduing Israel. Sometimes individual foreigners are envisioned. But a sense of the threatening character of such foreigners is often present. That is not always the case. There are several texts that do not show hostility to such foreigners but out of a prudential wisdom suggest that business deals with them are risky (Prov. 6:1; 11:15; 20:16; 27:13). In all the uses of *zar* there are none that refer to such persons as strangers among Israel to be received by them. The only explicitly legal text identifying a moral responsibility relative to a *zar* or foreigner is Deut. 25:5, which enjoins a widow against marrying an *'îsh zar*, "a foreign man," or "a foreigner."

The closely related terms, *nokrî* and *ben-(han)nekar*, which also can be translated as "foreigner," "stranger," or "outsider," can function in much the same way, referring to those foreigners who oppress and take over or with whom Israel is to have nothing to do. But these are generally, as is the case with the *zarîm*, those who are outside of Israel and stay that way. They may be encountered in war (e.g. Ps. 144:7,11) or commercial activity, with hostility or without it. But they are not, for the most part, those with whom one experiences a continuing existence unless forced to do so by subjugation and domination under a foreign country. With regard to the *nokrî*, there are explicit laws distinguishing the relation with such foreigners or strangers. Israel is prohibited from setting a foreigner (*nokri*), who is not a "brother," as king over them (Deut. 17:15). Food that Israelites are not allowed to eat may be sold to a foreigner (Deut. 14:21) and interest may be exacted of a foreigner but not a brother or sister Israelite. (Deut.15:63; 23:21 [Eng. 23:20]).[3] Priestly legislation forbids sacrifice of an animal gotten from a foreigner (Lev. 22:25) or the presence of uncircumcised foreigners in the temple (Ezek. 44:7,9) or at the Passover (Exodus 12:43). In 2 Samuel 15:19-20, we do find a case of a foreigner (*nokrî*), Ittai the Gittite, among the Israelites. But the story underscores the fact that he is not really at home among the Israelites, that he has come "only yesterday" and is an exile from his own home who by all rights should return home. A *nokrî*, therefore, is a foreigner who has not entered into any lasting relationship to the land or the people.[4] One deals with such persons at arm's length.[5] They are not involved in the daily life of the community and are only encountered for all intents and purposes in commercial activities or hostilities with other nations.

There are some cases where a foreigner, that is a *nokrî* or a *ben(han)nekar*, is viewed as having some positive relation to or involvement in Israel. In the later post-Exilic period, Third Isaiah testifies to the presence of "foreigners" who have "joined themselves to the Lord" (Isa. 56:3,6), that is, become proselytes to Yahwism. Indeed between the texts of Third Isaiah and Ezra 9 and Nehemiah 9 one can see the conflict within the community as to whether or not foreigners were to be a part of the cultic community. In Isaiah 56 they are clearly included whereas in the time of Ezra and Nehemiah, those who demand a total separation from foreigners are in control. The later Old Testament tradition thus shows here as in other matters a fundamental conflict that probably represents authentic differences and struggles within the community over whether being a foreigner is sufficient grounds for exclusion from the sacral community if one has converted or joined oneself to Yahweh. The prayer of Solomon at the dedication of the temple (1 Kings 8:41,43) also speaks positively about the Lord's response to the prayer of a foreigner who comes and prays to the Lord "for your name's sake." Some would regard this text as reflective of the same situation as Third Isaiah and the experience of proselytes in the post-Exilic community. Others have argued that these verses are pre-Exilic and as such "would refer, not to the later concept of the proselyte, but to foreigners on diplomatic missions like Naaman, as traders, or as artisans."[6]

The usage of the two sets of terms for foreigner just discussed, that is, *zar/zarîm* and *nokrî/ben(han)nekar*, indicates that there was in Israel's experience an encounter with foreign people and individuals that was experienced incidentally, in war, and in commercial or diplomatic activity. These tended not to be persons or groups with whom the community had an extended experience of living together unless it was a hostile one in which Israel was taken over or oppressed by foreign peoples. There are few legal requirements relative to the encounter. They tend to be primarily restrictions on the involvement of such foreigners in the sacral community and permission to engage foreign individuals or groups in commercial and financial activities that were not permissible among Israelites. The very fact that such strangers or foreigners as these terms designate were not persons or groups who stayed for prolonged periods of time in Israel reduced the need for much instruction about how to deal with them except to safeguard the purity of the religious community, a concern that permeates the moral and cultic instruction of Israel. When these foreigners were present for brief periods of time for non-hostile purposes, presumably the operative rules and practices were those that guided Israel in its relationship with those from outside who resided in Israel for extended periods or permanently.

It is this last group that is regularly designated by the term *ger* (singular) or *gerîm* (plural), commonly translated "sojourner(s)" or "stranger(s)," but sometimes translated as "foreigner(s)" (Jerusalem Bible and Today's English Version) or "alien(s)" (New American Bible and New English Bible). The verb *gûr*, from which the noun comes, means "to dwell for a (definite or indefinite) time, dwell as a new-comer without original rights."[7] The *ger*, therefore, is a resident of a community (which can be as small as a family unit, e.g., 1 Kings 17:20) who comes in from outside and lives on a temporary basis or settles in the community even though not a part of it. The sojourner or stranger may be one who is in a sense passing through, but most of the narratives in which someone is present as a sojourner/stranger and that give some indication of the extent of the sojourn suggest that the stranger in this sense was one who lived for an extended period of time in the community. In many instances it appears as if the outsider remains indefinitely or for good in the community. The messenger who brings to David the news of Saul's death identifies himself as one of the Amalekites (who elsewhere are regarded as Israel's paradigmatic and eternal enemies) who is a son of a sojourner. That is, the family has been living for a long time in the Israelite community and the son is even now a soldier in the Israelite militia (2 Sam. 1:13). The term "resident alien" may be the best way to convey the meaning of *ger* as it conveys both the notion of stranger and sojourner but also points us clearly to the fact that this is the outsider who comes into the midst of the community without the network of relationships that can be counted upon to insure care, protection, acceptance, the one who belongs to another group but now resides in the midst of the Israelite community.

The reasons for sojourning are varied. Famine and the search for food often send persons as *gerîm*, sojourners. Military conflicts or conflicts of other sorts force people to flee their home and reside as aliens or strangers among another people or in another community. The *ger* is thus an exile or immigrant in many of the instances in the Old Testament. Jacob and his sons went to Egypt to secure food, but their stay as sojourners and strangers lasted for generations. Indeed their sojourn in Egypt became a paradigm of inhospitality for Israel, the definitive story of how not to treat the stranger (see below). The Egyptians did not regard the Hebrews as belonging to their group and thought they might join with any enemies who came to do battle (Exod. 1:10) and coerced them into forced and hard labor, which David and Solomon also did with the aliens residing in Israel, according to 1 Chronicles 22:2 and 2 Chronicles 2:17ff.

To explore at more depth the status of the stranger, the resident alien, and the treatment of such in the Old Testament, one needs to turn to both the narratives or stories of persons in their experience as aliens and the laws and directive about how such individuals are to be treated.

Stories of Strangers and Sojourners

The story of Israel begins as a story of sojourners, of the Lord's people in a strange land and among a strange people. That history and that fact is determinative for Israel's treatment of strangers in the rest of the biblical story. The movement from the history of curse to the history of blessing, from the universal plane to the particular plane of Israel's history as the context in which God would work to overcome the human failure to live as God intended in the created order, begins in the call of Abraham to leave home, family, and kindred to become a stranger in an unknown land. The stories of Abraham and his descendants in Genesis become in effect a continuing story of living as resident aliens in a strange land.

The first instance is at the beginning of the patriarchal story when Abram and Sarah are forced to sojourn in Egypt for a period of time because of famine in the land of Canaan (Gen.12:10-20). Indeed that whole episode is a recounting of the ambiguity of life as a resident alien and the compromises into which such an existence may lead even God's faithful ones. For it is Abraham's status as a *ger* or sojourner that leads him to risk the promise and let his wife be taken into Pharaoh's harem, an act whose immorality is not commented upon in the text but is readily identifiable by the narrative's account of what is done to Sarah beyond her control, Abraham's motivation to save his own skin and the consequence of his action in securing great wealth by letting Sarah be taken, and especially the judgment of the Lord in afflicting Pharaoh and his house with great plagues.

The story is typical in some rather basic ways of the plight of the resident alien in a strange country: the necessity of immigrating in order to sustain life in the face of the exigencies of one's situation, the apparent ease with which the immigrants can be subject to the domination of the leaders of the land in which they are forced to dwell, and the tendency, which can be perceived as a necessity, to accommodate to the situation into which one is forced to go. These are elements of a quite specific incident, but they are not incidental to the story. They are characteristic of such sojourning stories. Indeed this very story is told two more times (Gen. 20; 26:1-11). In both the other occasions, the moral issue is more sharply identified, though in the last case, which has Isaac as the central figure instead of Abraham, the ruler—this time the king of Philistines, among whom Isaac is residing because of famine—perceives the wife/sister deception before anything can happen. Even then the moral failure is explicitly identified by the king. And in each case, there is a clear understanding in the story that the sojourners (Abraham/Isaac) feel themselves vulnerable as aliens among another people.

Especially to be noted in this instance—for one will see it as a regular theme of the biblical story—is the explicit protection of the sojourner by the Lord. In this case, the one protected is the Lord's chosen, but further texts will show that protection is not confined to the chosen ones. Or the protection of the chosen ones is an indicator of a wider divine propensity and an experience from which the chosen ones are meant to extrapolate fundamental directives for their own behavior (see below).

The story of Sodom and Gomorrah (Gen. 18:17-19:29) with its preface account of the visit of the three messengers to Abraham (Gen. 18:1-16) is at its most fundamental level a story of the experience of strangers in the midst of hospitality and inhospitality. At the beginning of the narrative, three strangers arrive unexpectedly at the entrance to Abraham's tent.[8] The Old Testament scholar, Claus Westermann, has commented with regard to this visit: "The visit of a stranger could be of vital, decisive importance for the one visited. The stranger comes from another world and has a message from it."[9] He goes on then to describe in some detail the dynamics of this occasion of hospitality to strangers:

> The haste is in deliberate contrast to the quiet beginning. It is worth noting that no one is in a hurry elsewhere in the patriarchal stories; here it is haste in the service of others: he saw . . . ran . . . bowed down . . . said. The following picture, the invitation, the acceptance, the entertainment is an element of early civilization whose proper meaning is for the most part misunderstood. We understand civilization primarily in relation to objects (products of civilization); early civilization looks to people; civilization unfolds itself in human relationships. Secondly hospitality in modern culture is practiced by and large with a chosen circle, whereas it is available in Gen. 18 to whomever needs it. The strangers are invited (see also Lk. 24:29) because they are weary from their journey, hungry, and thirsty, and need Abraham's hospitality. So Abraham is completely at their service; hence his availability, haste, and concern. This too is the context in which one is to understand Abraham's bowing down before the three men. Such a mark

5

of honor is something quite outside our understanding of the situation. Abraham does not know who the strangers are, but he cannot and will not exclude the possibility that they are worthy of honor. One who comes as a stranger is honored because a dignity may be his without there being need of any external sign thereof.[10]

The chapter provides what is the most extended account of the particularities of hospitality to strangers that we have in the Old Testament. These include courtesy and honor without reference to whether it is deserved or not, rest and washing, and food. The narrative emphasis of the story is clearly on the last item. For three verses the details of the food preparation are recounted. The meal is generous and includes some of the best that Abraham can provide of bread, meat, and milk. Again, as Westermann has indicated, elements of the story are not only that; they are reflections of a more pervasive practice and understanding of what it means to host strangers.

The point is sharpened by its comparison and contrast with what happens in Chapter 19. There Lot, Abraham's nephew, who lives in Sodom, extends to the men[11] who visited Abraham virtually the same acts of hospitality that Abraham had showed: honor, rest and washing, and food. He eventually goes beyond this in extreme acts (venturing outside and shutting the door behind him to talk to the mob of Sodomites) and words (offering his daughters to the mob in place of the strangers)[12] to try to protect the strangers who are under his roof. In his words to the citizens of Sodom, Lot assumes the relationship of brother rather than sojourner (v. 7). But this is rejected by the Sodomites, who remind him that he is a sojourner and threaten both the sojourner Lot and the strangers within.

The story in Chapter 19, thus, is set as a counterpoint to what we encounter in the previous chapter. The nephew of Abraham copies his uncle in the demonstration of hospitality. But the vulnerability of the stranger and sojourner is revealed in what the Sodomites seek to do. Here is a story, which, like many other of these stories, is not merely a recorded incident, but a lesson. The names of Sodom and Gomorrah continue in the Bible to exemplify inhumanity and violent oppression of others. The particular act that exemplifies their conduct—and it is the only one that we are given—is an act of hostility toward sojourners and strangers, one that is underscored by its contrast with the behavior of Abraham and Lot in the surrounding material. Inhospitality and rejection of strangers becomes the grounds for the paradigmatic act of divine destruction in the Old Testament (Isa. 13:19; Jer. 23:14; 49:18; 50:40; Lam. 4:6; Zeph. 2:9).

Two other stories in the Abraham cycle depict Israel's ancestor in the context of situations of hospitality to strangers. One of these is the account of the buying of a burial plot for Sarah from the Hittites (Genesis 23), a narrative from the Priestly stratum and perhaps reflective of an Exilic or post-Exilic setting. In the narrative, Abraham describes himself with the typical Priestly terminology as a stranger (*tôoshab*) and sojourner (*ger*). Approaching the Hittites (the indigenous population) in such a manner, he is greeted by them with honor and respect as he had greeted strangers earlier. What ensues is a rather complicated and subtle legal transaction, but in the context of this paper the primary thing to note is the positive response to Abraham on the part of the Hittites. His request is accepted and he is offered the choicest of grave sites. Once again, therefore, we find the one whom God calls living as a resident alien among a people not his own. Their behavior, however, unlike that of the Sodomites, typifies the welcome, respect, and assistance appropriate to those who are host to strangers, whether their sojourn is long or short. One sees afresh the universal character of the host responsibility and the frequency with which God's chosen ones are themselves strangers and sojourners in a strange land.

The last of the Abrahamic stories is also a narrative in which the actions rendered toward a stranger are a basic ingredient. In the story of the wooing of Rebekah as a bride for Isaac (Genesis 24), the servant Eliezer regards the response of a woman to his arrival as an omen of God identifying whom he should choose as Isaac's wife. What follows when he arrives at Nahor as a stranger is again a typical example of hospitality to strangers. The young woman Rebekah not only gives him water to drink at his request but offers to water his camels also and then gives a positive response to his inquiry about lodging and provision for the night. This is followed up by Laban's offer of straw and provender for the camels, water to wash, and food to eat, acts of hospitality to the stranger who has come to his door.

Moving beyond the Book of Genesis, one finds in Judges 19 a long narrative that revolves in ironic fashion almost entirely around events of hospitality and inhospitality to strangers. It is reminiscent in many ways of Genesis 19, but it is more horrible in its violence toward woman. At each stage of the story the principal figures are sojourning in a place: the Levite in the hill country of Ephraim (19:1); the Levite, his concubine, and his servant spending the night at Gibeah after turning away from Jebus because it was not an Israelite city (19:10-15); and finally the invitation of the old man to the Levite and his party to spend the night with him[13] where he provides provender for the animals, rest and washing, for the Levite and his party, and food and drink for them as well. As in Genesis 19, the story reaches its climax in an act of inhospitality as some hoodlums see the strangers as potential and eventually actual objects of their violent pleasure and desire, reminding the reader once more that hospitality to strangers is not automatic. Indeed, the vulnerability of strangers to hostility and oppression is clearly demonstrated by both these stories. In both the Genesis and Judges narratives, hospitality is not provided by the citizenry of the community but by persons (Lot and the old man, who are both sojourners; see Judg. 19:16) from outside who are themselves sojourners in the community. The failure of the people of Gibeah to provide hospitality for the Levite is explicitly indicated when he states that no one would take him in for the night.

The way in which everything in the story revolves around the issue of hospitality but in a highly ironic fashion is sharply indicated in the summary of Stuart Currie:

> It is the courteous urgings of the Levite's father-in-law which cause the delay in departure that prevents the party from reaching the safety of Ephraim by nightfall. The servant's advice to stop for the night in Jebus (a city outside the Israelite alliance) would if followed have averted the calamity. The disgraceful lack of hospitality by the Benjaminites is repaired through the offer of possibly the one

man in town the sanctity of whose hearth and board is not protected by fear of reprisal through blood-kinship and political ties within the city.[14]

One must not leave this story, however, without confronting the fact that both Genesis 19 and Judges 19 show, as Phyllis Trible has sharply underscored, that the rules of hospitality in Israel protect only males.[15] The hospitality of the host not only does not extend to the females, but they are easily given over to violence as a way of protecting the male stranger. In one case it is a concubine who is offered; in the other it is the daughters of the host (Lot) who are offered. In either case what we retrieve about hospitality to the stranger is placed under suspicion by what we encounter in the way of easy violence to women, whose only role in the stories is to be the objects of male violence that males may receive the hospitality of protection.

The Book of Ruth does give us a story of Israelite hospitality to a woman stranger who comes into the Israelite community from another country, one often at odds with Israel. The Moabite woman, Ruth, comes with her mother-in-law to Bethlehem where she goes into the fields of a kinsman of Naomi's by marriage, Boaz. There she gleans in the field "after the reapers," in accord with the gleaning laws of Israel that required those to whom the land had been allotted to leave the gleanings after the harvest for the poor and the sojourner (Lev.19:9-10; Deut. 24:19-22). In this case, not only is Ruth a sojourner, she actually describes herself as a "foreigner" (*nokrîyah*). Boaz not only affirms her right to glean after his gleaners but provides food and drink for her. Boaz's attraction to Ruth may account for the fact that he goes beyond the gleaning laws to let her participate more fully in the harvesting, but the basic act of hospitality is fully in accord with Israelite law and custom. Again, however, there is an explicit indication of the vulnerability of women in that Ruth's mother-in-law warns her to stay with the young women in Boaz's field lest she encounter (i.e., in a hostile way) someone in another field (2:22).

One should not leave the narrative texts of the Old Testament without calling attention to the paradigmatic salvation event of the Old Testament, which is a story of the experience of Israel as strangers and sojourners in Egypt. The tradition of Israel as sojourners in Egypt is pervasive in the biblical tradition. It is rooted back in the promise to Abraham (Gen. 15:13). It is widespread in the laws (e.g., Deut. 23:8; cf. the discussion below). The traditions of the Psalms and Second Isaiah remember Israel as sojourners in Egypt (Psalm 105:23; Isaiah 52:4). Israel's credo made the "sojourn" in Egypt a part of the Israelite's confession of faith. The Exodus event arose out of the migration of Jacob and his family to Egypt in the face of famine. While treated well at the beginning of their stay because of Joseph's position of honor and power, after a while the children of Israel found themselves forced into slave labor by the Egyptians. Moses's efforts to provide alleviation from the hard labor are met by a stone wall response on the part of the king of Egypt, who decrees heavier burdens and harder tasks than before. The story provides a cardinal example of the potential for tyranny and oppression on the part of a community or people over strangers and aliens who reside in their midst. It happens later on in Israel, according to the late tradition of Chronicles, who

8

ascribes such actions to both David (1 Chron. 22:2) and Solomon (2 Chron. 2:17ff.), as we have noted above.

In the case of Israel in Egypt, oppression of the sojourner becomes the ground for the delivering activity of God and the overthrow of the power of the Egyptian king. That such an act is meant to exemplify and influence the way in which the later community should deal with those who are slaves and sojourners is frequently indicated in the later biblical literature, particularly the legislative corpora (e.g., Exod. 22:21, 23:9; Lev. 19:33; Deut. 15:15, 16:12, 24:17-18; see below).

The story of the Hebrews in Egypt is really an *anti-sojourn* story, a depiction of in-hospitality to strangers. Fearfulness before the fact of an increasing immigrant population along with coercive and oppressive measures to restrain and restrict that population are some of the basic situational factors that lead to God's conflict with Pharaoh and the deliverance of the Hebrews. Exodus 1:8-11 are instructive in this regard:

> Now there arose a new king over Egypt who did not know Joseph. And he said to his people, "Behold, the people of Israel are too many and too mighty for us. Come, let us deal shrewdly with them, lest they multiply, and, if war befall us, they join our enemies and fight against us and escape from the land." Therefore they set taskmasters over them to afflict them with heavy burdens; and they built for Pharaoh store-cities, Pithom and Raamses.

Administrative "wisdom" or shrewdness at the top develops a scheme for keeping the immigrant people occupied. They are placed at hard labor in bureaucratic projects. This is a result of a decision on the part of the king and "his people." It is possible that this last expression refers to his advisors in his administration, but we can not be sure. At a minimum, it is his supporters and those who counsel with him and carry out his decisions.

The "we"/"they" language serves to set in the minds of Pharaoh's supporters a sense of the immigrant Hebrews as "other" and foreign. The Hebrews had done nothing against the Egyptians. They had not taken over economically. Their growing presence simply became grounds for suggesting possible ways in which they could become a threat, thus providing a rationale for bureaucratic wisdom to solve the apparent (not real) problem of a growing immigrant population: put them in slave labor on work projects for the government.

The final item in the king's rationale is especially interesting. He claims to be concerned that the immigrant Hebrews will grow too numerous and ally themselves with an enemy against Egypt. Such a justification demonstrates some "wisdom," as the king claimed, even to the reader of the text, who all too often shares the king's implicit fear that a growing immigrant population by definition poses a threat to the indigenous population. But Pharaoh's concluding remark seems contradictory and betrays a further motivation. One would think that the king feeling threatened by the growing Hebrew population would wish them to leave. But instead he expresses a fear that they will indeed leave the country. Presumably the king's advisors and supporters understood well this motivation. The disappearance of the Hebrews would destroy a ready source of cheap labor. (Admittedly the later part of the chapter with its account of the effort to destroy all the male children stands in tension with this plan, but it is given a rationale in the continued multiplication even when the governmental labor projects would seem to take their toll.[16])

The plan did not really work, of course, as is probably generally true of state efforts to restrict and restrain immigrant numbers and growth, and the end result was exactly what the king had feared. By the power of God, the Hebrews left the land and Egypt's cheap labor went with them. The experience marked forever Israel's understanding of what it meant to be a resident alien in a strange land. The laws protecting and providing for the sojourner (see below) were not unique to Israel. But in Israel they were stamped with the memory of slavery and oppressive life as immigrants in Egypt. The anti-sojourn in Egypt thus shaped in a marked way Israel's understanding of its responsibility to play host to strangers, not just in spontaneous moments but in the structure of society and over long periods of time.

Moral Requirements

Recognition of the relation between Israel's experience in Egypt as resident aliens and then slave laborers and the laws having to do with strangers and slaves opens the question of what specific moral directives were given to Israel for their treatment of strangers and sojourners in their midst. First of all, it should be noted that the sojourner or resident alien falls into a category with the widow, the orphan, and the poor. Rarely is the sojourner treated by herself or himself in the Old Testament laws. They are perceived as belonging to that group of marginal or weaker members of the community without the power or capability to ensure their own survival and well-being or without the structures to provide the same. The widow without a husband, the orphan without parent, and the poor without money or its equivalent were analogous to sojourners in their place in the community. The last did not belong to the community and its family and clan structures that provided the context in which protection and provision were guaranteed. So they were included with these other persons whose circumstances made their daily living perilous and crises more dangerous.

The laws in the Old Testament having to do with the sojourner or resident alien that are the most common are the gleaning laws, referred to above with reference to the story of Ruth and Boaz (Lev. 19:9-10, 23:22; Deut. 24:19-21) and the tithing laws (Deut. 14:28-29, 26:12). In the first case Israel is enjoined from picking up the remnants of the harvests of grain, olives, and grapes. In typical fashion, Deuteronomy gives specific examples of the kind of overly careful harvesting that is prohibited: going back to the grain fields to retrieve a forgotten sheaf, beating the olive branches a second time to get more olives, and going back through the vineyard a second time to pick any grapes missed on the first go-round. It was expected that widow, poor, and sojourner would avail themselves of these remnants so that they might have food to live on. The system is less haphazard than it might appear, and Ruth is a good example of its effectiveness. Even more controlled as a system for providing for the welfare of the resident alien and other such persons was the tithe. For it was given as a means of providing regular donations of food for these persons to eat.

Another set of laws that seems quite different at first glance nevertheless served the same purpose. These are the Deuteronomic laws directing the worship of Israel (Deut. 12:1-7,8-12,13-19,20-28,29-32; 14:22-29; 15:19-23; 16:1-17). A number of these laws have a characteristic structure consisting of the following elements: a prohibition (12:4,8,13,16-17), a command using the sanctuary formula, that is, the place where the Lord shall cause the Lord's name to dwell (12:5,11,14,18; 14:23a), the bringing of sacrifices and offerings (12:6,11b,14b; 14:23b,26,28), command to eat the tithes and offerings at the sanctuary (12:7,18-19; 14:23b,26b,29), rejoicing (12:7,12,18-19; 14:26b), an allusion to God's blessing (12:7,15; 14:24,29), and a concern for inclusiveness (12:7,12,18,19; 14:27,29). These statutes, therefore, called the community to gather with all its gifts before God at the place of worship to eat and rejoice and celebrate the blessing of God. And the laws made sure that no member of the community, including the resident alien, was left out or unprovided for. Here we see at the center of Israel's life a kind of anticipation of the messianic banquet where in thanksgiving and celebration all partake of the blessing of God. At this crucial point in Israel's regular life, anticipating implicitly an eschatological reality, the Israelite citizens rich and poor and those from outside who resided in Israel came together to worship God and enjoy God's benefits.

This series of statutes prescribes what we see in the narrative texts as one of the most characteristic acts of hospitality to strangers, the sharing of a meal, a simple act that more than any other in ordinary experience provides for human needs, builds friendship, and makes persons feel included in the community and at home. No meal takes place without human energy and labor. All meals have the potential to build intimacy and community. Thus Deuteronomy specifically makes the point that "the alien living among you" is included in the celebrative feasts of the family and the community. Precisely there where all the good gifts of God are celebrated and enjoyed is where there is a place at the table for the stranger and the poor.

Such statutes anticipate also the regular Priestly insistence in the Exilic and post-Exilic period that there shall be one law for the native-born Israelite and the stranger or sojourner. That is generally the case in Leviticus and the Priestly writings (Exod. 12: 43-49; Lev. 16:29; 18:26; 24:16; Num. 9:14; 15:15-16,29; 19:10; cf. Ezek. 14:7). The foreigner or stranger who was uncircumcised was excluded from Passover and the like, but whoever was circumcised, that is, bore the mark of belonging to the sacral community, was included.[17]

In Deut. 24:17, there is a statute, like many in the Old Testament, which prohibits Israel from perverting justice in the case of the sojourner in the courts. Similarly, in Num. 35:11-16 the resident aliens (ger and *tôshab*) are specifically mentioned along with the "people of Israel" in the laws of asylum that were meant to provide sanctuary against blood vengeance. Even more important in this connection is the slave law in Deut. 23:15-16: "You shall not hand over to his master a slave who seeks protection from his master with you; he shall dwell with you in your midst in the place which he shall choose within one of your towns, where it pleases him best; you shall not oppress him."[18] The term for "seeks protection" is the same verb used of God's delivering Israel from slavery. The slave is seeking deliverance and *may not be handed over*. For those who have already been set free by God, another person in bondage is a brother or sister, bound in a relationship of care and protection. And the fleeing slave is as free to choose a place to dwell as the Lord is free to choose a place for the Lord's name to dwell (the language is the same). There are no conditions here. The slave alone decides whether to continue in slavery or to break it off. While such laws still assume an institution of slavery, they also provide the seeds of its destruction. If such a statute perdures and is taken seriously, then slavery is on the way out.

Furthermore, here, even more than in the laws of asylum, is where sanctuary begins to come into the picture. One should note that in this instance sanctuary is not only provided for. It is obligatory. When the oppressed one comes for protection and deliverance, you must not hand him or her over. Rather the community shall make provision for the well-being of the one who flees oppression. In the present formulation of the law, it is envisioned that such fleeing slaves are refugees from outside the country who come into Israel seeking sanctuary. Protection and the opportunity to settle wherever the refugee slave desires are the specific safeguards of this statute.

The conclusion of this statute echoes one of the two kinds of more general directives about how the stranger is to be treated. In several places, as in Deut. 23:16, Israel is told not to oppress or wrong the stranger (e.g., Exod. 22:21; Lev. 19:33). Here is an all-inclusive demand for proper treatment of the stranger. The prohibition form is turned into a positive command in the form of the love command in Leviticus 19:34 and Deuteronomy 10:19. Israel is commanded to love the stranger or sojourner with all that that means by way of providing for the welfare and ensuring the good of this one who comes from outside and from another people and place. Such a form of the love command provides one of the earliest examples of its extension beyond the neighbor, or one might say that here the definition of the neighbor receives its extension. The sojourner may be a resident alien, but he or she is also a neighbor and due all the expressions of neighborliness that any native or member of the clan is due.

We should not leave the legal material of the Old Testament without taking note of one peculiarity, and that is the fact that one of the principal figures in the socio-cultic sphere, the Levite, is specifically given the role of sojourner in the Deuteronomic legislation.[19] The story of the Levite in Judges 19 shows the Levite as a sojourner, consistent with the Deuteronomic view that this office in Israel gave the people a chance to demonstrate hospitality on a regular basis to one of their central and continuing religious figures. The Levites were "brothers" who were also true sojourners in that they did not have claim on place and family and the provision and protection that such provided. What took place among the Levites thus exemplified the way it should be in Israelite society when Israel provided for the sojourner. J.G. McConville has described the place of the Levite as follows:

> The Levite in Deuteronomy is meant to be prosperous, therefore. His prosperity, however, is realized in dependence. He personifies the dependent spirit. His dependence on Yahweh is more conspicuous than that of his brethren, because he does not have private property in the same way that they do. His prosperity depends on the day-to-day factor of his brothers' continued obedient giving of

cultic offerings. His security is therefore less evident than that of his brethren, and yet in reality they too can only be prosperous in dependence. The Levite, whose perennial dependence is ever before his brethren's eyes, yet who is prosperous, is a constant reminder of this basic principle.[20]

The sojourning of the Levite in the midst of a people demonstrates the possibility of a communal life in which those whose circumstances keep them outside the usual structures of economic and social accessibility experience a well-being out of dependence, a dependence that is built into the system not as a necessary evil but rather as a reflection of the dependence of all the community. Israel's memory of a past as sojourners and the Levitical model in the present shape an orientation to the stranger that transcends the usual and modern fear of dependence on others to a recognition that such dependence is the nature of creaturehood and both a gift and a requirement of community, particularly as that is experienced in the complexity of plural and varied relationships. In any one-to-one or person-to-person relationship, the reality of dependence can be denied or indeed rejected. But the possibility of what Michael Welker has called a "security of expectations" requires a dependence whose character is shaped by such laws as these that let one know what to "expect."[21] The memory of the past and the example of the Levite in the present serve both to provide the security for the stranger and to acknowledge the dependence of every member of the community.

Theological and Anthropological Grounds

Examination of the various narratives and directives of the Old Testament about Israel's treatment of the stranger identifies several primary theological and anthropological grounds for the manifestation of hospitality to the stranger that ought to be lifted up to enable moral and ethical reflection. Some of these are explicit and already referred to in part. One is more implicit and an important connection to the New Testament.

Hospitality and caring of the stranger are given two of their basic grounds in Deuteronomy 10:17-19, a central text with echoes at other places in the Old Testament:

For the Lord your God is a God of gods and Lord of lords, the great, the mighty, and the terrible God, who is not partial and takes no bribe. He executes justice for the orphan and the widow, and loves the sojourner, giving him or her food and clothing. Love the sojourner therefore . . . .

In this context, Israel's conduct with the stranger or sojourner is both an *imitatio dei*, a reflection of God's way with sojourners, and the primary specific Old Testament manifestation of the Great Commandment to love the neighbor. One of the answers of the Old Testament to the question of how Israel is to live is that they are to walk in the way of the Lord. That is done both by obedience to the Lord's command and by imitation of God's own way with the stranger and sojourner. The fleshing out of the command to love the sojourner, the acts that are required and prohibited, are spelled out in the laws and exemplified in the stories. Israel also learns its way with strangers through the way that the Lord deals with them. That is very familiar to Israel because it is precisely as sojourners that the Lord has loved and delivered and cares for God's people. Psalm 146 praises the Lord as one who "watches over the sojourners," a reality perceived first in God's providing care of Abraham and Sarah and Rebekah and Isaac, and demonstrated especially in the deliverance of the Hebrew slaves from Egypt.[22]

Here, of course, is where also we encounter yet another moral ground for the love of the stranger. Israel's way of dealing with the aliens resident in their midst is given an empathetic moral incentive out of their own past and present experience as strangers and sojourners. This prominent theme, "You yourselves were strangers in the land of Egypt," has already been alluded to in the discussion of the laws. One of the more helpful analyses of its meaning and implications is provided by Michael Welker in his discussion of the theology of the law, a formulation worth presenting in some fullness:

> The attribution and identification "You were strangers in Egypt" is not self-evident. One can undermine it only too easily from the concrete perspective: "I myself was never in Egypt. Therefore the law of mercy, which is supposed to motivate me does not convince me at all!" Amazingly, the mercy code draws its strength precisely from this tension.
>
> First, Israel assumes this perspective on itself. It allows a history running from oppression to liberation to be attributed to it. Whatever individuals concretely and families and generations objectively have experienced and attributed to themselves as their history, all experiences and histories become centered on the attribution: "You were strangers in Egypt and are now addressed as those who have been liberated and led out. Your history bears the imprint of the transition from being strangers and oppressed to being at home and liberated."
>
> A differentiated social identity with far-reaching consequences is thereby formed and accepted. Not only is a communal history established that is publicly known and familiar, on which people can base appeals to each other, of which people can remind each other, and which people can communally celebrate and take as an occasion for assemblies and reconciliation. The history thus established also conditions an identity that encompasses opposing situations and apparently irreconcilable perspectives. "You were strangers—now you are no longer strangers." Israel is thus trusted and required to hold copresent two conflicting perspectives. "You can put yourselves in the shoes of the weak, and not just exteriorly and condescendingly. Rather, you know what it means to be a stranger. However, you do not thus become schizophrenic and disoriented, for you have gone through a process of liberation: you have left the oppression behind you; you can distinguish the development toward well-being and salvation from the

development toward sorrow and disaster." . . . If you take advantage of and exploit the stranger, then you repeat, then you reproduce, the sufferings that have been overcome. You reverse the process of liberation that is imprinted on your individual and social life.[23]

Welker suggests that not only does corporate memory, arising out of a corporate identity and an assumed perspective, shape the way in which we act in the present—it is surely axiomatic that having gone through an experience of oppression or suffering shapes the way one looks at anyone else going through the same experience but usually only if one has *come out of* or *through* that experience—but, at least in this case, it is a guard against the *reversion back* into the situation of suffering and oppression out of which one has come. Obedience to the Lord's instruction, therefore, arises out of an empathetic memory—both real and appropriated—that also protects the story of God's way from being undone and thus the social good from being undermined.

One needs to add to this claiming of an identity through memory and identification the further dimension that Israel in one sense continues to know itself as a community of resident aliens, but in a way that does not violate the history that has brought the people from oppression to liberation. Israel still lives as strangers and sojourners, not in relation to the Exodus experience and Egyptian slavery, but in relation to the Lord and the land:

> The land shall not be sold in perpetuity, for the land is mine and you are strangers and sojourners with me. (Lev. 25:23.)

Such a claim stands in the Holiness Code in the midst of the laws of the sabbatical year and the year of jubilee, one of the primary pieces of torah (also present in varying degrees in the Book of the Covenant [Exodus 21-23] and Deuteronomy) that seeks to provide for the welfare of the poor, the widow, the resident alien, those who through circumstances have lost access or lack access to the primary social and economic goods of the society. Israel's experience with sojourners in its midst is not apart from its own understanding that it lives in dependence on the Lord, without a final claim on the material good of this world. Whatever looseness the resident alien may feel to the land by virtue of his or her status may not be seen as a sharp contrast to an absolute claim on the land by the community of Israel. It is rather a reflection of Israel's own status as resident aliens given hospitality by the Lord.

Yet a further rationale for welcoming the stranger has been suggested from other perspectives and is confirmed by the biblical tradition, at times explicitly but often implicitly. That is the fact that hospitality to the stranger allows for surprising possibilities and wonderful happenings. The most explicit biblical text suggesting that implication is in the New Testament in the admonition of the writer of the Letter to the Hebrews: "Do not neglect to show hospitality to strangers, for thereby some have entertained angels unawares" (Heb. 13:2). As was noted above, this text has its source in the stories of Genesis 18 and 19 where Abraham graciously welcomes and entertains three men who come by his way and later in the story turn out to be messengers from God with the incredible news that Sarah will bear a child. Lot also welcomes them and more somberly discovers the surprising news that God is going to destroy Sodom.

The New Testament tells its own stories of what wonderful and surprising things may happen when strangers are welcomed and given hospitality. More specifically, it continues in the tradition of Genesis 18, where the messengers are divine messengers or even the Lord and the Lord's attendants (see Gen. 19:10 and 13), in claiming more than once that welcome to the stranger is hospitality rendered to the Lord. That is what we hear in Jesus' parable of the great judgment (Matt. 25:31-46) when the astonished folk gathered around the throne of the King wonder when it was they met him as a stranger and welcomed him, only to hear that it was as they met the stranger at their door that they showed hospitality to the one who is their Lord. In Luke 24 two disheartened disciples on the Emmaus road after the death of Jesus meet a stranger and offer him food and lodging at the end of the day only to discover that they have welcomed the risen Lord to their house and table. So the community of faith heard—and hears—of the possibility that in its hospitality to the stranger it may be extending an unintended and indeed unrealized welcome to the one who is host at all the banquets and feasts in the Kingdom of God.

As a final note, I want to call attention to the fact that the Old Testament, as it lays out in various ways Israel's responsibility and manner with strangers, guards against a tendency to see the whole matter simply on a highly individualized person-to-person scale. That way of dealing with strangers is integrally a part of what is intended. The welcome of strangers at a meal in the home of a family is a highly personal act between individuals and is of the essence in showing hospitality to strangers. But such hospitality, so singularly exemplified in the intimacy of a meal or a bed in a home is not confined to such acts or their legitimate and desirable spontaneity. The Old Testament material reveals that the hospitality of strangers is something that permeates the whole social structure of the community beginning with the most intimate family contexts but moving out to the various aspects of community and social life, incorporating the central economic sources, the protection of the court, and the worship activities of the people. No act is too small to demonstrate the love of the stranger. No small act is itself sufficient to insure that the alien in the midst of the community is protected, provided for, and given access to the possibilities for life available to others in the community.

Addendum

Two important and useful studies of the *gerîm* or sojourners came to my attention too late to be integrated into this study but will be of interest to the reader.

The point that Israel's story begins as a story of sojourners (cf. Exod. 6:4 and Ps. 105:12) is given a historical and social grounding in the important study of Frank Spina, "Israelites as *gerîm*, 'Sojourners,' in Social and Historical Context," in *The Word of the Lord Shall Go Forth*, edited by Carol L. Meyers and M. O'Connor (Winona Lake, IN: Eisenbrauns, 1983), pp. 322-35. Spina argues on various grounds that the tradition is consistent in portraying Israel before the settlement in Canaan—and only then—as *gerim* and that this tradition preserves a genuine historical memory. He further contends that the term "immigrant" best translates *gerim*, suggesting the situations of "war, famine, economic and social troubles, oppression, plague and other misfortunes that produced *gerîm*" (p. 324) and still produce emigration.

The most recent study of the sojourner in the Old Testament is an essay by Donald E. Gowan, "Wealth and Poverty in the Old Testament: The Case of the Widow, the Orphan, and the Sojourner," *Interpretation*, 41 (1987), pp. 341-53. In this context, the sojourner is treated as a part of a general category that includes the widow and the orphan, as has been noted above, and with Spina, is understood as an immigrant.

Both articles include helpful bibliographies.

NOTES

1. The noun *tôshab*, which appears only in the Priestly material, is often joined with ger, with which it shares the same basic meaning. Separate discussion of it is not required. Most of the texts in which it occurs receive attention in looking at the use of *ger*.

2. *Nekar* usually occurs in the expression *ben-(han)nekar*, which means literally "son of a foreigner," but more accurately should be understood as "belonging to the class/group, foreigner."

3. Isaiah 2:6 has been interpreted by some as referring to the people shaking hands with foreigners to seal an agreement, an act obviously castigated by the text. More recently, J.J.M. Roberts has plausibly suggested that the text is an attack on the Israelites of the northern kingdom for "joining their foreign allies in making derisive gestures toward Jerusalem" at the time of the Syro-Ephraimite war. J.J.M. Roberts, "Isaiah 2 and the Prophet's Message to the North," *The Jewish Quarterly Review*, 75 (Jan. 1985), pp. 290-308.

4. Cf. A. Bertholet, *Die Stellung der Israeliten und der Juden zu den Fremden* (Leipzig: J.C.B. Mohr, 1896), pp. 1-2.

5. So Paul Dion, "Israël et l'étranger dans le Deutéronome," *L'altérité vivre ensemble différents*, edited by M. Gourgues and G.-D. Mailhiot (Montreal: Editions Bellarmin, 1986), p. 222.

6. R.D. Nelson, *The Double Redaction of the Deuteronomistic History* (JSOT Supplement Series, 18; Sheffield: JSOT Press, 1981), p. 71.

7. W. Gesenius, *A Hebrew and English Lexicon to the Old Testament* (Oxford: Oxford University Press, 1959), p. 157.

8. One should note in this instance that the terminology talked about in the first part of the paper is not used here. The strangers are simply called "men." While the terminology is a primary indicator of the subject matter under discussion, this story shows that hospitality to strangers can be described in a story without any particular concern for so designating the persons involved.

9. C. Westermann, *Genesis 12-36*, trans. by John Scullion, S.J. (Minneapolis: Augsburg, 1985), pp. 276-77.

10. Ibid., pp. 277-78.

11. The men are here called "messengers," or "angels," as the Hebrew word is often translated, uncovering immediately, therefore, the background for the reference in Hebrews 13:2 where Christians are enjoined to show hospitality to strangers, "for thereby some have entertained angels unawares."

12. The morality of Lot's offer of his daughters is an immediate issue to the contemporary reader of the story and one that cannot be avoided. The story itself does not seem to judge or question his act as a part of the extreme effort proper to the protection of strangers. That such a handling of one's daughters can be in some sense justified in the practice of hospitality to strangers is itself worthy of consideration and very revealing of attitudes toward women in the practices of that time and the material before us (see note 15 below).

13. This story of a sojourner having difficulty finding lodging overnight provides a narrative background to one of Job's pleas of innocence: "The sojourner has not lodged in the street, I have opened my doors to the wayfarer" (Job 31:32).

14. S.D. Currie, "Biblical Studies for a Seminar on Sexuality and the Human Community," *Austin Seminary Bulletin*, 87 (1971), p. 14 (quoted in R. Boling, *Judges* ["The Anchor Bible," vol. 6a; Garden City, N.Y., 1975], pp. 277-78).

15. P. Trible, *Texts of Terror: Literary-Feminist Readings of Biblical Narratives* ("Overtures to Biblical Theology;" Philadelphia: Fortress, 1984), pp. 65-91. One key paragraph (pp. 75-76) is worth quoting:

> These two stories show that rules of hospitality in Israel protect only males. Though Lot entertained men alone, the old man also has a female guest, and no hospitality safeguards her. She is chosen as the victim for male lust. Further, in neither of these stories does the male host offer himself in place of his guests. Constant only is the use of innocent and helpless women to guard and gratify men of all sorts. Nonetheless, Lot's proposal was rejected, not out of concern for his virgin daughters but out of animosity that a sojourner should try to adjudicate the crisis (Gen. 19:9). Ironically, male anger against another male spared Lot's daughters the horrors for which he had volunteered them. Similarly, one line in our story reports the dissatisfaction of the Benjaminites with the proposal of the old man. "But the men would not listen to him" (19:25a, RSV). This time, however, male anger does not spare the female.

16. On the tensions within the chapter and the growth of the traditions out of which it was created, see B.S. Childs, *The Book of Exodus* (Philadelphia: Westminster Press, 1974) pp. 10-11.

17. Once again the statutes reveal a focus on the place of the male and a silence with regard to female members of the community. On the place of women in the cult of Israel, see P. Bird, "The Place of Women in the Israelite Cultus," *Ancient Israelite Religion*, ed. by P.D. Miller, P.D. Hanson, and S.D. McBride (Philadelphia: Fortress, 1987), pp. 397-419.

18. While this piece of legislation may have had in mind particularly male slaves, the characteristically masculine formulation of the statute does not necessarily mean that female slaves did not have the same protection. Presumably they did.

19. The Priestly stratum of material does not so view the Levites. There they are given an allotment of forty-eight cities in which to live. The Deuteronomic view is consistent with its program and polity whatever the actual realities of Levitical existence may have been.

20. J.G. McConville, *Law and Theology in Deuteronomy* (JSOT Supplement Series, 33; Sheffield: JSOT Press, 1984), p. 151.

21. M. Welker, "Security of Expectations: Reformulating the Theology of Law and Gospel," *The Journal of Religion*, 66 (1986), pp. 237-60.

22. One should mention in this context also the vivid picture of the Lord as host in the second part of the very familiar Psalm 23.

23. Welker, "Security of Expectations," pp. 252-53.

Israel Experiences Exile

Leslie J. Hoppe, OFM
Catholic Theological Union

Introduction: Israel Remembers

". . . a wandering Aramean was my father . . ." (Deut 26:5). So begins one of ancient Israel's most important creedal statements. This is the opening line of a prayer that the Israelite is to recite at the offering of first fruits. The prayer reminds the Israelites who are enjoying the benefits of God's gift of the land that their ancestors were, at one time, migrants in search of a place to settle. When ancient Israel told the story of its origins, it began with the divine command that ordered Abraham to take up a migrant's life: "Go from your country and your kindred and your father's house to the land that I will show you" (Gen 12:1). The Israelites celebrated God's care of their migrant ancestors in their hymns: "When they were few in number . . . wandering from nation to nation . . . [God] allowed no one to oppress them" (Ps 105:12). The Book of Deuteronomy, which is known more for its exclusivist tendencies, shows an uncharacteristic sympathy for Egypt, which offered Israel's ancestors refuge during a severe famine in Canaan: "You shall not abhor an Egyptian, because you were a sojourner in his land" (Deut 23:7b).[1] Reminders of the migrant's life were never far from the consciousness of the Israelites; they were deeply embedded in the collective memory of the Israelite community.

1. Migrations in the Late Bronze Age (1550-1200 B.C.E.)

The groups that eventually merged to form the Israelite community were part of the mass migrations into Canaan during the Late Bronze Age. During this period, Egypt was the dominant power. Its control and influence were widespread within Canaan, the future home of the Israelites. Canaan was Egyptian territory. During the Late Bronze Age the only other power that could rival Egypt was the Hittite Empire whose center was north of Canaan in Anatolia. Though they were rivals for some time, the Egyptian and Hittite empires did develop a pattern of peaceful co-existence.[2] At the end of the 13th century B.C.E., both empires had to deal with the effects of major population movements in the eastern Mediterranean region. From the northwest came Indo-European groups known as the "Sea Peoples." They disrupted the political status quo throughout most of the area controlled by Egypt to the extent that Egypt's hegemony over Canaan was in doubt. Canaan's fertile land attracted Semitic groups from the southeast. Its central hill country was only sparsely populated and this invited occupation by people looking to escape the harsh life on the fringes of the desert.

The population of Canaan became quite diverse as the migrations continued with the gradual unraveling of Egyptian control. The heterogenous character of the population of Canaan is evident from Egyptian sources themselves. In describing this population, one Egyptian text from the 15th century named Canaanites, the people of Retenu, Apiru, Shasu,

Kharu and Neges.[3] The Amarna Letters coming from a century later and written by vassal rulers in Canaan to their Egyptian overlords described the rivalries and battles among the various groups in Canaan.[4] At the end of the 12th century, the Assyrian king, Tiglath-Pileser I, suggested that the migrations of people that were going on in Syria were disrupting the stability of the entire region.[5] The collapse of Egyptian authority in Canaan led to very difficult and turbulent times as the diverse groups in the region withdrew their allegiance from old political powers and began their quest for control of their land and destiny.

The end of Egyptian authority in Canaan also meant the demise of the Canaanite city-states that controlled the region under Egyptian aegis. The politically marginalized and economically oppressed peasant population of Canaan was in a position to bring to an end the domination of the region's petty rulers who were able to rule only because of Egypt's support.[6] Migrants who came into the region looking for arable land on which to settle may have joined the peasants of Canaan. The spark igniting the revolt against the Canaanite city-states may have come from semitic migrants from Egypt who worshipped a God who took the side of the oppressed over their oppressors (the Exodus group). The worship of the God Yahweh who gave victory to the slaves from Egypt probably served as the theological support that the peasants' revolt needed.It was faith in a God who took the side of the oppressed, which helped forge a genuinely diverse group made up of escaped slaves from Egypt, migrants from Transjordan and elsewhere, along with Canaanite peasants into a force that eventually ended the Canaanite city-state system and replaced it with the national states of Edom, Moab, and Israel, the latter bifurcating into the Kingdoms of Judah and Israel after the death of Solomon.

Summary

At the end of the Bronze Age large empires and the old political coalitions in Canaan were becoming increasingly unable to deal with the influx of migrants into the region. These migrants merged with the indigenous peasant population of Canaan and successfully ended to the domination of the Canaanite city-states whose places were taken by small national states such as Israel. The villages and towns settled by the people coming into the central hill country looking for arable land along with the disaffected indigenous population may have provided the nucleus of the Israelite state.[8] Some of those who made up these migrant groups saw their success as the fulfillment of divine promises made to their ancestors. Those who gave literary and theological shape to the biblical traditions about the settlement considered the origin of the Israelite state to have been according to the divine will and so told the story of ancient Israel's origins accordingly. Even though these narratives were given their present shape much later than the period of the settlement, the story of Israel as emerging in part out of the migrations of the Late Bronze Age could not be forgotten.

22

2. The Importance of "The Land"

The Bible, which records the experience of some of these migrants to central Canaan, portrays ancient Israel's coming to possess the land where they settled as a divine gift to people who were at one time without a land of their own (Deut 26:5-10). Ancient Israel came to experience its God in this process. The land then became a genuine "sacrament" for the Israelites. Appreciating the central role of the land in Israel's religious experience is crucial for understanding Israel's experience of exile. This is sometimes difficult for Christians whose theology is not "land-based" like that of ancient Israel. It is not simply a matter of a material versus a spiritual notion of the divine-human encounter; rather, it is a question of the perspective from which one comes to have an experience of God.

The land became the locus of Israelite religious experience. According to the biblical faith, the land that ancient Israel came to control belongs to God. There are several texts in which God refers to the land as "my land," e.g., Isa 14:25; Jer 16:18; Ezek 36:5; Joel 1:6. The land is God's inheritance: 1 Sam 26:19; 2 Sam 14:16; Jer 2:7; 16:18; 50:11; Pss 68:9; 79:1. The Israelites were to consider themselves as merely temporary residents on "God's land": "The land shall not be sold in perpetuity, for the land is mine; for you are strangers and sojourners with me" (Lev 25:23). The biblical institutions of the Sabbath Year and the Jubilee Year (Lev 25) presuppose that the land belongs to God. Ancient Israel's infidelities pervert the sacred character of the land: ". . . when you came in you defiled my land and made my land an abomination" (Jer 2:7). God lives in the land and therefore in the midst of Israel: "You shall not defile the land in which you live; in the midst of which I dwell; for I the Lord dwell in the midst of the people of Israel" (Num 35:34). God, the land, and the people then belong together. The Book of Deuteronomy therefore feels free to assert that the land is the inheritance of Israel: 4:21,38; 12:9; 19:10; 20:16; 21:23; 24:4; 25:19. In describing the land, the Bible simply refers to it as good, but behind this simple expression is the belief that the land is the source of every blessing because of its fruitfulness, wealth, and beauty. The rhetoric of Deuteronomy can be quite prosaic but it is most eloquent and almost lyrical when it speaks about the land and its bounty:

> For the Lord your God is bringing you into a good land, a land of brooks of water, of fountains and springs, flowing forth in valleys and hills, a land of wheat and barley, of vines and fig trees and pomegranates, a land of olive trees and honey, a land in which you will eat bread without scarcity, in which you will lack nothing, a land whose stones are iron, and out of whose hills you can dig copper. And you shall eat and be full, and you shall bless the Lord your God for the good land God has given you (Deut 8:7-10).

> For the land which you are entering to take possession of it is not like the land of Egypt, from which you have come, where you sowed your seed and watered

it with your feet, like a garden of vegetables; but the land which you are going over to possess is a land of hills and valleys, which drinks water by the rain from heaven, a land which the Lord your God cares for; the eyes of the Lord your God care for; the eyes of the Lord your God are always upon it from the beginning of the year to end of the year (Deut 11:10-12).

Additional words of praise that the Bible heaps upon the land include the familiar "land of milk and honey" (Num 13:27; Deut 6:3 *et passim*; Jer 11:5; 32:22).[9] Another epithet describes the land as "broad" (Exod 3:8; Judg 18:10; Isa 22:18; Neh 9:35; 1 Chron 4:40).[10] The land is also called "precious" (Jer 3:19; Ps 106:24) and "glorious" (Dan 8:9; 11:16,41).

The Book of Deuteronomy, a type of "constitution" for Israel in its land, understands the land first as "the land of promise." A favorite Deuteronomic expression is "the land that the Lord swore to give to your [Israel's] ancestors (1:8,35; 6:10,18,23; 8:1; 10:11; 11:9; 19:8; 26:3; 30:20; 31:7,23). The book emphasizes that Israel came to own the land not because of its righteousness but in order that God could fulfill the promises made to Abraham, Isaac, and Jacob, the migrant ancestors of the Israelites.

A second Deuteronomic conception of the land is that it offers the proper setting for Israel's fulfillment of the law. There are a few ways that Deuteronomy makes this clear. For example, the text admonishes the Israelites to learn the law so that they might *keep it in the land* God is giving them (4:5,14; 5:31; 6:1; 11:31-32). The law code of Deuteronomy (Deut 12-26) begins as follows: "These are the statutes and ordinances which you shall be careful to do in the land which the Lord, the God of your ancestors has given you to possess . . ." (12:1). Obedience and disobedience have consequences for Israel's life in the land, e.g., the fourth commandment promises those who honor their parents long life *in the land* (5:16). Obedience brings God's blessings upon the land and its produce while disobedience call forth a curse (28:8-18). Expulsion from the land is the final curse. Moses warns the Israelites that disobedience will result in loss of the land:

> I call heaven and earth to witness against you this day, that you will soon utter-ly perish *from the land* which you are going over the Jordan to possess; you will not live long upon it, but will be utterly destroyed (4:26).

The ties between the land and Israel were so strong, possession of the land so important, living on the land so central to its identity that loss of it threatened Israel's very existence. Possession of the land was the only way that Israel could continue as a people.

Summary

Ancient Israel's experience of exile was made all the more acute because of its beliefs regarding the land. Israel believed that the gift of the land was the fulfillment of divine promises made to their migrant ancestors. The land was the source of Israel's prosperity and the locus of its encounter with God. Failure to remain faithful to God, however, would result in the forfeiture of that gift. Without the land, Israel's very existence was in doubt.

3. The Exile of Israel from Its Land

Introduction: From a Covenant Community to Nation-State

At first, the people of Israel lived in the land as a covenant community. A common commitment to the Lord Yahweh united the association of families, clans, and tribes that made up the people of Israel. They withheld allegiance from every human lord and submitted to God alone. The union of the groups that made up ancient Israel was loose and hardly able to withstand the pressures brought to bear upon it from several of its rivals for the possession of the land that Israel believed was its gift from God. The Philistines soon became Israel's principal rivals in Canaan. The military might and technological sophistication of the Philistines led many Israelites to conclude that the only way to effectively resist the Philistines was to unite behind the type of strong and permanent leadership that a monarchy provided. Israel began its experiment with the monarchy under Saul, but it was David who successfully transformed the covenant community into a national state. The centrifugal forces that were part of ancient Israel's early years were never successfully overcome by David or his immediate successor, Solomon. It was the failure of Solomon's son and successor Rehoboam to be sensitive to these forces that led to the breakup of the Davidic empire into two small kingdoms following Solomon's death (1 Kgs 12).[11]

These two Israelite kingdoms coexisted for some two hundred years. The hill country north of Jerusalem was the base of the Northern Kingdom, though it included the Jezreel Valley and Galilee as well. It adopted the name Israel. It was also known as Ephraim after its most dominant tribal group. The Southern Kingdom extended from Jerusalem southward to the Negev. It came to be known as Judah. These two kingdoms were sometimes rivals and occasionally partners, but their continued existence depended on the political climate created by the resurgence of the Mesopotamian empires of Assyria and Babylon. Once Assyria began to assert its power in the ancient Near East, it was just a matter of time before the two Israelite kingdoms would be caught up in the designs of the military and political power that was the neo-Assyrian empire. The Northern Kingdom did fall in 720 B.C.E. Miraculously the Southern Kingdom was able to maintain a semblance of independence during the period of Assyrian ascendancy although it was obviously a client state that had to pay a hugh tribute as the price of its nominal independence. Judah, however, could not withstand the Babylonians who brought an end to the Southern Kingdom in 587 B.C.E. The method both empires used to insure the pacification of conquered areas was to exile elements of the local population. It is to this policy and its effect upon the ancient Israelites that we now turn.

The Fall and Exile of the Northern Kingdom (Israel)

David was able to form the Israelite tribes into a stable and even powerful national state because the political climate in the ancient world was favorable to the formation of such small states during the early part of the Iron Age. The Egyptian and Hittite empires who had dominated the region lost their control and ceased to be effective forces in Canaan by David's day. The 8th century B.C.E. witnessed a revival of the phenomenon of ancient Near Eastern empires.[12] The Northern Kingdom was the first to fall to the power of a resurgent Assyria. Israel ceased to exist as an independent nation early during the period of Assyrian domination. The Assyrians captured Israel's capital Samaria in 721 B.C.E. and they incorporated the territory of the Northern Kingdom into their provincial system. It is not necessary to retrace the chain of events both in Israel and Assyria that led up to the fall of the Northern Kingdom. Though the fall of a small state such as Israel to the expansionist Assyrian Empire was probably inevitable, there was a combination of internal and external forces that came into play and together made any resistance to the Assyrians futile.[13]

The Bible does not contain too many details about what happened to the Northern Kingdom and its people following the fall of Samaria. The Deuteronomistic History of Israel[14] reports the fall of Samaria in summary fashion (2 Kgs 17:1-6) but then goes on at length to explain the reasons for the fall of the Northern Kingdom (2 Kgs 17:7-23, 34b-40). Since the interest of the Deuteronomistic author is theological rather than historical, the reasons given have nothing to do with the resurgence of Assyrian power in the 8th century B.C.E. The reason given for the fall are religious: Israel was not faithful to the worship of the Lord alone but "made Asherah, and worshipped all the host of heaven, and served Baal" (v. 16); Israel did not listen to the prophets God sent to it (v. 12) but "burned their sons and their daughters as offering, and used divination and sorcery. . ." (v. 17a) and Israel did not obey Torah (v. 13).

Assyrian texts offer some information that can help fill in the some of the details ignored by the biblical account. Sargon II, to whom Israel fell, left this description:

> I besieged the conquered Samaria, led away as booty 27,290 inhabitants of it. I formed from among them a contingent of 50 chariots and made the remaining population assume their social positions. I installed over them an officer of mine and imposed upon them the tribute of the former king.[15]

The most devastating of Sargon's actions was, of course, his deportation of a significant segment of the Israelite population and the resettlement of non-Israelites in the territory of the former Northern Kingdom. One reason for the deportation was to punish the Israelites for their foolish rebellion against Assyrian hegemony. Israel's ruling elite made up the major portion of the exiles in order to make future uprisings less likely. Another reason for the deportation was to supply population for other areas in the empire.[16] The Assyrians resettled the Israelite exiles in cities of their empire that experienced a loss of population due to war. The exiles worked in rural areas on agricultural projects. They plied their crafts and served as laborers where needed in the empire.

The Resettlement of Samaria

The Bible gives some specific information about the people with whom the Assyrians chose to replace the exiled Israelites in the territory of the former Northern Kingdom. According to 2 Kings 17:24 and 18:34, Samaria received people from Babylon, Cuthah (a site northeast of Babylon), Avva (location unknown); Hamath (northern Syria) and Sepharvaim (known as Sibraim in Ezekial 47:16 and located between Damascus and Hamath). The resettlement of new populations in Samaria continued throughout the Assyrian period. After his campaign of 716 B.C.E., Sargon settled some Arabs in Samaria. According to Ezra 4:2,10, the resettlement of foreigners were still taking place in Israel as late as the reign of Esarhaddon (680-669 B.C.E.) and Ashurbanipal (668-627 B.C.E.).[17]

The story of this resettlement as told in the Deuteronomistic History (2 Kgs 17:23-41) reflects popular imagination more than historical memory. The text intimates that the entire population of the defunct Northern Kingdom went into exile (2 Kgs 17:23) and that lions harassed the resettled population because the new settlers did not "know the way of the God of the land" (v. 26). To deal with this menace, the king of Assyria returned a single Israelite priest from exile in order to instruct the foreign settlers how "they should fear the Lord" (v. 28).

The Deuteronomistic History was written from a southern perspective and reflects the animosities that developed later between the Jews and the people who lived in Samaria. The people of Judah considered the population of Samaria to be a non-Israelite group that engaged in a hybrid form of worship and worshipped the gods of their native lands beside the God of Israel (2 Kgs 17:29-33). The text asserts: "To this day they do according to the former manner. They do not fear the Lord, and they do not follow . . . the Law . . ." (2 Kgs 17:34). This judgment is tendentious and provided theological support for the Jewish refusal to accept the people of Samaria as genuine worshippers of Israel's ancestral deity.

The foreigners who resettled in Samaria by orders of the Assyrian officials assimilated into the remaining Israelite population. During the period of the Judean restoration (late 6th and early 5th centuries B.C.E.), animosity developed between the people of Samaria and the people of Judah. The introduction of non-Israelites into the north and the assimilation that took place was the excuse by the Judean to reject the worshippers of Yahweh who lived in the territory of the former Northern Kingdom. The causes of the rift that grew between the Samaritans and the Jews are quite complex.[18] Justifying that rift based Ezra's requirement of endogamy (Ezra 9:1-15) was an anachronism. The breach between Jew and Samaritan temple on Mt. Gerezim by the Hasmonean king, John Hyrcanus, in 132 B.C.E.[19]

The religious conditions in the former Northern Kingdom may have been much different following the fall of Samaria than the Deuteronomist portrayed them [20] The new settlers brought their own religious traditions with them, but as was customary in the ancient Near East, they would have participated in the worship of Yahweh who was the God of the land in which they lived. In addition, since the Assyrians integrated Samaria into their provincial system, the people of that region had to observe the official state religion of Assyria to some extent. Despite this, it is probable that many Yahwistic shrines in the North survived the Assyrian onslaught without significant disruption since the Assyrian military centered its activities primarily on Samaria, the capital of the Northern Kingdom.[21] No doubt Samaria's Yahwistic temple suffered great damage and perhaps even destruction, but it is also likely that Sargon II restored it along with the rest of the city. In any case, it is a mistake to assume that the ancestral religion of Israel disappeared from the North.

Finally a significant portion of the northern population may have moved to Judah to avoid deportation. Hezekiah, the king of Judah during the last quarter of the 8th century, enlarged the area encompassed by the city walls of Jerusalem to accommodate the refugees from the North (2 Chron 32:5). It is likely that these refugees brought with them traditions such as the stories about Elijah and Elisha, two prophets who exercised their ministry in the North. These and other northern traditions were eventually incorporated into texts that formed the Hebrew Scriptures.

Conditions of Samaria's Exiles

Assyrian documents about the fate of exiled peoples makes it clear that they did not have to endure physical hardship nor did they have the status of slaves. Some became tenant farmers who received their land from the Assyrian government. Others served as craftsmen in various imperial projects. The exiles had certain rights and were able to enjoy economic security. Some even achieved a high social and political status in the empire. To make this possible the exiles had a certain measure of internal autonomy. Apparently most of the exiles from the former Northern Kingdom assimilated into their new milieu, though some probably tried to preserve their distinctive national character and to maintain connections with their homeland. When later prophets spoke about the Judean restoration following the Babylonian Exile, they sometimes spoke of a restoration of Samaria as well: "I will restore . . . the fortunes of Samaria and her daughters. . . . As for your sisters . . . Samaria and her daughters shall return to their former estate . . ." (Ezek 16:53,55).

Ezekiel even looked to an eventual restoration of the union between the two Israelite kingdoms (Ezek 37:15-16), a theme echoed later by Zachariah (8:13; 10:6-12), who believed that God was going to bring the exiles back from Assyria. These prophetic visions never turned into reality.

Over the centuries, all sorts of legends developed regarding the fate of the so-called Ten Lost Tribes as the exiles from the Northern Kingdom came to be known.[22] Unfortunately there is no definitive information available regarding the fate of the Israelite exiles who resettled following the fall of Samaria. There are some Assyrian documents from the 7th century B.C.E. that contain some personal names with the distinctively Israelite theophoric element *ya*.[23] The story found in the deuterocanonical book of Tobit has its setting in the Assyrian Exile. The book's hero is a member of the tribe of Naphtali who was supposedly deported in the days of Shalmeneser. Of course, the book is more of a popular legend than an historical text.[24] The author of 1 Chron 5:26 attests to the survival of the exiles from the North down to his own day (4th cent. B.C.E.) while Josephus mentions them as late as the 1st century of the Common Era (*Antiquities* xi.133). Another 1st century text, 4 Ezra states that those led into captivity by the Assyrians would one day rejoin the authentic worshippers of Yahweh (13:39-45). Both Act 26:6 and James 1:1 assume the existence of all twelve tribes. Despite the affirmations of these texts, the exiles from the Northern Kingdom have disappeared from the pages of history.

Summary

Because the political climate which allowed the Israelite covenant community to emerge at the end of the Late Bronze Age and David to unite the members of that community into a national state at the beginning of the Iron Age changed dramatically by the 8th century, the continued existence of the two Israelite kingdoms as independent national states was in doubt. The Northern Kingdom fell in 721 B.C.E. Many of the leading citizens of that kingdom went off to exile in various parts of the Assyrian Empire. Apparently these exiles assimilated into their new surroundings. The Assyrians brought in a non-Israelite population to resettle the territory of the former Northern Kingdom. These new settlers assimilated with the remnants of the indigenous population and adopted this worship of the Israelite ancestral deity. The people of the south regarded this assimilation as an evil accommodation and no longer considered the people of the North to be legitimate Yahwists and thus the rift between Jew and Samaritan began.

4. The Fall and Exile of Judah

The Rise of Babylon

Since the Bible represents the perspectives of the South for the most part, the text pays much more attention to the fall of the Southern Kingdom to Babylon and the exile that took place in the early part of the 6th century B.C.E. Though the Southern Kingdom felt the pressure that came with the resurgence of the Assyrian Empire in the 8th century, it was able to maintain its existence as a distinct political entity though its actual independence was severely curtailed by the Assyrians. Unlike the Northern Kingdom, the Assyrians did not annex Judah. Of course, Judah could not escape the effect of the Assyrian assault on Palestine. After his campaign in Judah that ended in 701 B.C.E., the Assyrian ruler Sennacherib claimed to have taken 200,150 people from Judah as booty.[25] These people must have resettled somewhere outside of Palestine (see Isa 6:13; 11:12-16; 27:8; Mic 1:16).

The Assyrian Empire fell to a coalition of Babylonians, Medes, and Scythians in 612 B.C.E. The prophet Nahum rejoiced over the sack of Nineveh, the Assyrian capital (1:15-3:19). The Babylonians, however, moved quickly to fill the vacuum of power and the Southern Kingdom soon passed from Assyrian to Babylonian control. The sudden rise of this new Mesopotamian power shocked the prophet Habakkuk (1:5-11). Jeremiah, on the other hand, believed that the Babylonians would rule for a long time and he suggested that Judah simply submit to the inevitable as God's will (25:12; 29:10).

The First Exile in 597 B.C.E.

In 601 B.C.E. Babylon suffered a setback in the plans to bring Egypt under its control. Encouraged by this demonstration of Babylon's vulnerability, Jehoiakim, king of Judah, decided to withhold tribute and thereby claim Judah's independence of its Babylonian overlord. In 597 B.C.E. Nebuchadnezzar, king of Babylon, brought an end to this short-lived revolt. The king who eventually surrendered to the Babylonians was Jehoiachin, who succeeded his father. There is some question about what fate befell Jehoiakim. 2 Kings 24:6 asserts that "he slept with his fathers" implying that the old king died a natural death and was buried in Jerusalem. By way of contrast, 2 Chron 36:6 reports that Jehoiakim went into exile in Babylon.[26] Josephus reports that Nebuchadnezzar executed Jehoiakim after the fall of Jerusalem (*Antiquities* x.96). The Babylonian Chronicles do not report any exile of Jehoiakim which makes the text from 2 Kings appear to be the most reliable.[27] Apparently Jehoiakim died waiting for the Egyptians to come to his aid. This left Jehoiachin to surrender Jerusalem to the Babylonians. Nebuchadnezzar immediately deposed and exiled the new king. Some relative and many leading citizens of Judah accompanied Jehoiachin into exile (2 Kgs 24:12; Jer 13:18-19; 2 Chron 36:9-10). The Babylonians replaced Jehoiachin with his uncle Mattaniah who took the throne name Zedekiah (2 Kgs 24:17; Ezek 17:11-14). The number of exiles is given twice—both times in round numbers: 10,000 men exclusive of artisans (2 Kgs 24:14) and 7,000 "men of valor" and 1,000 artisans (2 Kgs 24:16). Jerusalem itself escaped harm probably because the city surrendered promptly, thus obviating the need for a long, costly, and destructive siege.

The fall of Jerusalem and the exile of Jehoiachin was a shock to most of the people of Judah. It seemed inconceivable that God would allow that "place where God made God's name to dwell" to fall into the power of the Babylonians and that God would allow pagans to depose and exile the anointed king of Judah, a scion of the chosen Davidic dynasty. The official cult of Judah promoted the belief that God would never allow Jerusalem or the Davidic dynasty to fall (Pss 46; 48; 76). A fair number of people believed that what had happened to Jerusalem and its king was a terrible mistake that God soon would rectify. The preaching of prophets such as Hananiah encouraged this view. He proclaimed that the exile would last no more than two years (Jer 28:2-4). Prophets such as Ahab, Zedekiah, and Shemaiah who preached in Babylon, echoed the same message (Jer 29:21-32). Clearly many in Judah considered Jehoiachin to be the rightful king and looked forward to his return and the deposition of Zedekiah who owed his throne to the hated Babylonians.

The prophet Jeremiah did not share these views. He rejected the notion that Jerusalem was "inviolable" because of its status as God's chosen city (Jer 7:1-15; 26:4-6). He contradicted the prophecy of Hananiah with one of his own, which stated that God had given Nebuchadnezzar dominion (28:13-14). The prophet considered Jehoiachin totally unacceptable as king (22:24-30) and he sent a letter to the exiles advising them to prepare for a long stay in Babylon (29:1-32). Jeremiah considered the assurances that the people in Jerusalem and in Babylon were hearing about a quick end to Babylonian rule as completely baseless. He advised the people to submit completely to Babylon while others continued to look for deliverance with the help of Egypt. Despite this, Jeremiah believed that the exilic community would return one day (29:10-14) and become a faithful people while those remaining in Judah would face a terrible future because they ignored God's visitation.

The Second Exile in 587 B.C.E.

There was a second revolt against Babylonian hegemony over Judah in the late 590s or early 580s. The reasons for this rebellion are unclear though apparently Zedekiah gave into those elements in Judah who considered success foreordained by God. In addition, Egypt's success against Nubia may have impressed Zedekiah and he may have looked to the Pharaoh to come to Judah's aid against Babylon (Jer 37:5; Ezek 17:15; 29:6-7). That help was not forthcoming and Jerusalem had to endure a two-year siege. During the course of the siege an Egyptian army did appear in Palestine, which led to some relief (Jer 37:1-10). Consistent with his previous assessments of the circumstances, Jeremiah advised Zedekiah to submit and sue for peace (Jer 21:1-10). Royal officials arrested the prophet twice. They threatened him with execution but Zedekiah released him and even guaranteed his rations as long as there was any food in the besieged city (Jer 37:16-21).The prophet was arrested a third time and placed into a cistern. Again the king had Jeremiah released; nonetheless he persisted in calling for Zedekiah to surrender to the Babylonians (Jer 38:1-28). As Jerusalem's predicament became more desperate and its eventual fate was clear to all, Jeremiah began speaking about the eventual restoration of the city (Jer 32:1-44). Even though the prophet believed that the city would fall, he believed that God would someday make it possible for the people to live again in the land of their inheritance.

Eventually Jerusalem ran out of provisions and about the same time the Babylonians succeeded in breaching the city's defenses. Zedekiah and his family fled, but the Babylonian military captured them near Jericho. Judah's king was taken to Nebuchadnezzar who condemned his rebellious vassal. He ordered Zedekiah's sons killed in their father's sight. The Babylonians blinded Zedekiah and led him into exile. Other leaders of the Southern Kingdom had to face execution. The temple was looted before the shrine was set afire. All but the poorest were sent into exile (2 Kgs 25:1-21; Jer 39:10-10; 52:1-27; 2 Chron 36:11-21).

Archaeological excavation has revealed evidence that many of the Southern Kingdom's cities, towns and villages suffered destruction during the early part of the 6th century—a destruction that was probably due to Nebuchadnezzar's campaigns.[28] The devastation wrought by the Babylonians in Judah meant severe economic problems for the region. What were important commercial centers become subsistence-level villages. Agriculture again became the area's sole economic resource. Judah suffered many casualties during its wars with Babylon though there is no certain way to determine their numbers. The large group of Judeans who went into exile made the social dislocation even more acute. One effect was a redistribution of wealth since the people of lower socio-economic levels took over the property of the displaced upper classes. Debtors no longer had to deal with pressure from their creditors and the landless could take over the estates of those led off to Babylon (Ezek 11:15).

Unlike the Assyrians, the Babylonians did not resettle the regions they conquered with a new population. Nebuchadnezzar did not even place a Babylonian in charge of Judah; rather, he was content with an administration drawn from the local population. According to 2 Kgs 25:22 and Jer 40:7, Nebuchadnezzar appointed Gedeliah to an office of leadership.[29] Thus Babylon did not annex Judah but allowed it to continue in existence as a vassal state as was the case in the Assyrian period. Gedaliah established his capital at Mizpah, which was just north of Jerusalem in the territory of Benjamin. Though he tried to establish a semblance of normalcy after the fall of Jerusalem, disgruntled remnants of Judah's army assassinated Gedaliah (2 Kgs 25:25-26; Jer 40:13-41:3). The biblical text simply reports the assassination without any comment, but clearly it was a desperate act of nationalistic zealots who wished to reestablish an independent Judean state under a Davidic king—a wholly unrealistic dream. The general population of Judah did not back the assassins and further rebellious steps were not taken. Fearing Babylonian reprisals, many people fled to Egypt, taking with them the unwilling Jeremiah (Jer 41:17-43:7).[30] The conditions in Judah following Gedaliah's murder is difficult to determine since there is very little data that is helpful in historical reconstruction. There was a third exile according to Jeremiah 52:30 in 581 B.C.E., though Gedaliah's assassination took place shortly after the fall of Jerusalem in 587.

Reactions to the Exile

The end of the Judean state, the fall of the Davidic dynasty, the destruction of the Temple, and the exile to Babylon were genuinely shocking experiences for the people of Judah. One response was hope for revenge against Babylon (Isa 47; Jer 51; Ps 137) and against Edom which took a portion of Judah's territory during its time of weakness (Ezek 25:12-14; 35:1-2; Obad; Mal 1:3-5; Lam 4:21-22). It also caused feelings to sorrow and repentance (the Book of Lamentations) probably as a response to the prophetic interpretation of the exile as divine punishment for sin. Another response was a commemorative fast (Zech 7:1-7; 8:1B-19) and the desire reestablish Judah's relationship to God and to return to the land (Iam 3:40-86). The trauma of the exile also provided the impetus for the crystallization of some literary traditions. For example, the Deuteronomistic History took its final form during the exile as did the Priestly History.[31]

Life in Exile[32]

The deportation of the leading citizens of Judah to Babylon under Nebuchadnezzar added to the already large number of Israelites and Judeans who lived outside the boundaries of the old Davidic empire. What happened to most of these deportees is simply not known, though it is possible that the Jewish communities that dot the eastern Mediterranean region outside of Palestine may have been the result of these exiles. Some of them eventually returned to Judah following the fall of Babylon to the Persians in 539 B.C.E., but apparently most exiles never resettled in the territory of the former Southern Kingdom. Besides the deportees in Mesopotamia, there were Judean colonies in Egypt and in some of the states surrounding Judah (Jer 40:11-12; 41:15). In the later development of Jewish faith, the Mesopotamian groups were the most important.

The Situation in Babylon

The treatment accorded to the exiles sent to Babylon differed according to their previous status and role in Judean society. Both kings who were exiles, Jehoiachin and Zedekiah, went to Babylon in chains and lived in confinement. The same was probably true for members of the royal family, leading military officers, and those who were prominent in the two failed rebellions against Babylonian authority. Apparently their captors treated the former royal family of Judah humanely since Babylonian texts refer to supples of food that Jehoiachin, his family, and retainers received.[33] The Deuteronomistic History ends with an enigmatic description of what appears to be some sort of a parole given to Jehoiachin. Besides his release from confinement, he was given "a seat above the seats of the kings who were with him in Babylon" (2 Kgs 25:27-30). What the exact nature of Jehoiachin's new status was is unclear. Beyond this nothing is known of the fate of Judah's former rulers.

The vast majority of exiles were taken to Babylon in order to weaken Judah and thereby lessen the likelihood of still another rebellion. These exiles did nor suffer harsh treatment but had to provide some services for the Babylonian state. The letter which Jeremiah sent to the exiles intimates that they were able to lead a rather normal life in Babylon. It is clear from this text that the exiles had a measure of economic and social freedom:

> Build houses and live in them; plant gardens and eat their produce. Take wives and have sons and daughters; multiply there, and do not decrease. But seek the welfare of the city where I have sent you into exile, and pray to the Lord on its behalf, for in its welfare you will find your welfare (Jer 29:5-7).

The places where the Judean exiles settled were probably cities that had fallen into ruin and that the Babylonians wanted rebuilt.[34] Skilled builders, craftsmen, and artisans among the exiles worked on royal building projects. Similarly the exiles settled in areas that needed agricultural development as the Assyrian Rabshakeh states:

> Make peace with me and come out to me; then every one of you will eat of his own vine, and every one of his own fig tree, and every one of you will drink the water of his own cistern; until I come and take you away to a land like your own land, a land of grain and wine, a land of bread and vineyards, a land of olive trees and honey, that you may live and not die (2 Kgs 18:31-32).[35]

In addition, the Jewish names included in commercial documents from the 6th century in Babylon suggest that the exiles also lived in administrative centers of the empire and engaged in diverse commercial activities. They were able to own property (Jer 29:5) including slaves (Ezra 2:65). The result of this economic freedom was that several exiles became quite wealthy (Ezra 1:6; 2:68-69). Obviously then the exiles were not slaves though their freedom of movement was probably restricted to some extent.

The Judean exiles were not under any external pressure to assimilate to Babylonian religion and culture. During the exile, practices such as circumcision, Sabbath observance and the dietary laws became very important and successfully isolated the Judean exiles from the local culture. While some of the exiles used Babylonian names (e.g., Sheshbazzar [Ezra 1:8] and Zerubbabel and Bilshan [Ezra 2:2]), most of the exiles probably continued to give Hebrew names to their children. The exiles even maintained a modicum of communal structure in Babylon. References to the "elders of the exile" (Jer 29:1) show that traditional forms of communal leadership was probably the rule among the Jewish exiles in Babylon and may even suggest that they were able to have a limited form of self-government according to their traditional patterns. Finally, using Jehoiachin's accession to the throne of Jerusalem to count years shows an unwillingness to acquiesce to the finality of Babylonian domination.

In all likelihood, the exiles were able to practice their ancestral religion. The activity of the prophets Ezekiel and the anonymous prophet whose words make up Isaiah 40-65 is clear evidence of just that. There was, however, pressure to combine the worship of Yahweh with worship of local Babylonian deities—something roundly condemned by Ezekiel who disdainfully refers to Babylonian gods as "dung balls" (14:3).[36] Unfortunately little is known about the features of Yahwistic worship in Babylon. It is not clear whether Babylonian exiles built a temple for themselves in order to continue sacrificial worship. There are two very enigmatic texts which have led some to conclude that the Judeans did just that: Ezekial 11:16 and Ezra 8:17. The former refers to a "temporary sanctuary" and the latter uses the Hebrew word magom (place), which sometimes is a technical term for the temple area. The Ezra text also uses the expression "the house of our God." These two texts, however, do not supply the type of information that allows for anything more than a conjecture about the existence of a temple of Yahweh in Babylon. Of course, the Deuteronomistic History, which has as one of its theological premises the centralization of sacrificial worship in Jerusalem does not envision any temple in Babylon but suggests that the exiles ought to pray in the direction of where the Jerusalem temple had been:

> . . . if they repent with all their mind and with all their heart in the land of their enemies, who carried them captive, and pray to thee toward their land, which thou gavest to their ancestors, the city which thou hast chosen, and the house which I have built for thy name; then hear thou in heaven thy dwelling place their prayer and their supplication . . . " (1 Kgs 8:48-49).

There are those who maintain that the synagogue had it beginnings during the Babylonian exile to deal with the need to continue some form of public worship in the land of exile.[37]

Of course, some cultural assimilation did take place. Some Judean exiles adopted Babylonian names. Aramaic and its distinctive square script began to displace Hebrew and its characteristic script. The Babylonian names for the months replaced those used in Canaan for centuries. No doubt some of the exiles assimilated so completely that they lost their Jewish identity. The achievements of Mesopotamian culture must have impressed the exiles. The material culture of Judah even at the heights of its prosperity did not compare with that of Babylon. The pressures to assimilate were greater on those born in exile since they had no experiential bonds with their ancestral homeland.

A good part of the credit for preventing the total assimilation of the Judean exiles into Babylonian culture must be given to Ezekiel and Deutero-Isaiah. Ezekiel kept alive the hope of an eventual return. He believed that their experience would purge the people of Judah of their infidelity (Ezek 11:14-25). The prophet even drew up an elaborate and somewhat utopian blueprint for life in Judah following the return (Ezek 40-48). The contribution made by the other great exilic prophet was his unremitting monotheism that parodied all other gods and their worship as mere delusion:

> Thus says the Lord, the King of Israel and its Redeemer, the Lord of Hosts: "I am the first and I am the last; beside me there is no god" (Isa 44:6).

The exile lasted until 539 B.C.E. when the Persians under Cyrus brought an end to the Babylonian Empire. Cyrus allowed the peoples resettled by the Babylonians to return to their native lands if they so wished. A small minority of Judeans wished to do so. The Bible presents the problems and achievements of those who returned from exile (see Haggai, Zachariah 1-8, Ezra, Nehemiah, Isaiah 56-66). It considers the return, the reconstruction of the temple and Jerusalem's fortifications, and the religious reforms of Ezra and Nehemiah as events of momentous importance that brought to a close the sad and tragic era of exile.

Summary

After at least three ill-advised revolts against Babylonian hegemony, the fate of the Southern Kingdom was not in doubt. Jerusalem fell, the temple was in ruins, the rule of the Davidic dynasty came to an end and many Judeans went into exile.The conditions of the exile limited the freedom of the exiles yet was not unusually cruel. Though some exiles did assimilate, many preserved their identity as Jews and were willing to return to Judah and re-establish their religious community in their homeland following the victory of Cyrus over Babylon.

5. The Exiles in Egypt

Compared with the predicament of the exiles in Babylon, much less is known about the people of Judah who were living in Egypt. They were not, of course, forced into exile. They sought refuge in Egypt during times of economic and political dislocation in Judah. The only

35

literary sources that illuminate the circumstances in Egypt are Jeremiah 43, 44, and 46 and documents from thearchives of a Jewish military colony at Elephantine.[38] There were other Jewish military colonies in Egypt besides the one at Elephantine: Migdol, Memphis, and Tahpanes (Jer 46:14). The Judean soldiers served as mercenaries protecting Nile commerce for the Egyptians. These colonies included women and children besides the soldiers themselves. Assimilation and intermarriage were not unusual. This meant that some Jews became part of the Egyptian community, but also that some Egyptians became part of the Jewish community. As happened with Judeans in Babylon, some Jews in Egypt were very successful commercially and became quite wealthy. They also were able to rise to high positions in governmental administration. They enjoyed a high degree of autonomy and were able to govern their lives according to their own customs and traditions. They observed distinctive religious practices such as the celebration of Passover and the Sabbath. What is striking about the Elephantine colony was that it had its own temple where people worshipped Yahu (a shortened form of Yahweh) with prayer and sacrifice.[39] The worship of the Judeans in Egypt was syncretistic and that may be the reason whey Jeremiah is quite negative towards members of the Jewish community in Egypt:

> . . . all the men of Judah who are in the land of Egypt shall be consumed by the sword and by famine, until there is an end of them. And those who escape the sword shall return from the land of Egypt to the land of Judah, few in number (Jer 44:27-28).

The temple at Elephantine was destroyed during political unrest in 410 B.C.E. Three years later, the Jews of Elephantine wrote to the governor of Judah for permission to rebuild. The letter also refers to other contacts that this community had with the Jewish community of Jerusalem.[40] Obviously then the Jews in Egypt wished to maintain their contacts with their fellow Jews in Palestine and recognized Jerusalem's authority in religious matters. There does not appear to have been an organized return to Judah from Egypt since the Jews continued to find a comfortable home in Egypt until by the end of the 1st century B.C.E. they made up 12 percent of Egypt's population.

6. The Significance of the Exile for Israel's Faith

In coming to grips with the tragedy of exile, ancient Israel not only believed that it was divine retribution for its infidelity to the covenant, but that if accepted in faith this punishment would result in a revelation of God's love and commitment that would be eternal (Isa 54:9-10; Jer 31:2-3). Once this sad and tragic era was past, God would conclude with Israel a new covenant that would be such that further rebellion simply would not be possible. God was going to write the Torah on the people's heart (Jer 31:31-34). Following the exile, there would be a restoration that would bind Judah to God in an entirely new way (Ezek 36:22-26). Even in exile, Judah had an important function since it played the role of the Lord's servant who is a witness to God's sovereignty to the world (Isa 43:10; 49:6).

There are two prophetic texts that illustrate the importance that the exile was to have in the theological thinking of a restored Judah:

> So, the days are coming—oracle of the Lord—when it shall no longer be said: As the Lord lives who brought up the Israelites from the land of Egypt, but as the Lord lives who brought up the Israelites from the north-land and from the land into which the Lord has driven them. And I will bring them back upon the land which I gave to their ancestors (Jer 16:14-15).

> Remember not the former things, nor consider the things of old. Behold, I am doing a new thing; now it springs forth, do you not perceive it? (Isa 43:18-19).

Both prophets say that the restoration following the exile will eclipse the divine favor shown to Israel through the Exodus.

Other confessional statements are not so grandiose in their evaluations of the exile's meaning, but they affirm God's continuing love for Israel:

> So you gave them into the power of foreign peoples, but in your great mercy you did not make an end of them nor forsake them, for you are a God merciful and gracious (Neh 9:30-31).

Here the return from exile is seen as a continuation of God's love for Israel even though its infidelities should have led to the destruction of the people.

It is possible to understand the exile as a great divide, which Judah had to cross if a new day was to dawn—a day characterized by fidelity. In a sense the exile had to happen for it was the final repudiation by both God and Israel of the evils that had threatened God's relationship with Israel. The exile was the Day of the Lord that prophets such as Amos spoke of (6:18). It was the consequence of Israel's breach of faith. It was as inevitable from a theological perspective as it was from a political perspective.

Above all, the exile was a lesson for ancient Israel about God's sovereignty. Israel cannot treat the land that was its inheritance from God as if it were a mere possession. For God can and has broken all ties with the land and its people (Jer 14:9). Post-exilic piety came to see the people of Israel not as possessors of the land but as no more than resident aliens: "For we are strangers before thee, and sojourners, as all our ancestors were . . ." (1 Chron 29:15).

Finally, there is a line of interpretation which sees the Book of Jonah as an allegory of the exile: Jonah is Judah and the great fish is Babylon. As God led the prophet to the fulfillment of his true mission by his being first swallowed and then regurgitated by the fish, so God was calling Judah back to its mission to the nations through the degradation of the exile. Its infidelity rendered Judah an unfit instrument of blessing. The exile transformed Judah and made it possible once again for it to fulfill the promise made it to migrant ancestor:

God from your country and your kindred and your father's house to the land that I will show you. And I will make of you a great nation, and I will bless you, and make your name great so that you will be a blessing. I will bless those who bless you, and him who curses you I will curse; and by you all the families of the earth shall bless themselves (Gen 12:1-3).

7. Implications for the Pastoral Care of Immigrants

Reflection on the biblical tradition makes it clear that concern for the migrant and the exile is not something peripheral in that tradition. A good portion of the First Testament deals with the concerns of the migrant and the exile. It contains promises made to the migrant ancestors of ancient Israel, Abraham, Isaac, and Jacob. God promises a great posterity and a bountiful land. The people of ancient Israel believed that they were the fulfillment of those promises. Their land became a great sacrament of encounter with their God for it was the revelation of God's love and fidelity. The loss of that land was so threatening that it had the potential for destroying the people God had called into existence in fulfillment of the promises made to the patriarchs. When the loss of the land became not a threat but a reality, the biblical tradition describes the attempts made by the people and their prophets to make some sense out of a disaster and thereby survive it.

The Church has a responsibility to help today's migrants and exiles cope with the dislocation that comes with a life in a new land as the prophets did for the people of ancient Israel. The Church ought to do what is necessary to help the migrants and exiles resist the type of assimilation that eradicates their unique cultural identity, for it was from within their native culture that today's migrants—like those of ancient Israel—came to encounter God. Without those cultural moorings not only is the migrants' identity threatened but so is their life with God. What the Church needs to do through its pastoral ministry to today's migrants and exiles is turn this potentially disastrous experience into a time of grace and recommitment to God. What is especially crucial to note is that the biblical tradition locates the migrant and exile at the very center of its concern. The Church should do likewise.

Notes

1. The story of Jacob and his family and their stay in Egypt (Gen 46-50) to which the Deuteronomic text refers reflects a common occurrence in the relationships between Canaan and Egypt. When the farmers of Canaan suffered through a severe drought and their land could not support them, they went to Egypt where agricultural pursuits were not subject to the climatic vagaries characteristic of Canaan. What the Book of Exodus describes as Egypt's enslavement of Jacob's descendants may have been no more than the usual contribution that foreign residents were expected to make to Egypt's building projects. This may explain Deuteronomy's uncharacteristically beneficent attitude toward Egypt.

2. See James Pritchard, *Ancient Near Eastern Texts Relating to the Old Testament, 3d edition [ANET]* (Princeton, NJ: Princeton University Press, 1975), 199-203, for treaties between the Egyptian and Hittite Empires dating from the Late Bronze Age.

3. Ibid., 245-247.

4. Ibid., 483-490.

5. Ibid., 275.

6. The rulers of the Canaanite city-states had Indo-European names and therefore were not of the same ethnic stock as the semitic groups that they ruled. This may have added to the resentment of the Canaanite peasants toward their rulers.

7. That ancient Israel emerged in the course of a peasants' revolt was first suggested by George E. Mendenhall in "The Hebrew Conquest of Palestine," *Biblical Archeologist* 25 (1962) 66-87 [slightly revised and reprinted in *The Biblical Archeologist Reader 3*, ed. E.F. Campbell, Jr. and D.N. Freedman (Garden City, NY: Doubleday, 1970), 100-120.].

This hypothesis has been developed by Norman K. Gottwald through the use of anthropological and sociological analysis along with a Marxian hermeneutic. See his *The Tribes of Yahweh: A Sociology of the Religion of Liberated Israel, 1250-1050 B.C.E.* (Maryknoll, NY: Orbis, 1979).

Mendenhall has repudiated Gottwald's development of his hypothesis principally because of Gottwald's Marxian analysis, which Mendenhall considers to be an inappropriate projection of modern ideology into biblical antiquity. See his "Ancient Israel's Hyphenated History," in *Palestine in Transition*, ed. D.N. Freedman and D.F. Graf (Sheffield: Almond Press, 1983), 91-103.

For a discussion and evaluation of the various hypotheses regarding the Israelite settlement in Canaan, see Marvin L. Chaney, "Ancient Palestinian Peasant Movements and the Formation of Premonarchic Israel," in *Palestine in Transition*, pp. 39-94, and *The Journal for the Study of the Old Testament* 7 (1978). The entire issue of this journal was devoted to a discussion of the settlement question.

8. Volkmar Fritz describes the relationship between the Israelite settlers and the indigenous population of Canaan as a "symbiosis." See his "Conquest or Settlement?," *Biblical Archaeologist* 50/2 (June 1987) 84-100.

9. This expression may have a mythological background referring to the land as paradise. See Magnus Ottosson, "*'erets*" *Theological Dictionary of the Old Testament [TDOT]*, ed. G.J. Botterweck and H. Ringgren (Grand Rapids, MI: Eerdmans, 1974), 1:403.

10. The description of the land as "broad" does not refer to its geographical extent but to the unlimited possibilities it offers to the migrants who settle in it.

11. The biblical account of the breakup of the Davidic Empire was written from a perspective that was quite sympathetic to the Davidic dynasty and so it portrayed the breakup as resulting from an act of rebellion against the divine will. The two kingdoms are presented as an anomaly. In reality, the group that made up the Davidic-Solomonic Empire were returning to a semblance of their original independence. Actually the coalition that David and Solomon managed to keep together was more of an anomaly.

12. A succession of empires have ruled the region almost continuously until the beginning of this century: Assyria (8th-6th cent. B.C.E.); Babylon (6th cent. B.C.E.); Persian (4th cent. B.C.E.); Hellenistic Empires (4th-2nd cent. B.C.E.); Rome-Byzantium (1st cent. B.C.E.-7th cent. C.E.); Arabs (7-16th cent. C.E.); Ottoman Turks (16th-20th cent. C.E.). From 164-63 B.C.E. the Jews were independent under the rule of the Hasmoneans.

13. For a presentation of these details see any history of Israel, e.g., J. Maxwell Miller and John H. Hayes, *A History of Ancient Israel* (Philadelphia: Westminster, 1986), 314-339.

14. The Deuteronomistic History is the story of Israel in its land from the settlement to the Babylonian Exile. It is made up of the Books of Joshua, Judges, Samuel, and Kings. The Book of Deuteronomy supplies the basic theological principles used to interpret Israel's history. Martin Noth was the first to propose the Deuteronomistic theory. See his *Deuteronomistic History*, Journal for the Study of the Old Testament, Supplement 15 (Sheffield: University of Sheffield, 1981). Though there have been a number of developments of Noth's theory since it was first proposed in 1943, most interpreters use Noth's theory as a working hypothesis in their own study of these books.

15. Pritchard, *ANET*, 284-285. The deportation that Sargon refers to here was actually the second one imposed upon Israel. The first took place during the revolt of the Syro-Ephraimite coalition against Assyria. Tiglath-Pileser III led the campaign against the coalition from 734-732 B.C.E. As a result of his victories, he deported a number of people from Gilead (1 Chron 5:6,26). Tiglath-Pileser's own inscriptions assert that he deported a number of people from eight cities in Galilee, see *ANET*, 282-284.

16. According to 2 Kgs 17:6, the deportees from Israel were resettled in "Halah, and on the Habor, the river of Gozan, and in the cities of the Medes."

17. Ezra 4:10 calls Ashurbanipal "Osnappar.

18. For a discussion of the origins of Samaritanism, see R.J. Coggins, *Samaritans and Jews* (Atlanta: John Knox Press, 1975), and Frank Moore Cross, "Aspects of Samaritan and Jewish History in the Late Persian and Hellenistic Times," *Harvard Theological Review* 59 (1966) 201-211.

19. This conflict between the Jews and the Samaritans continued into the New Testament period as is evident from the Gospels (e.g., John 4:9,20). There is still a small group of Samaritans left, many of whom live in the city of Nablus near the site of ancient Samaria. They follow their own distinctive religious traditions.

20. See S. Talmon, "Polemics and Apology in Biblical Historiography--2 Kings 17:24-41," in *The Creation of Sacred Literature: Composition and Redaction of the Biblical Text*, ed. R.E. Friedman (Berkeley: University of California, 1981), 57-68.

21. 2 Kgs 23:15-20 has Josiah engaging in a sweep of the former Northern Kingdom's territory in order to destroy the Yahwistic shrines at Bethel and other cities in the course of his attempt to centralize Yahwistic worship in Jerusalem. Josiah's move against these shrines took place some one hundred years *after* the fall of the Northern Kingdom.

22. Many different ethnic groups have been identified with the Lost Tribes, from the people of Great Britain to Native Americans. Of course, all these identifications are fanciful and without any basis in fact. See L.I. Rabinowitz, "Ten Lost Tribes," *Encyclopedia Judaica*, 15:1003-1006.

23. See A. Malamat, "Exile, Assyrian," Encyclopedia Judaica, 6:1036.

24. No historical texts have been found from the reign of Shalmeneser who ruled Assyria during the final revolt of Israel. Tobit's usefulness as a source for reconstructing the situation faced by the exiles from the North is questionable. It is not even familiar with the sequence of Assyrian kings (1:15).

25. *ANET*, 288.

26. Both Dan 1:1-2 and 1 Esdras 1:39 also make this assertion, though both are probably dependent on the text from Chronicles and therefore provide no independent confirmation.

27. See Pritchard, *ANET*, 564.

28. Miller and Hayes, *History of Ancient Israel*, 416-417.

29. The exact nature of this office is not certain though it has been suggested that Gedaliah was made king by the Babylonians but that the Deuteronomistic editors of the Book of Kings did not wish to reveal his true title out of concern for the promises made to David (2 Sam 7). See Ibid., 423.

30. Egypt had frequently been a place of refuge for the pople of Palestine even before the problems following the assassination of Gedaliah. See Isa 11:11; Jer 46:14. Even before the problems with Babylon there was a sizeable number of people from Judah residing in Egypt. Judean troops wnt to Egypt during the reign of Manasseh. See Pritchard, *ANET*, 294. The Letter of Aristeas (par. 13) asserts that here were Judean mercenaries in the Egyptian army in the 7th century B.C.E.

31. For a discussion of the different literary responses to the fall of Jerusalem and the exile see Peter R. Ackroyd, *Exile and Restoration: A study of Hebrew Thought of the Sixth Century B.C.*, Old Testament Library (Philadelphia: Westminster, 1968).

32. There is very little biblical material that describes life in exile. The primary sources are the Books of Jeremiah, Ezekiel, and Isaiah 40-55. The two historical sources covering the period (the Deuteronomistic History and the Chronicler's History) do not concern themselves with the situation outside of Palestine. There are some nonbiblical texts that have shed some light on the role and status of Jews living outside Palestine. For a description of these nonbiblical sources, see Miller and Hayes, *History of Ancient Israel*, 431-432.

33. Pritchard, *ANET*, 308.

34. Some of the places where the Judean exiles lived were Tel Melah (Ezra 2:59), Tel Harsha (Neh 7:61), and Tel Abib (Ezek 3:15). The word "tel" in these names refers to the artificial mound created by the debris of cities abandoned over a long period of time.

35. Though these words are placed on the lips of an Assyrian official, they probably reflect the citation of the Babylonian exile which was part of the Deuteronomist's own experience.

36. The translation of *gillulim* as "idols" is correct though it fails to reflect the scatological metaphor that the prophet uses some forty times when referring to Babylonian gods.

37. Joseph Gutmann, "Synagogue Origins: Theories and Facts," in *Ancient Synagogues: The State of the Research*, ed. Joseph Gutmann, Brown Judaic Studies 22 (Chico, CA: Scholars Press, 1981), 1. Practically nothing is known about synagogues until the 1st century C.E. There are some earlier references but these come from Egypt in the hellenistic period. See Lee I. Levine, "The Second Temple Synagogue: The Formative Years," in *The Synagogue in Late Antiquity*, ed. Lee I. Levine (Philadelphia: American Schools of Oriental Research, 1987), 9.

38. Pritchard, *ANET*, 491-492, 548-549. Though these documents date from the Persian period (late 6th to the late 4th centuries B.C.E.), they are useful in understanding the position of Jewish exiles in Egypt during the exilic period as well.

39. The Jewish community at Elephantine either did not know the Deuteronomic prohibition of sacrificial worship outside of the "one place" God has chosen in Canaan (Deut 12:1,10) or its members did not feel bound by it. In any case, there is a text in Isaiah (19:19) that speaks about an altar to Yahweh in Egypt and apparently endorses sacrificial worship outside of Palestine. Perhaps this tradition was more well known that the Deuteronomic prohibition.

40. Pritchard, *ANET*, 492.

The Incorporation of Immigrants into the American Catholic Community (1790-1990)

Dolores Liptak, RSM, Ph.D.

When Balboa viewed the American continent from the Straits of Darien, he saw its narrowest point, bounded by both Atlantic and Pacific. Perhaps to him it appeared a diminished thing. But for the European explorers and adventurers, especially those from Portugal, Spain, England, or France who had sought its shores from the sixteenth century onward, it was an endless land, sparsely populated and underdeveloped: a land full of challenge, full of promise. For them, its vast network of waterways and river highways meant access to treasure; even its deserts led to the rocky promise of precious minerals. From sea to shining sea, from highland to the Gulf Stream waters, from sandy shore to prairies and oceans white with foam, it presented a world ready for the taking. For the missionaries who accompanied these adventurous bands, it meant even more: the planting of the faith, the harvest of souls. And so it has been for some five hundred years; as Pope John Paul recently reminded his San Antonio audience, our continent continues to be a crossroads which beckons succeeding generations in search of treasure, freedom, even faith expression.

If some Americans today seem to view the promise of the land according to the myopic vision of Balboa and if an unwanted stream of migrants and refugees now tends to apologize for intruding, there was a time in which even the poorest immigrants, regardless of aims, were received with far greater warmth and grace. Especially during the century after 1820 which marked the large-scale development of new world industrialization, over thirty million Europeans alone sought out and settled in the rapidly expanding United States. With each succeeding decade, furthermore, more and more of the newcomers came—not because of the lure and promise which motivated those earlier voyagers—but in order to escape the bitter economic or political realities which had beset them in their native lands. In the last forty years of that period, twenty-three million of these arrived mostly from southern and eastern Europe. The largest number overcrowded the new world's industrial and commercial northeast and middle west. Some moved farther west, reinforcing the immigrant character of the frontier as well. No longer predominantly from Ireland and Germany, these so-called "new" immigrants were to change the face of American society, creating a widespread network of immigrant institutions and implanting a complex ethnic character upon the Catholic Church in the United States. In the southwest, a Hispanic culture perdured despite Yankee power and an ecclesiastical administration largely evangelized by immigrant clergy. As today's Catholics face the latest social justice issues of the sanctuary movement and immigration legislation, it is essential that they consider the monumental role played by these immigrant forebears in the making of the Catholic culture in the United States.

The Catholic Church in the United States was, from the start, a church shaped by ethnic leaders and textured with ethnic strands. After 1790, its rapid development, especially in the northeast and midwest, came largely as a result of the increase of immigration from Germany, France, Ireland, and, to a limited degree, from the Caribbean and Azores islands. For the native-born John Carroll (1735-1815), appointed first Bishop of Baltimore in 1789, the need to supply pastors for a church which had not yet been able to develop a native clergy was, undoubtedly, a serious concern. In fact, from the start, Carroll wrestled with the uncomfortable fact that, outside of his native Maryland, most of his fellow Catholics—clergy and laity alike—did not present the kind of appearance which he thought essential for the building of an American Catholic Church. But he had no alternative. Almost all of his first clergy were emigres who had either fled the French revolution or were mission-minded priests who had voluntarily left their European homelands for the sake of ministry. Six of the emigres he early appointed his co-bishops. In 1808, Benedict J. Flaget (1763-1851), as Bishop of frontier Bardstown, and Jean de Cheverus (1768-1836), as Bishop of Yankee Boston, began administrations that transformed the Catholic image in their respective episcopal regions. Another six rendered service as remarkable in missions extending from Kentucky, Michigan, and Indiana to points farther west and northwest.[1]

In a generally anti-papist, anti-ethnic climate charged with ethnic overtones and exacerbated by the foreign background of most of the presiding clergy, it is not surprising that Carroll continued to express his earlier hope that "all would lay aside national distinctions & attachments & strive to form not Irish, or English, or French Congregations & Churches, but Catholic-American Congregations and Churches."[2] It is also easy to understand why some of the early missionaries, especially those of German or Slavic background, readily anglicized their names. Thus, the Russian Prince, Demitri Gallitzin, changed his name to "Smith" while the German missionary, Father Steinmeyer, preferred to be known as "Farmer." Still Carroll and his fellow bishops came to recognize—albeit reluctantly—that without an immigrant clergy and a committed membership that also reflected a rich ethnic Catholic heritage there would be little chance for the Catholic Church to maintain even a tenuous hold in this Protestant stronghold. Despite attempts to downplay the immigrant background of both clergy and membership and to champion democratic traditions wherever possible, Catholic leaders knew they had to compromise American expectations for the realities of a church led and peopled primarily by immigrants.

As much as forty years after its establishment (i.e., 1830) the foreign appearance of the Catholic Church still remained distinct. At that point, more than half of the 232 priests were still immigrants, mainly French, German, or Irish-born. During the same period, newly-organized religious congregations of women had also begun to develop rapidly. Even if three of the original eight native foundations had native-born co-founders—the Sisters of Charity of St. Joseph, in Emmitsburg, Maryland, as well as the Kentucky-based Sisters of Charity of Nazareth, and the Sisters of Loretto—they, too, showed all the signs of European influence. From the start, these congregations were to derive many of their recruits from the available ranks of transplanted daughters of Erin. After 1830, moreover, communities originally founded in France, Germany, and Ireland began to share the adventure of the

44

American mission; they, too, quickly expanded their membership in the new land. Together with increasing numbers of German- and Irish-American Catholics, the nation's bishops, clergy, and religious women shared in the tremendous work of building the U.S. Catholic Church. Their multi-ethnic diversity became an unmistakable, distinguishing factor identifying both the leader-ship and membership of the church.

By the 1850s, moreover, the American Catholic Church had taken on a certain numerical and geographic significance which newly threatened the Protestant elite. It had, in fact, become the largest single religious denomination in the United States, its membership more than a million and a half members, its churches and missions stretching from Florida to Texas and California and from Maine to Oregon. If the Church had earlier been attractive to some Protestants, especially Episcopalians, because of its claims of unity and tradition, most of its uniqueness now seemed lost in a maze of geographic and ethnic sprawl. A renewed, virulent anti-Catholicism, politically fuelled by Native-Americanism and Know-nothingism resulted, underscored dramatically by Isaac Hecker, the impressionable son of Prussian immigrants and future founder of the Paulist community, when he wrote:

> I am not prepared to enter the Roman Catholic Church at present. The Roman Catholic Church is not natural with us, hence it does not meet our wants, nor does it fully understand and sympathize with the experience and disposition of our people. It is principally made up of adopted and foreign individuals.[3]

The Civil War proved the first substantial reprieve for Catholics as the patriotism of Irish-American regiments and nursing sisters dealt nativism a substantial blow. Anti-Catholic sentiments were never again to hold sway either to the degree or to the extent that they had in the pre-war years. More than that, the southern Irish- and Anglo-Catholic elite community, once personified by the Carrolls, Fenwicks, Mattinglys, or Spaldings, gave way to a northern predominance involving Irish- or German-Americans whose hard work and business ability could bring them wealth and reputation. The center of Catholic episcopal strength also shifted north; moreover, its Irish complexion became more obvious as well. More than half of the nation's hierarchy in 1866 had Irish backgrounds; sixteen of the bishops present at the second Plenary Council, held that year, were Irish or Anglo-Irish Americans; another nine were Irish immigrants. The once dominant French now numbered only twelve, or one-fourth of the bishops; only three of the bishops were German. Representing over three million members in the 1860s and expanding by millions each decade, both church leaders and members reflected the ever-strengthening Gaelic-American appearance.[4]

Especially after the 1880s, however, as Irish-Americans gathered distinction and influence, especially on the episcopal level, other dramatic changes were taking place. With the floodtides of immigration shifting to southern and eastern Europe, the church's newest membership began to reflect a more multi-ethnic appearance. Then, too, the elementary dynamics of church organization and policy formation began to undergo sophistication and nuance. As newcomers sensed their less-favored status and sought recourse, they perceived little sympathy for their plight. Only among Europe's Catholic leadership did their disadvantage seem worthy of redress. Following the historic example set by the German-Americans, these newer immigrant priests and laity made demands of the bishops in the dioceses in which they had settled for special consideration. If their repeated efforts failed to achieve a fair hearing, they brought their concerns to church leaders abroad. How would a predominantly Irish-American church react to their complaint? Were they ready to accommodate the newcomer according to their needs and on their own terms?

The Third Plenary Council, which met in Baltimore in 1884, marked the first occasion in which a joint meeting of the American bishops had been called upon officially to discuss jointly the problems attendant upon immigrants—a matter of particular concern to the Holy See because of grievances presented with regard to Italian immigrants. Typical of first approaches to difficult considerations, and despite some reflection on the pastoral care of immigrants, the bishops demurred. In fact, the one chapter of the Council's *Acts and Decrees* that dealt with immigrants did not even address such issues as the authorization of parishes for immigrants. Instead, the bishops spoke of the plight of immigrants and made general suggestions, such as having "prudent priests" made available, devising a seminary education that included the teaching at least one other modern language, and providing religious education for the children of immigrants. The reasons why this meeting of bishops failed to address adequately the matter of incorporating immigrants were complicated by other problems, not the least of which was the missionary status of the church, which called into question the very right of bishops to structure the local church. Thus, the bishops preferred to view the problem of immigrants as "diocesan" concerns that could be dealt with in their respective dioceses.[5]

But the sensitive issues remained. In particular, the bishops were fully aware of the diverse needs of immigrants. They were also personally bothered by what they considered unwarranted complaints about their own handling of the so-called "immigrant problem"; some were annoyed by the Holy See's suggestion that the needs of Italian immigrants, in particular, were not being properly met. Realistically, the bishops knew that the Roman concern expressed too narrow an understanding of the condition facing immigrants to the United States and underscored a lack of comprehension of American diocesan arrangements. More, since the greater majority of the bishops were already first or second generation Irish-Americans, the criticism seemed almost a reproach. Had it not been their special Irish-American gifts of organization as well as their stubborn tenacity to the faith during times of nativist excess that had made possible the present favorable reputation of the church in the first place? For other church pioneers as well, including the few French-, German-, and Spanish-American prelates represented at the council, attention to the Italian problem also seemed exaggerated. Sensitive to their own immigrant background, these prelates found the emphasis on the needs of any one particular ethnic group unwarranted. Besides, as Wilmington's Bishop, Thomas A. Becker (1832-1899), put it, another sensitive issue was at stake: "It is a very delicate matter to tell the Sovereign Pontiff how utterly faithless the specimens of his country coming here really are."[6]

In addressing the Roman proposal, therefore, the bishops chose to join it to the actual situation of massive Catholic immigration. As a consequence, they implicitly validated what was already in existence: the establishment of parishes specifically for separate immigrant groups within the boundaries of territorial parishes. These "national" or "language" parishes, they admitted, were parochial accommodations which suited the situation; by means of them the new waves of immigrants found religious solace; in such churches they were able to express their faith through their own language and customs as full-fledged members of the U.S. Catholic church.

The national parish was, indeed, a *fait accompli* in several dioceses Since the first generations of American Catholics, especially in the northeast and midwest, immigrants who insisted upon special status had been allowed to develop their own parishes and, wherever possible, priests of the same ethnic background had been assigned. Within these parishes, the language and customs of the gathered community were basic elements of devotional life and worship. Depending upon the numbers of newcomers, the strength and viability of the request, the availability of priests who could relate to the immigrant group in question, but, most importantly, depending upon the perspective of the bishop of the diocese in which the newcomers were seeking special status, the development of parishes for immigrants had occurred. This was particularly the case in those dioceses where there were large German populations; in other instances, *de facto* French-Canadian congregations had been organized.

Philadelphia's Germans had been the first ethnic group to convince the early church of the need for national parishes. Thus, Bishop John Carroll had permitted the establishment of Holy Trinity parish for the Germans in 1789. From that time on, German-Americans aggressively pursued similar tactics in other areas of the country. Because of the cooperation of the Irish- born Bishop of Cincinnati, John Baptist Purcell (1800-1883), for example, the first parish for Germans in the west was established in 1833; within a generation, a dozen more autonomous German national parishes had been founded there. As early as 1842, moreover, Purcell was also pursuing his concept that a seminary be established in Germany to train Germans for the American mission. St. Louis provided still another early nineteenth century example of accommodation to Germans through national parish development; by 1842, separate churches for Germans—albeit subject to the authority of the territorial parish—has been organized. The sense of subordination implicit in this latter model, however, only highlighted the reason why the status of national parishes needed further consideration by the later decades of the nineteenth century.[7]

By the 1890s, then, a general plan of national parish development had emerged to satisfy differing immigrant needs. But its primary goal was the preservation of the faith. In order to provide more effectively for Catholic immigrants, furthermore, church leaders strove sedulously to avoid any show of preference or alignment. Within their respective dioceses, they attempted to develop strategies of accommodation suitable for every group. Increasingly necessary because of massive immigration and outside pressures, the establishment of national parishes were founded within the territorial boundaries of other parishes; however, they remained exceptions to the ordinary rule for church organization. Moreover, their establishment remained a diocesan concern, the direct outcome of collaboration between bishop and the immigrant clergy or laity who initiated the request. But, once founded, national parishes became symbolic of the accord reached by the American Church and developed within dioceses. By this means American bishops gave evidence that they at least comprehended the "immigrant problem" and were willing to share in the creation of a multiethnic church which could be viewed as neither "American" or "foreign."

A cursory reading of U.S. Catholic directories for these critical years of immigration reveals that this national parish alternative to the regular territorial parish model proliferated in the turn-of-the-century years, especially in the urban northeast and midwest. This is true not only in such key immigrant centers as New York, Pennsylvania, Massachusetts, Ohio, Illinois, Michigan, and Wisconsin, but it also became a significant factor of development in the smaller states which bordered metropolitan port-cities, especially Connecticut, Rhode Island, and New Jersey. Thus, in the major industrial areas of the nation, distinctively designed, even grandiose, parish churches emerged, sometimes within blocks of one another, as the Catholic sign of the ethnic transformation. Complete with wayside shrines or ornate statuary, they became focal points for a variety of immigrant communities. Around these churches, social work and educational facilities, staffed largely by religious congregations of women or men who had also emigrated, became the means of social, intellectual, and spiritual growth for the immigrant membership. In this setting, the germ of migrant and refugee policy for the Catholic Church was planted. Within the ethno-cultural milieu of these dioceses, the pastoral strategies that the nation's bishops had been asked to consider jointly in 1884 began to be separately developed.

By 1910 estimates, there were already 408 Polish, 223 Italian, 188 French, 85 Slovak, 54 Bohemian (Czech), and 55 Lithuanian national parishes, functioning largely in the northeast sector of the United States. This figure does not include those parishes in which more than one foreign language was used or in which some foreign language services were interspersed with English. According to the United States Census (1916), there were 2,230 churches nationwide which used foreign languages exclusively, with another 2,535 in which both English and foreign languages were spoken. By the 1930s, there were 2,000 German-language parishes, 1,700 Polish parishes, and more than 1,000 Italian parishes. In at least half of these parishes, furthermore, schools had also been established; among Poles and such less numerous but equally convinced minorities as the Slovaks and French-Canadians, the number of schools ran particularly high. As a result, the establishment of churches and schools became the means of measuring the breadth and depth of Catholic ethnicity within a given region. The immigrant concern over establishing schools, ironically, concurred with the major theme of the 1884 Plenary Council, which had reviewed the practice of establishing national parishes but had paid particular emphasis on the need to secure Catholic educations for their children.[8]

But such statistics merely indicate that Catholic leaders were willing to assume responsibility with regard to assisting immigrants in developing their own institutions. They do not indicate the degree to which the majority Irish-American Catholic leaders either empathized or willingly initiated ways of assistance, nor does it clarify whether newcomers themselves felt incorporated as co-equal members of the church. Were there other measures taken during these crucial turn-of-the-century decades so that immigrants sensed belonging as well? The remainder of this paper will review some of the explicit ways in which a predominantly Irish-American Catholic leadership attempted to go beyond rhetorical statements of support and expediency in complying with immigrant requests so that their actions conveyed a deeper understanding of an appropriate Catholic response to these strangers in the land.

The Archdiocese of Chicago provides one example of a diocese which persuasively addressed the issue of accommodating immigrants during the crucial years of massive immigration. This was especially the case during the episcopacies of two Irish-Americans, Bishops Patrick A. Feehan (1829-1902) and James Edward Quigley (1855-1915). Under Bishop Feehan, a network of national parishes, especially for the amazingly large numbers of Slavic newcomers in the Chicago environs, was created, and priests avidly sought. Much of the initial phase of Polish development was the product of cooperative action between the bishop and the Reverend Vincent Barzynski, a Resurrectionist immigrant pastor, who was encouraged by Feehan to create what became a gigantic community-parish system in the city itself. Despite criticism and problems emanating from the nationalistic posturing of some German- and Irish-American groups, as well as threats of schism by some Poles, Feehan maintained an even-handed policy which fostered resolution of conflict among immigrants and general respect for the cultural traditions of his diverse Catholic population. Because of his patience during disputes which ultimately did divide the Polish community into competing parishes and caused tension among German congregations, he succeeded in gaining the respect of ethnic leaders who accepted his "fatherly admonitions," and even praised him for his "kindly advice" and willingness to confront the recalcitrance of schismatic groups.[9]

Both Feehan's policies and disposition toward understanding continued during the administration of his successor, Bishop Quigley, who gained the title "Bishop of the immigrants" largely because of his perfecting the coalition of nationalities begun by Feehan. Under Quigley, church policy was to "treasure diversity as a mosaic, because cultural differences reflect the various features of Christ himself."[10] During his administration, the Polish Catholic population alone more than doubled to 230,000; this immigrant group was enabled to develop twenty-three national parishes—thirteen of these administered to by the same religious community. The example of successful incorporation proved instructive for other immigrants as well; by the end of his tenure, there were more Irish immigrants living in Chicago than in Dublin, more Poles than in Warsaw, more Bohemians than in Prague, and more Italians than in Pisa. In fact, twenty distinct nationality groups, including Lithuanians, Croatians, and Slovenes, developed churches and increased rapidly. But it was not enough for Quigley to establish ethnic parishes, schools, and other organizations or to seek out immigrant clergy; his interaction with immigrants clearly proved his deep respect for them as well as his desire to build up their sense of belonging as American Catholics. Sensitive to the complaints of Polish Catholics that there had never been a Polish member of the clergy among the ranks of the hierarchy, for example, Quigley initiated the move to nominate a Polish-American as bishop; it was largely because of his continuing efforts in this regard that the Polish immigrant Paul P. Rhode was appointed auxiliary Bishop of

Chicago in 1908—a post in which he remained for seven years until his appointment as ordinary of the Diocese of Green Bay, Wisconsin.

The kind of leadership provided by both Feehan and Quigley made a significant difference both within the Archdiocese of Chicago and beyond. Its national parishes functioned as "corridors to the future" in which the Catholic faith of immigrants was conserved culturally intact until immigrants could adjust to the new American environment.[11] As a result of their episcopal efforts, ethnic pride continues to typify Chicago's Catholics. In fact, despite the development of tensions, even schism, and despite subsequent efforts on the part of Cardinal George Mundelein (1872-1939) to break down national boundaries among Chicago's Catholics, the acceptance of pluralism inaugurated under Feehan and Quigley managed to prevail to such an extent that, even to this day, Chicago's national parishes have been cited as major factors in the continuing fidelity of its Catholic population.

Newark, New Jersey, is another diocese where the evidence is clear that constructive episcopal action from the nineteenth century made an important difference for immigrants and led to solid growth for the church. A German-American, Winand Michael Wigger (1841-1901), who presided over the diocese from 1881 until his death in 1901, set the tone: he consistently looked for ways to prove by his actions that immigrants not only should be given special status in his diocese but that they should receive the same respectful treatment given to other Catholics by both clergy and laity. In affairs beyond the diocese, Wigger publicly championed aid for immigrants; in 1883, he became the first president of the St. Raphael Society, the American branch of an international immigrant aid society especially aimed at improving the situation of German immigrants. With his assistance, the St. Leo House was established in New York City specifically as a Catholic hostel for immigrants. But it was on the diocesan level that Wigger was able to work consistently to convey his interest in, and concern for, immigrants. One of his first episcopal acts, in fact, related to this desire: the conversion of the parish school hall in Newark into a temporary chapel for Italian immigrants. Repeatedly Wigger acknowledged his deep commitment to, and anxiety over, the impoverished conditions of the Italians. To assist immigrants materially and spiritually, he not only saw to the establishing of several parishes for Italians but he even insisted upon the founding of three parochial schools. Over five hundred Italian children attended Catholic schools in the Newark area alone by 1900—a particularly impressive fact in the face of historical evidence that Italian-American communities did not lend full support to the concept of parochial education until after the First World War.[12]

Just as Wigger watched carefully over his Italian population, he sought ways to assist other immigrant groups as well. Because of his persistence, Polish immigrants also became convinced that Wigger was actively concerned for their welfare. As a sign of support, for example, he early made it a practice of attending their organizing meetings. According to Polish clergy of the diocese, Wigger actively participated in discussions and encouraged them in their search for appropriate property. As Polish communities developed, moreover, Wigger followed their progress, frequently offered the liturgy, and joined them for the dedication of their churches. He also tried to inculcate the same attitude among the diocesan clergy. When the Irish-American pastor of St. Nicholas in Passaic welcomed Polish immigrants within his own parish and then supported them in their efforts to establish a parish of their own, Wigger was among the first to express his gratitude. Later, he encouraged the same priest to recruit Polish children to attend his parochial school. Greek-rite Catholics, including Ruthenians, as well as such less numerous Roman Catholic immigrants as the Slovaks, Hungarians, and Lithuanians, also found a receptive climate for their efforts to establish themselves in New Jersey. In fact, with his co-operation, Elizabeth's tiny Lithuanian community was able to establish what would be designated its pioneer national parish in the United States.

By the time of Wigger's death in 1901, the multi-ethnic diversity of the Newark diocese was well established. From a diocese which had no national parishes for its new immigrant Catholics, there were thirty-five for these newcomers: nine for the Italians, four for the Polish, three for Slovaks, two for Greek-rite Catholics, and one each for Lithuanian and Hungarian immigrants. During the twenty years of his administration, the tiny diocese had grown to number 362,000 Catholics. An eight-fold increase over a fifty-year span, this was undoubtedly the result of immigrants' search of work. But would New Jersey's Catholic census have been as large if the thirty-five language parishes that were established during Wigger's episcopacy had not materialized? Would Catholicism in New Jersey have been so strengthened if the performance of the bishop and his clergy was as questionable as that which motivated anti-Catholic maneuverings on the part of other churchmen in the APA hysteria of the 1890s? Evidently, Wigger had begun a trend that would, in fact, characterize the diocese under his Irish-American successors. The pattern of national parish development which continued under them was a clear indication that his perspectives about immigrants was understood as contributing to the good of the church. His policies, in fact, remained diocesan guidelines. Thus, during the twenty-five years of Bishop John J. O'Connor's administration (1855-1927), an average of two national parishes was added per year. Under O'Connor's successor, Thomas J. Walsh (1873-1952), the Diocese of Newark's serious commitment of assisting Italian immigrants and the newer minorities was further extended.[13]

Walsh clearly took the initiative in finding ways to ease the way of the diocese's newest immigrants. His sponsorship of a struggling group of Italian women religious, the *Maestre Pie Filippini* (Religious Teachers Filippini), was to make a critical difference not only for the Italian immigrants of the Diocese of Newark but beyond. As Bishop of Trenton (1918-1928), Walsh had already become convinced of the contribution these sisters could make to the Italian community. Especially after he took charge of Newark, he not only became the benefactor of the congregation in many ways but he guided the establishment of an Americans headquarters so that the sisters could more freely provide educational and social services for Italians. Walsh's concerns embraced other minority groups as well; he was responsible for important outreach programs on behalf of the diocese's newly settled Hispanic and Black Catholics. Because of his endeavors, large-scale evangelization took place. Not only were six parishes or parish centers for Blacks established during Walsh's administration but great increases of membership among Blacks were recorded. In 1935, Walsh was singly honored as being the first American bishop to receive a member of the

Black community into the church—this when he baptized the thousandth convert at Queen of Angels Black Catholic parish. This same concern for the welfare of the diocese's Black Catholics was greatly expanded during the episcopacy of Peter L. Gerety (1912-   ) when he became Bishop of Newark in 1972.[14]

Since the days of Bishop Wigger, the Newark diocese had grown stronger as a result of its attentiveness to both European and other ethnic minority concerns. As indications of this, as early as the 1930s the diocese could point not only to an impressive number of national parishes among a population still largely Irish-American but to high numbers of conversions, especially among Blacks. It could also illustrate that incorporation of immigrants had occurred even in the ranks of the diocesan clergy: almost 19 percent were of the same immigrant background as were the newest European immigrants in the diocese. Perhaps the highest percentage of any diocese in the United States at that time, this statistic regarding the ethnic diversity of diocesan personnel represented the truest sign of the commitment to incorporation of immigrant minorities into the mainstream of the church.[15]

Few other dioceses, however, were to develop an episcopal policy as committed to immigrants as the one which began to develop as early as the 1860s in the Diocese of Hartford, Connecticut. First initiated by two of its Irish-American bishops, Francis Patrick McFarland (1819-1874) and Lawrence J. McMahon (1835-1893), it would take firm shape under the inspiration of Michael Tierney (1839-1908). To the formation of national parishes already in practice, Tierney added other important ways of assuring immigrants that they were integral parts of the diocese. Under this creative bishop, the recruitment and training of priests to serve the various ethnic groups and the celebration of ethnicity by means of both the preached and written word became important features of a distinct immigrant program.[16]

Almost immediately upon assuming the episcopate in 1894, Bishop Tierney began a series of measures designed to insure the incorporation of ethnics into the Diocese of Hartford. To find priests to assist the Polish membership of the Hartford dioceses, for example, Tierney encouraged Polish pastors to recruit fellow Polish clergy and corresponded with Polish religious communities both in the United States and abroad. In 1903 he travelled extensively throughout Europe in search of either seminarians or clergy; during that visit, he managed to persuade one Polish-based religious congregation, the Vincentians, to establish parishes in his diocese. Further, he encouraged immigrant seminarians who were studying in American dioceses to consider joining the Diocese of Hartford and he sought ways to provide a broader education for his own seminarians. Each year he assigned some priestly candidates to selected central and eastern European seminaries at Tarnow, Cracow, Lemberg, Eichstadt, Guyla-Fehervar, and Budapest as well as to less renowned provincial Italian seminaries in Bedonia, Piacenza, and Nepi. Blessed with an abundance of Irish-American seminarians, he utilized American seminaries in the same way, sending some even to the Polish seminary of Saints Cyril and Methodius (then in Detroit) or otherwise encouraging them to develop the tools of language and cultural study for future pastoral ministry. Still other students were assigned to major seminaries in Louvain, Issy, and Rome. There, in the style of his contemporaries, he attempted to influence European seminarians to join his diocese as well. His aim in every case was to develop a corps of priests, regardless of ethnic background, who would be familiar with both the language and culture of the diocese's newest membership so that they could assist immigrant clergy in their work among immigrants. Except for a brief period during the First World War, the assignment of seminarians to many of these schools continued well into the 1930s.

Besides the concerted effort of training personnel on the theologate level along these specialized lines, Tierney had locally-based strategies for relating to the expanding multi-ethnic population in Connecticut. In 1987, he established a minor seminary (high school and first two years of college) in Hartford for beginning diocesan candidates where the teaching of German, Italian, and French was particularly emphasized. Furthermore, he assumed official sponsorship of the diocesan paper as a means of raising the consciousness of Catholics in Connecticut to the full breadth of their membership. From a newspaper whose articles often identified being Catholic with being Irish, the *Catholic Transcript* rapidly became a paper which consistently distinguished between the two. Throughout his administration, Tierney utilized both the diocesan press and his frequent parochial visits to remind Catholics of the richness of ethnic diversity, the universality of the church and the contribution which each group of immigrants was making to the advancement of the Catholic Church. No ethnic ceremony or parade was too insignificant an event for Tierney to attend. He seemed to relish each command performance; these were carefully elaborated upon in the diocesan paper.

By the time of his death, Tierney's "progressive immigrant policy" was well known far beyond the diocese. It was commented upon with awe in the eulogy delivered by Bishop Matthew Harkins of nearby Providence, Rhode Island. It was mentioned in the tributes given by the area's most prominent ministers as well as in the editorials of the state's secular newspapers and in the Catholic newspapers across the nation. By then, even the most widely-discussed problems between immigrants and their bishop, which had received their share of publicity during his tenure, paled to insignificance. Instead Tierney received the praise that was his due for his remarkable insight into, and work on behalf of, the nation's and the church's most "pressing problem."

What Tierney had begun was followed without exception by his successor, John J. Nilan (1855-1934). Less charismatic, Nilan nevertheless had learned his lesson well; he recognized the value of continued outreach to newcomers. He, too, worked to incorporate the tide of immigrants which continued to stream into industrial Connecticut in the early decades of the twentieth century. For one thing, Nilan made sure that national parishes were added to the diocese: one third of the parishes founded during his administration of twenty-four years were for ethnic minorities. He also kept up Tierney's plan of sending seminarians to be educated abroad. Despite the possibility of misunderstandings over delays in the assigning of priests and the establishment of new parishes, he specifically waited for the ordination of Connecticut-born non-Irish candidates so that he could send them, sometimes even as pastors, to their native parishes or to parishes where Catholics of their own nationality worshipped. Folklore had it that Nilan sedulously lived by the maxim which he often repeated to his fellow clergy: "A priest who can speak two languages is worth two priests."[17]

Throughout his administration, Nilan showed concern over the place which his multi-ethnic Catholics had to assume in a society which was growing increasingly nativist. During the First World War, especially when the "alien" image of Slovaks and Hungarian factory workers in the state's munitions plants was questioned, Nilan led his diocese in developing a rhetoric of respect for the opposing European sides. Through his diocesan paper, he supported both the parishioners of national parishes and those priests who worked to ease the tensions which could emerge between allied nations and those in collaboration with the German and Austro-Hungarian empires. In terms of diverse rites, Nilan found areas of accommodation and accord, providing parishes for Slavonic Catholics of the Greek Rite, Syrians of the Melkite Rite, as well as Byzantine and Ukrainian Catholics; each of these established churches in the key cities and towns of the state. In one creative move, for example, he inaugurated a diocesan plan which authorized a corps of public school teachers to teach catechism to Italian immigrant children whose parents were not churchgoers. By the time of his death in 1934, the Diocese of Hartford, which had almost doubled in population, had expanded its institutions widely and increased its ethnic personnel and national parishes as well. By then, there were twelve additional Polish, ten more Italian, and two more Lithuanian and Slovak parishes each, while 91 of the diocese's 529 priests (17.2 percent) claimed southern or eastern European background. Following in the footsteps of his predecessor, Nilan had done his appropriate share to incorporate immigrants.

From such diocesan studies, one can conclude that there were U.S. Catholic Church leaders in the crucial decades surrounding the turn of the twentieth century who recognized the need to develop policies and practices which would incorporated immigrants into the American Catholic Church. At first, the means taken to accomplish this had been simple: the location of clergy or religious congregations to assist immigrants and the establishment of parishes in which the language and customs of the new members would be honored. But, as has been noted, further measures were developed, at least in some dioceses, which were aimed at more fully incorporating ethnic minorities into the mainstream of Catholic life. Besides Chicago, Newark, and Hartford, other dioceses with large numbers of immigrants took sincere, constructive steps to care for newcomers and went well beyond the minimum of accommodation. This is not to suggest that the record of incorporation of European immigrants was without blemish; in fact, the darker side of the story of accommodation has been the more prevailing description of the U.S. Catholic Church experience during the peak years of immigration. Without denying that insensitivity on the part of both Catholic leaders and members to the needs of immigrants wrought considerable distress, it is important to remind ourselves of the actions of dioceses in which clergy, religious, and laity did make a positive difference. One can, in fact, argue that, despite some evidence to the contrary, the twentieth century U.S. Catholic Church stands as a proof that its earlier leadership—in the most crucial decades of massive immigration—had largely succeeded in their initial efforts of accommodation and incorporation. The policies developed on behalf of immigrants eventually guaranteed the solid growth of the American Catholic Church and the continuation not only of ethnic policy but of an ethnic or "immigrant" identification for the church. In fact, these efforts even perdured beyond the first generations and renewed bouts of nativism. Wherever the successful incorporation of immigrants had occurred, in particular, the church represented an especially strong, impressive front. Even as Irish-Americans retained a predominance in the hierarchy, a healthy and ethnically diverse church multiplied in numbers. In 1925, when Gerald Shaughnessy asked *Has the Immigrant Kept the Faith?*, the U.S. Catholic population had already reached twenty million members. Despite loss, the church had come to be impressive even to outside observers. In the aftermath of world war, it was seen as a patriotic partner, an ally to American culture, and a magnet in terms of certain political issues. In this way, the U.S. Catholic Church gained steadily in numbers and stature well into the mid-twentieth century. Even in the second half-century, the national parish has retained its attractiveness and its signature as a continuing feature of Catholic membership. By this period as well, interest in finding ways to incorporate newcomers did not diminish. In a number of significant ways, in fact, the church began to move beyond incorporation on the local diocesan level to lead in the advocacy of immigrant rights and as the initiator of new ways to address contemporary problems.[18]

While maintaining the same philosophical attitudes towards immigrants, however, twentieth century Catholic immigrant policy had undergone some important shifts in understanding and methodology. As national coordinating committees and commissions of bishops gradually assumed authority in the two post-war periods to plan jointly, the issues of appropriate care for immigrants moved beyond the sense of structural incorporation to a wider awareness of the meaning of incorporation and a search for new methodologies. For the first time since the proposal of the 1884 Plenary Council, the combined action of bishops could be invoked on behalf of ethnic minorities struggling within their adopted land. In the 1920s a National Catholic Welfare Conference office of the Bureau of Immigration was established in Washington, with branches in New York and El Paso, to coordinate and cooperate with the work of Catholic immigrant aid agencies. Because of its existence, a concerted effort to influence immigration legislation could finally be made. Even before the end of World War II, the Catholic Action Department of the same NCWC held its first regional meeting, convened specifically on behalf of the economic plight of the Spanish-speaking people of the Southwest. Two years later a bishop's committee for the Spanish-speaking was formed to provide for the religious, social, economic, educational, and cultural advancement of Mexican-Americans.[19]

Supported by the backing of bishops' commissions, furthermore, the creative work of clergy, religious men and women, as well as a newly-inspired laity continued on the diocesan and local levels. Some of the dominant preoccupations which have particularly affected the Hispanic minority were the development of educational programs and social justice pursuits, including education for promoting legislative action, as well as resettlement, counselling, and spiritual programs. Celebrated outcomes have been joint episcopal support given migrant workers, the formation of the National Farm Workers Association, and the endorsement of Cesar Chavez or other Catholic labor activists. Programs to enhance the spiritual life of Hispanic newcomers were also advanced. A National Secretariat for Hispanic Affairs was begun in 1974; it attended to the development of new models for the integration of immigrants into the church. Since that time, national and international meetings of Hispanic

Catholics have worked out procedures to help raise the consciousness of Hispanics; they have also developed policies and activities to improve opportunities and enhance power within both church and society.

On a lesser scale but also on a national basis, church leaders began to respond, especially through the offices of the United States Catholic Conference and Catholic Charities, to other recent refugees and immigrants. In order to begin the pro-cess of Catholic community building, for example, resettlement programs, under the auspices of national bishops' committees, were inaugurated from Texas and California to Michigan, Illinois, and the New England states. Experiments in creating pastoral resource centers or other models of Catholic immigrant communi- ties as alternatives to national parishes were also attempted, especially for Vietnamese and Cambodian refugees. From coast to coast, Catholic Charities offices engaged in the daily, practical aspects of incorporating newcomers into neighborhoods and churches. National conferences and diocesan pastoral institutes have been organized for the sake of bringing together isolated immigrant communities and finding ways to incorporate newcomers appropriately. Diocesan priests and religious congregations of men and women have been asked to dedicate their expertise to these enterprises and immigrant clergy have been recruited as well. Most recently, in May of 1987, the celebration of Black Catholicism took on new momentum through the sponsorship of the National Office of Black Catholics when the first national Black Congress to be held in the twentieth century was convened.

As Black, Hispanic, Asian, and Third World Catholics seek admittance to the Church in the United States in the wake of renewed commitment to refugees, migrants, and minorities, they find a committed host church ready to assist them in their present need. Yet they might be surprised to know that the beginning stages upon which present action has taken place had its origins even in the days when the church was still considered a "despised" minority. Coordinated programs to incorporate immigrants into the church, such as the one Michael Tierney devised for Hartford, were not commonplace, to be sure; but the historical record does give evidence that in many of the areas where immigrants had settled in large numbers the first outreach to immigrants had occurred. These efforts could be dismissed as insignificant, yet they were aimed at developing a sense of belonging among Catholics. Present-day Catholics are in a far better place to continue what was properly begun and to ameliorate what was done poorly. After all, as descendants of immigrants, they have all the more reason to be in the vanguard of immigrant assistance. Their ability to coordinate projects on the national level and allow for a deepening of policies begun decades ago is clear as well. Today's Catholics, laity and clergy alike, are also in a secure position concerning their own status as both Americans and American Catholics; their very commitment may even extend from the fact that they recognize, consciously or otherwise, the legacy of generations of Catholics who previously opened their arms in welcome to the teeming masses of immigrants.

It is this tradition of openness to ethnic concerns, in particular, which must be remembered and celebrated as an intrinsic characteristic of the American Catholic Church as the church plans for the future. The record of American Catholic attentiveness to the immigrant has been a good one which stands ready for improvement in these enlightened, activist times. The successes that resulted in an multi-ethnic church should encourage today's clergy and laity to go forth with the same sense of commitment to address the current problems facing immigrants and refugees in the American context. Practical questions remain, to be sure. Should the pluralistic approach which has protected immigrant groups in the past from losing the most endearing aspects of their religious expression extend so far that old patterns of ethnicity are reinforced for their own sake and new islands of separatism are drawn? Will these questions of incorporation divert Catholics from more important social and economic issues also facing immigrants?

The chances that the situation for Catholic immigrants will be bleak seem minimal after the story of the American Catholic Church's response to the immigrant has been reviewed. Clearly policy has evolved since the 1800s; it has deepened its perspective over the generations; both its aims and intentions have improved. Perhaps, as the noted historian of immigration, John Higham, has recently suggested in terms of American society, new directions must now be considered. Perhaps the church must admit to the limits of pluralism for the next generation. Is it time, for example, for Catholic leaders to present the issue of the incorporation of immigrants not in terms of cultural pluralism but rather in terms of a pluralistic integration of all God's people? Today's immigrant policy may be due for a substantial reevaluation; under the auspices of bishops and with the full collaboration of laity this new challenge can readily be met.

Notes

1. There are two noteworthy recent histories of U.S. Catholicism: James Hennesey, S.J., *American Catholics: A History of the Roman Catholic Community in the United States* (New York: Oxford University Press, 1983) and Jay P. Dolan, *The American Catholic Experience: A History from Colonial Times to the Present* (New York: Doubleday and Co., 1985). Dolan's emphasis on the place of immigrants in the American Catholic experience makes his book the more useful for this paper.

2. Thomas O'Brien Hanley, S.J. (ed.), *The John Carroll Papers: Vol. II, 1792-1806* (Notre Dame: University of Notre Dame Press, 1976), quoted in Dolan, *American Catholic Experience*, p. 79.

3. Robert Leckie, *American and Catholic* (New York: Doubleday and Co., 1970), p. 144.

4. *Sermons Delivered During the Second Plenary Council of Baltimore, October, 1866 and Pastoral Letter of the Hierarchy of the United States together with the Papal Rescript and Letters of the Council. A Complete List of Dignitaries and Officers of the Council* (Baltimore: Kelly & Piet, 1866).

5. Joseph E. Ciesluk, *National Parishes in the United States* (Washington, D.C.: Catholic University Press, 1944), pp. 45ff.

6. Quoted in Hennessey, *American Catholics*, p. 174.

7. For a detailed discussion of Purcell's accomplishment regarding Cincinnati's Germans, see Joseph M. White, "From Home Town to Congregation: Cincinnati Germans, 1814-1870" (Working Papers Series, Charles and Mary Cushwa Center, Notre Dame, November, 1982), passim.

8. *Catholic Directory* (Hoffmann and Co., 1910); and U.S. Government Publications, *Bureau of Census: Religious Bodies, 1916,* 2 vols. (Washington, D.C., 1919).

9. Charles Shanabruch, *Chicago's Catholics* (Notre Dame: University of Notre Dame Press, 1981), pp. 97ff.

10. Shanabruch, Chicago's Catholics, pp. 12ff; see also Silvano M. Tomasi, C.S. "The Response of the Catholic Church in the United States to Immigrants and Refugees" (CMS Occasional Papers: Pastoral Series, 3, August, 1984), p. 16.

11. Of the recent studies of Chicago's immigrant church the author who has interpreted the church's achievements with respect to immigrants in the most positive light is Stephen Joseph Shaw, "Chicago's Germans and Italians: the Catholic Parish As a Way-Station of Ethnicity and Americanization" (Ph.D. diss., University of Chicago, 1981).

12. Carl D. Hinrichsen, "The History of the Diocese of Newark, 1873-1901" (Ph.D diss., Catholic University of America, 1963), pp. 291-327.

13. Ibid.; see also New Jersey Catholic Records Commission, *The Bishops of Newark, 1853-1978* (South Orange: Seton Hall University Press, 1978), pp. 59-74.

14. New Jersey Catholic Records Commission, *Bishops*, pp. 98-123.

15. Dolores Ann Liptak, *European Immigrants and the Catholic Church in Connecticut, 1870-1920* (Staten Island: Center for Migration Studies, 1987), p. 70; see also Hinrichsen, "Diocese of Newark," pp. 335ff.

16. Liptak, *European Immigrants*, pp. 45-54.

17. *Ibid.*, pp. 45-59, table, p. 70.

18. Shaughnessy's investigation was prompted by fears of great losses among immigrants, estimated in the millions; see Gerald Shaughnessy, *Has the Immigrant Kept the Faith?: A Study of Immigration and Catholic Growth in the United States*, 1790-1920 (New York: MacMillan Co., 1925), pp. 223-245.

19. Tomasi, "Response to Immigrants and Refugees," passim.

Faith and Culture in the Pastoral Care of Immigrants

Joseph P. Fitzpatrick, SJ
Professor Emeritus
Fordham University

Faith and Culture in the Pastoral Care of Immigrants[1]

No faith can exist outside the context of a culture, and all immigrants live their lives within the context of a culture. Therefore, the relation of faith to culture is an essential consideration in the pastoral care of immigrants. What I would like to do in this article, therefore, is: (1) provide some background particularly to Christian faith and culture; (2) describe a variety of ways in which the Church has sought to adapt its ministry to different cultures; and (3) look at the contemporary issue of faith and culture in the United States, particularly in reference to the pastoral care of immigrants and refugees.

The mission that Jesus gave to His Apostles was a mission "to the world." "Go, therefore, make disciples of all nations" (Mt. 28:19).[2] The world into which He sent them was neither remote nor abstract. It was the busy, active, turbulent, joyful, and sorrowful actuality in which God's children were born, grew up, sought to find and fulfill an ultimate meaning in their lives, married, had children, grew old, and died. Within that world, God expected all persons to express in themselves the image of God created in all of them. It was in their day-to-day activities, their relationships to each other, their efforts and achievements, that the spirit of God living within them would have to be expressed. Ministry and pastoral care are the tasks of assisting them to do this.

The context then of ministries and pastoral care is the total social, economic, political, cultural, and religious reality within which we seek to bear witness to the life and teachings of Jesus. All of these day-to-day activities are touched by the meaning people find in their lives. Religious beliefs penetrate this social reality. At the same time, the social reality penetrates the religious beliefs. The beliefs themselves become elements of the total social experience of the people who are members of a particular society. In the present case, that society is the United States. However, we are also concerned about the relevance the U.S. experience has for other areas of the world. In order to analyze the interrelationship of religion and culture in the United States in relation to the pastoral care of immigrants, some attention must be given to the larger issue, the relationship of religion to culture in general.

Inculturation of Faith[3]

This interpenetration of a culture by a religious faith is called, in more technical terms, "inculturation." The word of God, the promises of the Messiah, the life of Jesus; these must express themselves in the particular way of life of a people, their social institutions, their political and economic activities. This interrelationship of all aspects of a society to a set of ultimate meanings and values is called the "culture." Therefore, the study of inculturation is central to a study of the context of ministries and pastoral care.

"Culture"[4] has many different definitions. In this article, we understand culture as the ways of believing, thinking, feeling, and acting that constitute what a person calls "my way of life." Culture constitutes the way of life of an Italian in contrast to that of a Japanese, the way of life of a person from India in contrast to that of a person from Mexico. It involves the ways people make their living, the food they eat and the ways they prepare it, the ways they clothe and shelter themselves. It involves the ways they relate as persons to each other, the political and economic institutions they create for their own mutual development and protection, and the art, poetry and music whereby they express themselves and symbolize their values and their feelings.

At the heart of every culture are the ultimate meanings, the response of the people to the ultimate mysteries of life: where I came from, where I am going, how I should get there. This is their faith. And faith penetrates every aspect of life, from the bow or kiss that means respect, to a legal system that defines the rights of citizens or the rules that govern the purchase and sale of food in the market; from the role of women in relation to men, to the ultimate understanding of the meaning of pain or evil or death.

Historical Development

Historically, the inculturation of faith appears to take a variety of evolving forms. At early stages of social and cultural development, the expression of religious belief tends to become rigidly associated with particular forms of behavior. This is seen in the faith of the ancient Hebrews. Fidelity to the Lord required strict adherence to the Mosaic law. But the Mosaic law was actually a culture. Apart from circumcision, it specified in detail what the faithful could eat and how it was to be cooked, when they could work or travel. It specified the relations between masters and servants and between husbands and wives, even such details as when they could have sexual relations. It restricted relationships with Gentiles and governed the broad range of ritual and religious practices. To participate in the promise, to be faithful to the covenant, one was obligated to observe the law strictly. In other words, God had integrated the faith of the ancient Hebrews with a culture in the sense that fidelity to the faith required that one live according to the Hebrew culture, the Hebrew way of life. Inculturation was integralist; faith and culture were one.

In the New Testament, God did just the opposite. He instructed Peter (Acts 10) that the faith of Jesus was never to be identified with a particular culture. It was to be kath'-holos (catholic), capable of expressing itself in any culture or way of life in which men and women sought the will of God and did what piety demands. "I have come to realize" Peter said, "that God does not have any favorites, but that anybody of any nationality [culture] who fears God and does what is right is acceptable to him" (Acts 10:35). In other words, the Romans (in the Acts account, Cornelius and his household) were not to be required to observe the

Mosaic law, to follow the Hebrew way of life in order to be Christians. They were to remain Romans; Greeks were to remain Greeks; and Egyptians were to remain Egyptians. Within the style and practice of their own culture, they were to give expression to the faith they shared in Jesus. The great confrontation of Paul and Peter at Antioch was centered on this very issue: "I said to Cephas in front of everyone, 'In spite of being a Jew, you live like the pagans and not like the Jews, so you have no right to make the pagans copy Jewish ways' " (Galatians 2:14). One main feature of Paul's vocation was the defense of the freedom of the Gentiles of many different cultures to "be themselves," to express the faith of Jesus within their own style of life, provided that they sought the will of God and did what piety demands.

The problem of the relationship of faith to culture has been a challenge to the Church throughout its history, from the days of Paul to the days of Cyril and Methodius, who resisted the attempt to Romanize the Slavonic Rite; through the sad history of the condemnation of the Chinese Rites to the Second Vatican Council.[5] During the Council, African bishops criticized a missionary strategy that claimed to be communicating the faith of Jesus while, in actuality, it was communicating a particular cultural expression of it as it occurred in Western Europe. Thus the *Pastoral Constitution of the Church in the Modern World*, chapter 2, has a long discussion about faith and culture, reasserting the need for the faith to be responsive to different cultures and to changes in culture. "For God, revealing Himself to His people to the extent of a full manifestation of Himself in His Incarnate Son, has spoken to the culture proper to different ages."

Since Vatican II, the problem of inculturation has been actively discussed by officials of the Church, theologians, and a variety of people concerned about ministry and pastoral care. The Third Synod of Bishops (1976)[6] issued an important statement about it, but, more importantly, it prompted the remarkable exhortation of Pope Paul VI, *Evangelization in the Modern World (Evangelii Nuntiandi).*[7] This is one of the most important statements about the problem, described as follows by the Pope:

> The Gospel, and therefore evangelization as well, *cannot be identified with any particular culture but it is independent of all cultures.* On the other hand, the reign of God which the Gospel proclaims takes concrete form in the lives of men [and women] who are profoundly shaped by their particular culture. It is also a fact that the elements of man's culture and cultures must be used in building the kingdom of God. Therefore, although the Gospel and evangelization do not properly belong to any culture, neither are they incompatible with any. On the contrary, they can enter into all of them without being subservient to any[8] [Emphasis added.]

Every possible aspect of the relationship of the Catholic faith to the cultures of the world is discussed in the letter. It is, without a doubt, the definitive document thus far on the issue.

Many other discussions of the issue are in the context, not of bringing the faith to a non-Christian people, but of revitalizing the faith in the Christian lands where its influence had been lost in situations of oppression and injustice. The Second General Assembly of the

Synod of Bishops (1971) issued their famous statement *Justice in the World*,[9] on the problems of the faith in nations, particularly Christian nations, where situations of injustice and oppression prevail.

> Action on behalf of justice and participation in the transformation of the world fully appear to us as a *constitutive dimension* of the preaching of the Gospel, or, in other words, the Church's mission for the redemption of the human race and its liberation from every oppressive situation. . . . For unless the Christian message of love and justice shows its effectiveness through action in the cause of justice in the world, it will only with difficulty gain credibility with the men [and women] of our times.[10] [Emphasis added.]

The "preferential option for the poor," so widely publicized after the Second Conference of Latin American Bishops at Medellin (1968)[11] and reaffirmed at the Third Conference at Puebla (1979),[12] has been a guideline for the involvement of Catholics in the pursuit of justice and liberation for the poor and oppressed, not only in Latin America, but throughout the world.

The issue, therefore, of faith and culture is a central topic of discussion and dialogue within the Church. In the process, the need for a thorough familiarity with cultures is emphasized, so that we may know what aspects of the culture are a suitable context for the manifestation of the faith, what aspects of the cultures impede or corrupt it. The Church has spoken clearly and emphatically that, in the pastoral care of all peoples, the relation of faith to culture is a central and critical issue.

Three problems develop as the Church seeks to relate ministry and pastoral care to different cultures. First there is the critical problem of determining which features of a culture are compatible with Christian faith and values and which are not. Paul and the Apostles certainly found serious moral problems with Roman society. The severe condemnations in the Letter to the Romans indicates what Paul found to be "unclean" and immoral and irreconcilable with a Christian way of life. This is a critical issue with which the Church continually wrestles. For example, Matteo Ricci found the ancestral rites of the Chinese compatible with Christianity but the rites were condemned as pagan worship by the Church in the eighteenth century; nevertheless Pius XI in the twentieth century declared the rites to be a form of social practice compatible with Christian faith.[13] Patterns of popular religiosity that had been repeatedly condemned in the past have been hailed by Paul VI in *Evangelii Nuntiandi* as a fertile ground for the Christian faith.[14]

Therefore, in relating ministry to culture, the first task is to determine the features of the culture that are compatible with Christianity. In other words, the missionary must search out the *meaning* that things have for the members of the culture. This is why the social sciences have become an important element in ministry. They help to reveal what things mean in a particular culture. In light of this a more reliable judgment can be made as to what is acceptable to Christian faith and practice.

The second problem is one of ethnocentrism. Once people of a particular culture have developed a manifestation of the life and word of Jesus in the context of their culture, they tend to identify the faith with their culture. In communicating the faith to others, they may actually be communicating their particular expression of the faith rather than the faith itself. As indicated above, the complaint of the African Bishops at Vatican II was that European missionaries, thinking they were bringing the Gospel to African peoples, were actually imposing on Africans the cultural styles of Western European Christianity.

Finally, there is the problem also mentioned above of the corruption of the faith in so-called Christian lands, in the patterns of social injustice, oppression, and violent subjection of the poor, a distortion of the faith that must be corrected by radical social change and that requires a new adaptation of the culture to Christian faith.

Adaptations of Ministry to Different Cultures

From the time of Saint Paul and the struggle to secure the freedom of the Gentiles from the Mosaic Law and the religious traditions of the Hebrews, the Church has sought to respect the culture of peoples in its ministry to them.

The first example of this occurred in the early Church in the controversy about circumcision and the Mosaic Law. God had instructed Peter that the Mosaic Law was not to be imposed on the Gentiles who wished to follow Jesus. And Peter clearly followed this instruction in dealing with the Roman officer, Cornelius, and his family. As this practice became widespread among the Gentile Christians at Antioch, some Jewish Christians who were dedicated to the Law and to Hebrew religious traditions began to create problems for the Gentile Christians by insisting that they follow the Mosaic Law.

The meeting of the Elders of the Church at Jerusalem (Acts 15), the first Council of the Church, was really a pastoral council. What patterns of religious practice must the Gentiles follow? What patterns of behavior would be permissible or forbidden? Following the advice of Peter, the Council did not place any burdens of the Mosaic Law upon the Gentiles. It simply asked them to "abstain from what is contaminated by idolatry, from fornication, and from meat which has been strangled or had blood in it." The Council put their instructions in writing and sent chosen messengers with Paul and Barnabas to carry the message to the Gentile Christians at Antioch.

Karl Rahner calls this decision "The Great Caesura," the cutting away of the Church from attachment to the Hebrew religious tradition. Rahner thinks a similar great caesura is needed today to cut the Church away from its attachment to Western European cultural and religious styles. More about this later.[15]

The Church has had an impressive tradition of adaptation to local cultures, customs, languages, and styles. When one looks at the varieties of rites in the Church, it is remarkable how careful the Church was to respect local customs and languages. From Coptic and Ethiopian to Syrian and Malabar, to the numerous subdivisions in the Byzantine rites, to the Chaldean, the Armenian, the and Latin, the evidence is impressive of a Church *circumdata varietate*, surrounded by a rich variety.

In these diverse rites are found different languages; in some rites a married clergy, in others, like the Latin, a requirement of celibacy for priesthood; in some a close relationship to local governments; in others, such as the United States, a Constitutional separation of Church and State; and of course a variety of liturgical styles. Furthermore, the Church has been very emphatic in its determination to protect the autonomy of these rites. Beginning with the decision in the thirteenth century down to more recent decisions about the protection of the rites, the Church has used its influence to assure them of their right to exist and to continue as a particular cultural expression of the life and word of Jesus; a genuine "catholicity," one Church capable of expressing the richness of its life in a wide variety of cultures, but without becoming identified with any one.[16]

This has not been without its conflicts and its struggles. Many of the heresies and schisms in the history of the Church have really stemmed from intercultural misunderstanding or conflict. As Christopher Dawson remarked, "Most of the great schisms and heresies in the history of the Christian Church have had their roots in social and national antipathies, and if this had been clearly recognized by the theologians, the history of Christianity would have been a different one."[17]

The problem of relating the faith to cultural differences remains one of the greatest challenges to the Church. It is now called "inculturation," the penetration of a particular culture by the faith and the penetration of the faith by a particular culture. The impressive statements of the Church in recent years reflect the keen awareness that has developed, particularly among Christian religious leaders and theologians, of the importance of the cultural context of Christian faith and practice. The encouragement of indigenous styles in Africa and Asia and the increasing respect for popular religiosity also reflect this.

One of the most striking approvals of this appears in the remarks of John Paul II on the occasion of the celebration of the four-hundredth anniversary of the arrival of Matteo Ricci in China. Speaking of the daring adaptations of the Church to Chinese culture in the Chinese Rites,[18] the Pope said:

> . . . Matteo Ricci was the first who succeeded in inserting himself into the full life of Chinese culture and society, bringing to that great people so much of the science and technology of Europe, and bringing to the West the civilization and the cultural richness of the Chinese people. . . . .

> It was thanks to this kind of an effort of inculturation that Father Matteo Ricci, with the assistance of his Chinese collaborators, achieved a task that seemed impossible to work out, that is, a Chinese terminology of Catholic theology and liturgy and, in this way, to create the conditions to make Christ known and to incarnate His evangelical message of the Church within the context of Chinese culture. . . . .

In the light of the spirit of dialogue and of the openness which was characteristic of the Second Vatican Council, the missionary method of Father Ricci appears so much more alive and contemporary.

This was an extraordinary approval of missionary methods that had been condemned in the seventeenth century and remained so until the condemnation was finally terminated by Pius XI in the instruction, *Pluries Instanterque*, on May 26, 1936.[19]

This is a brief review of the background of the question of faith and culture in the history of the Church. What follows is a more detailed examination of the contemporary challenge of ministry to immigrants and refugees and the efforts of the Church, particularly in the United States, to respond to it.

The Pastoral Care of Immigrants and Refugees in the United States of America[20]

The United States is a nation that has been made up of immigrants and refugees. It is also a nation where, over the years, the Church has flourished.[21] From this point of view, it would appear that the pastoral care of immigrants was successful. This does not mean that the experience of the United States can be used as an example for other nations. But certain features of the U.S. experience do have a wide, if not universal, significance. These can at least be described and analyzed. In the United States the Catholic Church faced two situations that it had not faced before: (1) This was a nation that recognized no national religion, but guaranteed freedom to all religions. Religious pluralism was a new social and religious experience; the Church had had no preparation for this. (2) The Church would face the challenge of the relationship to each other of Catholics of many different ethnic and cultural backgrounds. Out of this new experience have come a few principles of pastoral care that may be helpful elsewhere.

Catholics were a small minority in Colonial America, but a minority of elite people. Highly educated, politically sophisticated, and in many cases wealthy, they were very different from the waves of poverty stricken immigrants who were to come later. One Catholic, Charles Carroll of Carrollton, signed the Declaration of Independence. His relative, John Carroll, became the first Bishop in the United States. This small group was determined to adapt the Catholic Church as completely as possible to the democratic ideals that were being fulfilled in the new nation—a vernacular liturgy; the democratic election of Bishops; a great deal of autonomy from Europe—a Church that would have the characteristics of American society. The early Catholics had a keen sense of cultural adaptation. The cultural ideals of the new nation were to give a specific character to the Church. It was anticipated that, by doing so, the Church would be able to influence American life religiously as she would not be able to influence it if her life were guided by norms too different from those of the new nation.

It was not long before this ideal of an American Church was to be severely challenged. Following the establishment of the nation, the immigration of poor Catholics from Europe began; in a few years millions of them were to arrive. Their life and culture were not only different from the pattern of life of the United States, they were strikingly different among themselves. Thus, the problem of the relationship of Catholics to Catholics was to be almost as important as the problem of the Catholic Church to a Protestant world.

In the one hundred years between 1820 and 1920, more than forty million immigrants poured into the United States. Large numbers were Catholics who came from many different European nations and many different cultural backgrounds. The Irish were poor peasants who had endured two centuries of persecution from the English; the Germans were farmers and craftsmen who had lost their land or their occupation and came to the United States to seek better economic conditions. Scandinavians, mostly Protestant, came with the hope of land and a new life. Most of the French went to Canada where they established the Province of Quebec, but large numbers also came to the United States. The Bishop of New York from 1826 to 1842 was a Frenchman, Bishop John Dubois. It was not long, however, before the Irish began to dominate the life of the Church in the United States. Their dedication to the Church, European style, their faithfulness to Rome and the Pope, their own suffering at the hands of American Protestants, left them with little sympathy for the American Church of the Colonial period. They brought a European-type Church to the United States. One characteristic that the Irish had above all others was a remarkable ability for political and social organization, a skill they had developed in order to survive two centuries of harsh persecution by the English. It was a skill superbly suited to the ideals and political processes of the United States. The Irish were to use it to maximum advantage for themselves, and particularly for the Church.[22]

The religious impact of the Irish immigrants was not a carefully planned pastoral program of the Church. It was simply the spontaneous response of the Irish to the opportunities of American political and religious institutions; it resulted in a strong and viable Catholic Church which was to have characteristics very different from those envisioned by the Colonial Catholics. As has been mentioned by historians of the Irish experience in America, the Irish immigrants, the moment they left the boats, were "Irish, Catholic, and Democrats." They brought with them a fierce sense of their identity as Catholics, which they were determined to keep. What a blessing it was, as they saw it, to have their religion politically protected in the United States after years of attempted suppression of it in Ireland. And, despite the persecution they suffered here at the hands of Protestants, they used the political institutions of the United States to secure the rights guaranteed to them by the Constitution. In a surprisingly short time, they began to dominate the political scene in the American cities, as they were beginning to dominate the Catholic Church.

Irish Catholics politically active as Democrats became a perfect American element. They took advantage of their rights to participate in political life and they used the political power they gained to secure their rights and privileges as Catholics in a religiously pluralistic society. In this way they established an authentically American Catholicism.

However, in the process, they established an American Catholicism that retained many of the European characteristics. They retained the liturgical styles of Ireland as they had been practiced for decades; they manifested a determined loyalty to the Pope in Rome and a disposition to accept the instructions that came from Rome. In contrast to the Colonial Catholics, the Irish established a European Catholicism in a decidedly American context.

The heart of this Catholic life was the immigrant community; and the parish was the heart of this immigrant community. Irish immigrants settled together in neighborhoods, generally poor and often in inhuman conditions. The immigrant community was the firm basis for a continuing sense of solidarity, a deep sense of identity, of social and psychological support. The Church and the parish were the solid rock on which this rested, a transfer to the new world of the central institutions of their lives in the old world. The parish was the main reference point for the immigrants; when asked where they resided, they would generally respond, not by mentioning the street address, but by the parish to which they belonged.[23]

The immigrant community, solidly based in the parish, became the base also of political power. To be a Catholic meant to be a Democrat. And religious identity became a firm base of political power. Local politicians, the "Ward Bosses" of early American political life, became the liaison between the immigrant community and political officials. The Boss delivered the vote to the political leaders and, in turn, provided the favors which political leaders made available to their constituencies in the parish. It was an extraordinary relationship of religion to political activity in a society of religious pluralism and the Constitutional protection of religious freedom. This was the first time in history that any such "institutionalization" of the Catholic Church occurred. It has given its specific identity to the American Church as a religious institution, an extraordinary adaptation of the Church to American culture and political life.

As indicated above, this was not the result of a planned program of pastoral care. The clergy and religious, who came in large numbers with the immigrant poor, simply transferred to the United States the Catholic life and identity of the Irish poor. They built magnificent Churches; they provided the spiritual and religious care that was common in the old country; they supported their people in their social and political activity. The people, poor as they were, gave generously to support the Church. They later developed the parochial schools because the public schools did not permit the teaching of religion. But the creation of a separate school system was another example of the ability of the Irish to take advantage of the freedom of American society to advance their own religious interests. It was a heavy financial burden, but it likewise became an integral part of Catholic life in the United States. As some historians have remarked: The Catholic Church in the United States is a massive school system interspersed by occasional churches.

This was a remarkably creative adaptation of Catholicism to American society and culture. Outside of the political framework of the United States, this would not have been possible. The particular political skill of the Irish was also a factor unique to the experience. However, there were some features of the experience that are important for ministry and pastoral care of immigrants and refugees in general. Let me indicate a few.

The Immigrant Community

There is no substitute for the immigrant community for the social and religious support of a people seeking to adjust as strangers in a new land. And the Catholic parish or religious congregation is an ideal basis for the immigrant community. Not only for the Irish, but for all the immigrants who came to the United States, the ability to cluster in their own neighborhoods, their ability to develop their own organizations, their own business enterprises from the local stores to the immigrant newspapers, to the small political clubs, to recreational, educational, and cultural centers, all of this provided a sense of identity, of security, a support for social and psychological satisfaction that enabled them to develop a community strength in the process of their adjustment to a new way of life. "One integrates from a position of strength, not from a position of weakness." And the strength of the immigrants is rooted in the immigrant community.[24]

The important point here is this: pastoral care and ministry to immigrants should seek, in every possible way, to support the effort of immigrants to develop the immigrant community. In the history of immigrants in the United States, there has always been resistance to the immigrant community. Established Americans tended to see it as a basis for division, as a form of voluntary segregation that would delay adjustment to American life. The history of immigration provides no evidence of this. On the contrary, it was the strength and stability of the immigrant community that enabled the immigrants to retain a well controlled and well organized social life. It became the basis of political activity which, more than anything else, brings newcomers into the mainstream of American society. Without the strength and support of the immigrant community, the immigrant can become marginal to American society, lost without support, alienated and helpless. It is the rare immigrant who can make his or her way alone into the mainstream. The immigrant community is their best support and the most important institution to hasten their adjustment to American life.[25]

As a general principle, therefore, this indicates that, in their transition to a new society anywhere, immigrants must have the opportunity to retain their own identity, the support of family and friends in a community that helps them retain their sense of identity and provides them with a sense of security. This is the pluralism that is essential for immigrants anywhere, the retention of their own culture and way of life while they face the process of adjustment to a new way of life. Whether this cultural pluralism can continue to exist over generations is another issue and will be discussed later. But for the newly arriving immigrant or refugee, it is essential.

A Class Identity

Ideally, clergy and religious of the same ethnic background and class as the immigrants are the most helpful in the establishment of the immigrant community. They have the same sense of cultural identity as the immigrants. More importantly, they have a sense of class identity. They share the same experience, are sensitive to the interests of the immigrants, share the same style of life. They relate to the immigrants as "one of their own." In the case of the Irish, the priests had suffered the same persecution in Ireland as the immigrant poor; they came over on the same converted lumber and fish boats and many died in passage or of the same diseases after arriving here; they were close to their families and friends who were often living in inhuman conditions. They had the same sense of political organization as their people. In fact the rectories often appeared like political clubs. This close sense of identity and solidarity enabled the Church to be a strong support of the people in their political and social struggles. It was the clergy who were most influential in the development of the parochial schools.

In the absence of an immigrant clergy, it is difficult for a non-immigrant clergy to supply the deficiencies. It means that American clergy must learn the language of the newcomers; learn the culture and develop the ability to respond in a familiar way to the immigrants; they must be able to create a situation in which the immigrants feel "at home" in a parish directed by priests who are foreign to them. The achievement of this is not impossible. The response of many American clergy to Hispanics, for example, has been marked by a remarkable sense of identity between American clergy and the Hispanic community.

In any event, if their own clergy accompany the immigrants, they are the ones ideally suited to support the effort of the immigrants to establish the immigrant community, with the parish at the heart of it. If an immigrant clergy is not available, the clergy of the host culture must make the effort to establish as close an identity as possible to the immigrants and to provide a ministry and pastoral care in the language and cultural style that make sense to the immigrants. This will support the immigrant community, which is a source of strength to the immigrants as well as a secure basis for the continuation of their Catholic life. One problem that complicates this is the difference of social class which may prevail if the host clergy are middle or higher class and the immigrants are lower class. Difference of class is more difficult to bridge than difference of culture. More will be said of this in a discussion of the pastoral care of Hispanics in the United States.

The National or Language Parish

Most of the immigrants coming to the United States were not Irish, nor were they English-speaking. In fact, among the early immigrants, German Catholics and French Catholics were numerous. Both French and German immigrants were also accompanied by priests and religious of their own nationality and ethnic and language background. Again, not as a result of a carefully planned pastoral program, the Germans and French spontaneously established their own parishes, with their own clergy, and their parish life became the heart of their immigrant communities. Their religious practice was the one thing that immigrants could bring with them that could serve, in the United States, as a perfect institution of transition. It was a large part of the old world reproduced almost intact in the new: the same clergy, the same language, the religious practices with which they were familiar. The national or language parish did for Germans, French, and others the same thing it did for the Irish. It was the basis for a continuing sense of identity in a strange world, a sense of solidarity and security. It provided a sense of social and psychological satisfaction, a small piece of America where the immigrants were at home among their own. Whether in an English-speaking territorial parish, or a national or language parish, the immigrant community was a source of strength for the immigrants and for the Church.

The New Immigration

Large scale immigration of Irish and Germans tended to slacken after the Civil War (1865). But a new wave of immigration began from Central and Southern Europe. This brought another variety of languages and ethnic groups to the United States: Polish, Lithuanian, Italian, Greek, Slovak, Russian, etc. The new immigrants did not come into a nation where the Church was not established. They came to a nation where the earlier immigrants had established the Church and constituted a religious context to which the new immigrants had to adjust. It was at this time that the need for a Church policy began to emerge. Italians, Polish, etc., were moving into areas where Irish, German and French parishes already existed and were well established. What was to be done with the more recent newcomers? This required some policy decisions on the part of existing bishops and a pastoral plan which would respond effectively to the immigrants. The principle of the language or national parish was established and became the ordinary response of the Church to the immigrants.

There was a recognition on the part of the Church that, in their adjustment to American society and culture, immigrants must be able to retain the cultural and religious experience of their traditional culture. The significance of American society was the fact that it made this possible. Despite the harassment of immigrants by the dominant Protestant majority, and despite the efforts of many to impose American language and culture on the newcomers, the American nation made it possible for newcomers to retain many aspects of their cultural past while they began to participate in American life. The most acceptable and viable aspect of that past was the religious life and practice of the immigrants. The religious pluralism of the nation and the acceptance of this initial cultural pluralism constituted a most favorable environment for the continuation of their religious practice by the immigrants and enabled them to contribute to a new and culturally diversified Catholicism in America.

Gradually all these newcomers went through a surprisingly similar transition to American society and culture. Their immediate involvement in American life was their occupation, their place of work. Most of them had come here seeking better economic opportunities. They suffered in many cases from discrimination and exploitation, but over a period of three generations had arrived at an adjustment to American life and culture that enabled them to feel at home in the mainstream of American society.

The Process of Assimilation

As indicated above, the term "assimilation" has many definitions and is a point of controversy among scholars and leaders of immigrant communities. It is frequently criticized and rejected as a process whereby the immigrants are stripped of their culture and are absorbed completely into the dominant way of life of the United States. I use the term here not as the statement of a social policy or ideal, but simply as a description of the process which has taken place historically in the case of most of the immigrants. Over the course of three generations, the immigrants had lost their language and improved their educational levels; many had achieved professional careers, advanced socially and economically, and moved to the suburbs of American cities. In the process, they had become part of suburban Catholic parishes with members of mixed nationalities and cultural backgrounds. Widespread inter-marriage had taken place between descendants of different ethnic and cultural groups: Irish with German, Italian with Polish, etc. Third generation Catholics had assimilated the dominant styles of American life.[26] There has always been a reflection back to ancestry, in Irish celebrations or Italian or Polish, etc., of what one sociologist calls "symbolic ethnicity," but for practical purposes, a common pattern of American life and culture and a common pattern of parish life became the characteristics of American Catholics. They and the Church with them had become decidedly American middle-class or working class. There were many aspects of discrimination and prejudice involved in this history, often a good deal of suffer-ing, particularly for Black Americans. But, nevertheless, the national ideal of an open society with upward mobility has been surprisingly fulfilled.

This represents an extraordinary adaptation of the Church to American society and cul-ture. The initial adaptation of the nation and the Church to the culture and language of the immigrants enabled them to take advantage of the process whereby they gradually moved into the mainstream of American society. In other words, the initial adaptation of pastoral care to the culture of the immigrants enabled them to develop a Catholic life that was decidedly American.

A number of things made this possible. Some of them were particular features of American society which may or may not be present in the experience of immigrants else-where. The open class ideal of the American nation and the effort to provide the opportunity for upward social and economic mobility; the system of universal education, whether in public or parochial schools, brought the children and grandchildren of immigrants to levels of education far beyond that of their immigrant forebears. The numbers of third generation in the professions, teaching, nursing, law and even medicine are impressive. The immigrants took advantage of the opportunities America offered them.

The immigrant parish served as the basis for the immigrant community. In the case of the European immigrants—Italian, Polish, etc.—the presence of their own clergy and religious with them contributed to the strength of the immigrant community. This essential element was solidly in place. From a position of strength the immigrants moved into the mainstream of American life and culture.

This process has not been without its problems and its difficulties. The economic burden alone of building and maintaining Catholic parishes and schools in the suburbs has been heavy. And the problem of the initial national or language Church, when its parishioners have moved away, leaves a different kind of burden on the parish and the diocese. Further-more, the loss of language and of many of the values of the immigrant cultures are a great loss to Church, nation, and immigrants. Nevertheless, in totality, it reflects a remarkable creative ability to adapt the Church to American life and culture.

Other problems are involved for the Church in this adaptation to American culture. Many of the deeply rooted American values are not a favorable environment for a vigorous Catholic life. The focus on social and economic advancement; the emphasis on the possession of the luxuries of a wealthy nation, the so-called "consumer society"; the preoccupation with security and well-being, the pursuit of wealth and the symbols of middle or upper class status; the support of a militaristic government—all these create an environment that is not favorable to the fulfillment of basic Christian values. The recent letters of the American Bishops—*The Challenge of Peace* on peace and disarmament;[27] *Economic Justice for All* on the American economy,[28] which is so critical of the neglect of the poor; *Brothers and Sisters to Us*,[29] about the importance of justice for Black Catholics and Americans; and *The Hispanic Presence: Challenge and Commitment*,[30] about the importance of respect for and acceptance of Hispanic newcomers--indicate the concern of Catholics with some of the unfavorable dominant values of American life and culture, and the need for Catholics to challenge this dominant culture in their own lives. It is a recognition by Catholics of aspects of American culture that are not conducive to "seeking God and doing what piety demands." In other words, the third problem mentioned earlier—the loss of Christian values in professedly Christian nations and the appearance of injustice, oppression, and violence—creates a situation where the Church must struggle for a new enculturation of the faith which will bring about justice and peace.

The Contemporary Scene and the Contemporary Challenge

The post-World War II immigrants are largely from Central and South America, the Caribbean, and Asia. They are largely Hispanic, from Puerto Rico, Mexico, the Dominican Republic, and Central and South America. Blacks from the Caribbean, particularly Haitian and Jamaican, also come in large numbers. Immigrants from Asia come largely from the Philippines, India, East Asia, Japan, and Korea. This constitutes a migration equal to that of previous waves of newcomers from Europe. It constitutes a new situation and a new challenge.

Puerto Ricans numbered 2,600,000 in 1985. Technically they are not immigrants. They are born American citizens, but they come from a language and cultural area different from those on the Mainland; their experience is similar to that of immigrants. Mexicans and persons of Mexican background are the largest group, counted at 10.3 million in 1985. There were one million Cubans; 1.7 million from Central and South America; and 1.4 million other Hispanics. Hispanics now constitute forty percent of all Catholics in the United States; if current trends continue, they will be the dominant Catholic population by the year 2050. There were an estimated 3,660,000 Asians in 1985 and numerous Haitians and Jamaicans. The great majority of Hispanics are Catholics; the Haitians are Catholics; many of the Asians, especially from the Philippines, Southeast Asia, and Korea, are Catholics. This constitutes a major challenge to the Church in its effort to provide pastoral care for these new-comers.

The Hispanic Challenge[31]

In this paper I am going to focus on the Hispanic challenge since it is the largest and most important for the future of the Church. Although Hispanics have a common language, Spanish, there are many racial and cultural differences among them. Mexicans are largely *Mestizo*, the offspring of unions of indigenous persons and Europeans; Puerto Ricans and Dominicans consist of persons who range from completely Caucasoid to completely Black with many varieties in between, the offspring of Europeans, African Blacks, and the remnants of indigenous populations. Mexicans, Puerto Ricans, and Dominicans have large numbers of the very poor; refugees and immigrants from Cuba and Central and South America tend to be Caucasoid and middle class. Puerto Ricans and Dominicans are located predominantly in the Northeast, Mexicans in the West, and Cubans in Florida and Northern New Jersey.

There is a certain irony in speaking of Hispanics as immigrants. Hispanics were the first settlers in Florida where the first Mass on what is now American soil was offered at Saint Augustine in 1565. The West was part of Mexico until it was annexed by the United States after the Mexican-American War in 1848. The descendants of these Mexicans numbered close to a million. However, the challenge of today is the great increase of Spanish-speaking persons from all the above mentioned areas. Demographers suggest that Hispanics will outnumber American Blacks by the year 2000.

In December 1985, the Bishops of the United States issued the pastoral letter, *The Hispanic Presence: Challenge and Commitment*. After describing the size of the Hispanic population and particularly its poverty and deprivation, the Bishops speak of the impressive Christian values of the Hispanic newcomers. They refer to their presence as a "Blessing from God," capable of making a great contribution to the vitality of the Church in the United States. They call for a policy of "cultural pluralism," namely, a respect for the language and culture of the Hispanics, and a policy which would enable them to retain their language and culture as a large Hispanic element in the Church and the nation. The letter outlines the aspects of an apostolate to Hispanics and the Bishops pledge the resources of the Church that are necessary to enable Hispanics to develop as a significant Catholic presence.

The Hispanics have followed patterns of settlement similar to that of earlier immigrants. They have settled in neighborhoods that have become in many instances Spanish speaking communities or *barrios*. The East Harlem section of New York City is called *El Barrio*, and the large market area nearby is called *La Marqueta*. Cubans have transformed Miami into an active international Hispanic business center. Central and South Americans are in clearly recognized neighborhoods in Queens and Long Island. Northern Manhattan in New York City is almost entirely Dominican. Entire towns in Texas and New Mexico are Hispanic, while large sections of cities like Los Angeles are Mexican. Therefore, the settlement pattern is favorable to the immigrant community.

However, it is not clear whether the Church will play the same role for Hispanics that it played for earlier immigrant groups. For one thing, Hispanics have not brought their own clergy and religious with them as the European immigrants did. Furthermore, they came into areas of American cities where parishes and parochial schools already existed, staffed by American priests and nuns. And they came at a time when the former parishioners were moving to other areas.

In order to meet the challenge of pastoral care to the large number of newcomers, a common arrangement was what the Bishops called an "integrated" parish. The existing clergy learned Spanish, sought to familiarize themselves with Hispanic culture, and made an effort to minister to Hispanics in the same parish with Catholics of older ethnic or national or racial backgrounds. Eventually many of these parishes became entirely Hispanic and really serve as a national or language parish for the Hispanics.

This has required a massive effort on the part of the Church to prepare American priests, religious, and lay persons in the Spanish language and in the cultural background and religious styles of Hispanics. Centers such as the Institute of Intercultural Communication, which flourished in Ponce, Puerto Rico, from 1957-72, and the Mexican American Cultural Center, which still flourishes in San Antonio, Texas, are two of the better known centers where thousands of Americans have been trained for work with Hispanics.

Thus the principle of pastoral care officially stated by the American Bishops is the right of Hispanics for a ministry in their own language and according to their own cultural background. This is one aspect of the effort on a larger scale to enable Hispanics to retain their language and culture while they learn English and adapt to an American way of life.

One major difficulty in this process is the problem of the class difference between a middle class clergy and a middle class Catholic Church in relation to a very poor population of Hispanics. As indicated above, as the immigrants moved into middle and upper middle class status in the United States, they brought the Church with them. As a result, the Church has developed the characteristics of American middle class life in its organization and its policies and in the attitudes and behavior of clergy and faithful. The clergy have not suffered with the immigrants; they have not walked across the border with illegals or fled from revolutions, oppression, and injustice in Central America; although many have made a great effort to share the life of the poor, to be their advocates, the difference between a predominantly middle class Church and a population of poor immigrants or refugees is more difficult to bridge than the difference between cultures. This may become the most serious challenge to the Church in its pastoral care of Hispanics.

Nevertheless, the official policy is in place and a remarkable effort has been made by clergy, religious, and lay persons to minister to Hispanics in their own language and in a cultural style that is familiar to them. An extensive effort is in progress to enable the Hispanics to retain their language and their culture as they settle in the United States.

Meanwhile, a vigorous involvement of Hispanic clergy has taken place. Although limited in size in contrast to the need, the Hispanic effort has been impressive and promising. There is a vitality in Hispanic parishes that is not often found in the middle class American parishes. Organizationally, Hispanics have already had three National Assemblies, two of them before the only assembly of American Catholics at Detroit in 1976. The *Cursillos*, the *encuentro familial*, the charismatic movement, the involvement of the laity in general are all signs of a vitality which prompted the Bishops to call the Hispanic migration "The Blessing from God."

What the future of the Hispanic experience and influence will be for the Church is still a matter of prophecy. To what extent will the presence of Hispanics result in an adaptation of Hispanics to American culture as creative as that of earlier Catholic immigrants? Will Hispanics be able to retain a cultural pluralism more successfully than previous immigrant groups were able to do? The evidence is already strong that the same process of adjustment that marked the life of earlier immigrants is occurring with Hispanics.[32] The language is being lost among second and third generation; intermarriage with non-Hispanics is widespread and increasing; despite the extensive poverty, there is evidence of substantial socio-economic advancement in the second and third generation. These are signs of an adjustment to middle class American life and Catholicism.

On the other hand, there is evidence that the Hispanic experience may be different. Hispanics are close to their lands of origin, and movement back and forth is very active, a contact and communication with their traditional culture that earlier immigrants did not have. The philosophy of the nation has also changed. The 1965 amendments to the immigration laws of the United States did away with cultural preferences; it has acknowledged the right of people of all nations and cultures to have equal access to the United States. There has been a substantial growth of intercultural understanding and sensitivity generally and an increase in respect for persons of different cultures. Hispanics are the first immigrants to make a major issue of bilingual education; through their influence they were successful in getting the Bilingual Education Act passed by Congress. This may result in a more successful effort to retain language and culture than occurred among earlier immigrants.

Thus the Church faces a new challenge in the development of pastoral care in the presence of a new cultural challenge. In the experience of Hispanics, the emphasis has been the maintenance of language and culture in the presence of the dominant influence of the United States. There is the other dimension of the adjustment of Hispanics to a middle class Catholic Church in the United States, and an American society and culture which is creating serious problems for all Catholics. Hispanics in the post-World War II period have been outstanding in their challenge to the injustice and oppression of existing cultures and societies. It is possible that they may manifest this spirit in the United States. In so doing they may bring a new vitality to the prophetic witness of the Church and a more effective challenge to the secular features of American culture. If this occurs in even modest ways, it would constitute the "blessing" of the Hispanic presence. What is clear is that this new experience for the Church will be a test of traditional methods of pastoral care, and possibly the development of more creative kinds of ministry for all Catholics in the United States and the world.

Notes

1. There is a growing literature about the problem of the Church and cultures. Pastoral institutes have developed throughout the world studying local or regional cultures, popular religiosity, and the possible adaptations of Catholic belief and practice to differing cultures. In the United States, one of the best known is the Mexican American Cultural Center (MACC) in San Antonio, Texas, which studies the expression of the faith in Hispanic cultures and the possibilities of cultural pluralism in the Church of the United States. On a more sophisticated and academic level, the Institute for Ecumenical and Cultural Research at Collegeville, Minnesota, is a center for research and publications about the relation of the Church to differing cultures and differing religious beliefs. International conferences occur regularly, such as the conference in the summer of 1985 at Tontur in Israel at which theologians and social scientists discussed the issue of cultural differences and the Church. Where appropriate, reference will be made to relevant publications or conferences. The definitive reference work is *Bibliografia Missionaria* (Rome: Pontifical Mission Library), which annually publishes titles of publications about Asia, Africa, Oceania, etc., from all European languages.

2. Scriptural quotations are from *The Jerusalem Bible*.

3. For a more extensive treatment of inculturation, see Joseph P. Fitzpatrick, S.J., *One Church, Many Cultures: The Challenge of Diversity* (Kansas City, Mo.: Sheed and Ward, 1987).

4. Ibid, Chapter 2, "Culture." See also the remarkable statement on "The Proper Development of Cultures" in *The Pastoral Constitution on the Church in the Modern World (Gaudium et Spes)*, Part 2, Chapter 2, *The Documents of Vatican II*, ed. Walter M. Abbott, S.J. (New York: Herder and Herder, 1966).

5. See Fitzpatrick, *One Church, Many Cultures*, Chapters 3 and 6.

6. The most important official statement on inculturation is found in the apostolic exhortation of Pope Paul VI, *Evangelii Nuntiandi (Evangelization in the Modern World)*, December 8, 1975, AAS 68 (1/31/76), 5-76. The English translation is published in *The Pope Speaks*, V.21, n.1 (1976), 4-51. This has extensive documentation. This was followed by a statement from the IV Synod of Bishops (1977), *Message to the People of God*, *Origins*, V.7, n.21 (Nov. 10, 1977), 321ff. The standard reference source is found in *Bibliografia Missionaria*.

8. *Evangelii Nuntiandi*, par. 20.

9. *Justice in the World*, Synod of Bishops, Second General Assembly (November 30, 1971), reprinted in *The Gospel of Peace and Justice*, ed. J. Gremillion (Maryknoll, New York: Orbis Press, 1976), 513-29.

10. Ibid, par. 6.

11. Conference of Latin American Bishops (CELAM), *The Church in the Present Day Transformation of Latin America in the Light of the Council* (Aptdo. Aereo 5278, Bogota, D.E. Colombia, South America, 1970).

12. *Puebla and Beyond*, ed. John Eagleson and Philip Sharper (Maryknoll, New York: Orbis Books, 1979).

13. Fitzpatrick, *One Church, Many Cultures*, Chapter 3.

14. *Evangelii Nuntiandi*, par. 48.

15. Karl Rahner, "Towards a Fundamental Theological Interpretation of Vatican II," *Theological Studies* 40 (December, 1979): 716-27.

16. Decree on Eastern Catholic Churches (Orientalium Ecclesiarum), *The Documents of Vatican II*, ed. Walter Abbott , S.J. (New York: Herder and Herder, 1966) .

17. Christopher Dawson, "Sociology as a Science," in *Dynamics of World History*, ed. John J. Mulloy (New York: Sheed and Ward, 1956), 31.

18. Pope John Paul II, "Address to the Participants at the Gregorian University on the Occasion of the 400th Anniversary of the Arrival of Father Matthew Ricci in China," October 26, 1982, in *Acta Romana: Societatis Iesu* (Rome: Curia of the General of the Society of Jesus, 1983), V.18, n. 3, 740-747.

19. Propaganda Fidei, Instructio: *Pluries instanterque*, May 26, 1936, AAS 28 (1936), 406-9.

20. There is an abundant literature on the history of immigration to the United States. The definitive reference work on the subject is *The Harvard Encyclopedia of American Ethnic Groups*, ed. Stephen Thornstrom, Ann Orlov, and Oscar Handlin (Cambridge, Massachusetts: Harvard University Press, 1980). This has an account of each of the ethnic groups together with topical articles about the many aspects of the study of immigration. There are also very good studies of each of the ethnic groups. Cecil Woodham Smith, *The Great Hunger* (New York: Harper and Row, 1963), gives the background to the Irish migration at the time of the famine; William Shannon, *The American Irish* (New York: MacMillan, 1962), is an excellent study of Irish experience and the Irish character in America; Oscar Handlin, *Boston's Immigrants* (Cambridge, Massachusetts: Harvard University Press, rev. ed. 1969), examines the adjustment of the Irish to the Boston area. The background of the Germans is found in Albert B. Faust, *The German Element in the United States*, two volumes, reprint (New York, 1968). Richard O'Connor, *The German Americans* (New York, 1968), describes the Germans in the United States; Philip Gleason, *The Conservative Reformers: German-American Catholics and the Social Order* (Notre Dame: Notre Dame University Press, 1968), provides information about the role of the Germans in the Catholic Church. For the Italians, Robert F. Foerster, *The Italian Emigration in Our Time*, reprint (New York, 1968), provides the background of the Italians before they came; Alexander De Conde, *Half Bitter, Half Sweet: An Excursion into Italian-American History* (New York,

1971), provides the history of Italians in the United States; Silvano Tomasi, *Piety and Power: The Role of Italian Parishes in the New York Metropolitan Area, 1830-1930* (Staten Island, New York: Center for Migration Studies), is a study of the Catholic experience of the Italians in New York.

21. Two excellent histories of the Catholic Church in the United States have appeared in recent years: James Hennessey, S.J., *American Catholics: A History of the Roman Catholic Community in the United States* (New York: Oxford, 1981), and Jay Dolan, *The American Catholic Experience: A History from Colonial Times to the Present* (New York: Doubleday, 1985). Both have extensive bibliographic notes which are helpful.

22. See Nathan Glazer and Daniel Patrick Moynihan, *Beyond the Melting Pot* (Cambridge, Massachusetts: MIT Press, 2d ed., 1970), "The Irish."

23. Joseph P. Fitzpatrick, "The Role of the Parish in the Spiritual Care of New Immigrants," *Studi Emigrazione* (Via della Scrafa 70, Rome, Italy), V.III, n.7 (Oct. 1966) 1-28.

24. The process of integration or assimilation is the object of different definitions and controversies. More will be said of this later. At this point, the term "integration" is used simply as a designation of a successful adjustment to American life.

25. See Milton Gordon, *Assimilation in American Life* (New York: Oxford, 1964). This is still the definitive work on the adjustment of immigrants to American life.

26. Richard D. Alba, "Social Assimilation among American Catholic Nationality Groups," *American Sociological Review*, 41:1030-46.

27. National Conference of Catholic Bishops, *The Challenge of Peace: God's Promise and Our Response, A Pastoral Letter on War and Peace* (Washington, D.C.: United States Catholic Conference, 1983).

28. National Conference of Catholic Bishops, *Economic Justice for All: Pastoral Letter on Catholic Social Teaching and the U.S. Economy* (Washington, D.C.: U.S. Catholic Conference, 1986).

29. National Conference of Catholic Bishops, *Brothers and Sisters to Us* (Washington, D.C.: U.S. Catholic Conference, 1978).

30. National Conference of Catholic Bishops, *The Hispanic Presence: Challenge and Commitment* (Washington, D.C.: U.S. Catholic Conference, 1984).

31. Fitzpatrick, *One Church, Many Cultures*, Chapter 5, "Hispanics in the United States."

32. The most extensive and penetrating analysis of the Hispanic population in the United States is found in A. J. Jaffe, Ruth M. Gullen, and Thomas D. Boswell, *The Changing Demography of Spanish Americans* (New York: Academic Press, 1980). Although based on 1970 Census data, the analysis still provides the best insight into the characters of Hispanics in the United States. For reliable information about Hispanics on the local New

York City levels, see Joseph P. Fitzpatrick and Douglas Gurak, *Hispanic Intermarriage in New York City: 1975* (Hispanic Research Center, Fordham University, Bronx, New York 10458). Data for this study were taken from 1975 marriage records in the Office of the City Clerk.

Sacrament of Unity: Ethical Issues in Pastoral Care of Migrants and Refugees

Drew Christiansen, SJ
University of Notre Dame

A note to the reader on Annotations: To make source references more accessible to the reader, I have listed the section/paragraph numbers used in well-known church social documents in parenthesis. I have followed the same procedure for primary statements on care of migrants and refugees; but ad-hoc statements, papal homilies, etc. are listed in the endnotes.

Two months ago Pope John Paul II caused a stir at a Mass in San Antonio when, during his homily, he had words of praise for men and women who worked for migrants from Mexico and Central America. "Among you are people of great courage and generosity," said the pope, "who have been doing much on behalf of the suffering brothers and sisters among you from the south. They have sought to show compassion in the midst of complex human, social and political realities."[1] The pope's words were strong, but general. In the last century, or even in earlier decades in this century, there would have been no need to be more specific. Papal statements were general in formulation but specific in their intentions, and everyone would have understood whom he intended to praise. But such subtleties, while they may be acceptable elsewhere and at other times, are lost on contemporary Americans. The Holy Father's words immediately became an occasion for a conflict of interpretations.

On one side, workers in the Sanctuary Movement took the Holy Father's words as an endorsement of their work. On the other, the Immigration and Naturalization Service asked the Vatican press office for a clarification. Pressured for a statement, Vatican spokesman Joaquin Navarro-Vals offered a plausible denial. Local people responded that, in any case, their bishop had consistently supported sanctuary workers.

The mini-drama in San Antonio is a kind of parable of the ethical issues in the Church's pastoral care of migrants and refugees. In matters of principle, Church teaching is clear. In the words of the Holy Father's address to Catholic Charities in San Antonio, "The aim of Christian solidarity and service is to defend and promote, in the name of Jesus Christ, the dignity and fundamental rights of every person."[2] But the teaching does not translate directly into a single strategy or policy because, to cite the pope's phrase once more, Christians must exercise their compassion "in the face of complex human, social and political realities." To determine just how those high moral principles are to be applied in the midst of those complex realities is the function of ethics.

In the tradition of Catholic moral theology, ethics consists in working out with greater precision what moral principle requires of conscientious persons in real-life circumstances. With respect to the rights of migrants and refugees, the task of ethics is to determine how the church's defense of human rights of peoples may be implemented in a world-system of nation-states. For the church's teaching on the rights of migrants is a global ethic that looks to the well-being of all persons and every person, while the international system, with a plurality of sovereign states, treats human movement not as a right but as a matter of state policy. There are other factors, of course—the so-called international labor market, for example—but none has the controlling influence over both problems of human movement and the avenues of relief or solution of those problems as do nation-states. The context of the pastoral care of migrants, therefore, is set by "the complex realities" of the nation-state system.

In the paper that follows, I shall argue that the ethical issues in pastoral care of migrants and refugees arise to a significant degree because of the intersection of the global human rights ethic found in Catholic social teaching with the political realities of the nation-state system. I assume, in keeping with the consistent teaching of the church, that "pastoral care" does not refer simply to evangelization and ministration of the sacraments, nor even to relief of suffering and misery, but extends also to the defense and promotion of the human rights of migrants as those rights are articulated in official Catholic social teaching. Catholic social teaching views even the religious rights of people to worship, to hear the word of God preached to them, and to live their faith life without interference as human rights. Thus, pastoral care cannot be separated from a broader defense and promotion of human rights.[3]

To be specific, in our American context ethical dilemmas arise for the pastoral care of peoples-in-movement out of the tensions between Catholic teaching on human rights and U.S. government policies. The distinction between political and economic refugees, selective definition of political refugees, admission on the basis of individual standing rather than on family status, customary employment of migrant farm labor—these policies are representative of the issues presented to American Catholics by U.S. immigration law.

My remarks will fall in three parts. First, I shall delineate the church's general teaching on the rights of migrants in light of the basic social theology of the post-Vatican II church. I shall argue that the church's pastoral concern for the rights of migrants is rooted in the very catholicity of the church, which is itself a sign and instrument of the unity of the human family. I shall further contend that in a world of sovereign nation-states the catholicity of the church's teaching on human rights serves both as an effective symbol of political transformation and a sign of contradiction to henotheistic nationalism.

Secondly, I shall examine in detail the specific rights and ethical obligations stipulated in church social teaching as well as some that are implied by statements on pastoral care. I shall distinguish between those moral principles that can be fulfilled *within the parameters of U.S. law* and those that can only be respected *at the limits of U.S. law*. These borderline cases involve obligations to work to change both law and public policy, and at the extreme they include the duty to provide safe haven to those in serious need whose rights are not respected by current government practice.

Thirdly, I shall return to the controversy over the Holy Father's remarks in San Antonio. I shall ask how Catholics ought to proceed when, due to political considerations or other constraints, magisterial teaching seems to become exhortative rather than prescriptive. I shall suggest that there are at present at least three models of Christian involvement in public issues in the contemporary church, and that the one appropriate to immigration issues is "the community of discernment." Finally, I shall advance some hermeneutical principles for the interpretation of social teaching in communities of discernment.

Part I
The Church: Sacrament of the Unity of Mankind

The unity of the human family in God's redemptive plan is at the heart of the life of the church. "Christ," declared Lumen Gentium, Vatican II's Dogmatic Constitution on the Church, "is the light of all nations." The church sheds Christ's light "by proclaiming the gospel to every creature." On the basis of this relationship to Christ, the Council Fathers defined the church as "a kind of sacrament or sign of intimate union with God, and of the unity of all [human]kind" (1).

The Council summed up its belief in the church's global mission when it announced that "the promotion of unity belongs to the innermost mission of the church" (42). Following the traditional notion of sacrament as an efficacious sign, the Council added, the church "is also an instrument for the achievement of such union and unity" (1). The means by which the church is an effective instrument of the unity of the human family is elaborated in *Gaudium et Spes*, the *Pastoral Constitution on the Church in the Modern World*. Returning to the church's reflection of Christ to the world, the Council announced:

> This she does *most of all by her healing and elevating impact on the dignity of the human person, by the way in which she strengthens the seams of human society* and imbues the everyday activity of men [*sic*] with a deeper meaning and importance (40). [Emphasis added.]

"By virtue of the gospel committed to her," declared the Council, "the Church proclaims the rights of man [*sic*]" (41). From the church's fundamental religious mission, it added, "come a function, a light and an energy which can serve to structure and consolidate the human community.... As a matter of fact, when circumstances of time and place create the need, she can and indeed should initiate activities on behalf of all men [*sic*]." In the advancement of universal human rights, the two services the church offers the world—the defense of the dignity of the person and the building up of the unity of the human family—converge. "Promoting the rights of all persons, irrespective of nationality," the Council declared, "is accordingly of the essence of the church's mission in the world" (42).

One of the areas in which the church has most persistently advanced the cause of human solidarity is the defense of rights of migrants and refugees. Pope John XXIII defined the right to freedom of movement to include both the right to emigrate *and* the less well-recognized right to immigrate.

Every human being has the right to freedom of movement and of residence within the confines of his own country; and, when there are just reasons for it, the right to emigrate to other countries and to take up residence there (*Pacem in terris* 25).

Paul VI identified specific rights of migrants that need legal guarantees. "It is urgently necessary for people to go beyond a narrowly nationalistic attitude [toward migrant workers]," Paul wrote, "and to give them a charter which will assure their right to emigrate, favor their integration, facilitate their professional advancement and give them access to decent housing where . . . their families can join them" (A Call to Action 17). In the magisterial reasoning, nationality, including statelessness, is no bar to the full enjoyment of human rights. As Pope John wrote in *Pacem in terris*: "The fact that one is a citizen of a particular state does not detract in any way from his [sic] membership in the human family as a whole, nor from his citizenship in the world community" (25).

Human Rights and the Universal Common Good

John XXIII: Both Nationals and World Citizens

In recent Catholic social teaching, *Pacem in terris* stands as the basic charter of human rights. For the first time in a papal document, Pope John in that encyclical explained the moral order in terms of human rights, linked the common good to guarantees of human rights, and prescribed the promotion of personal rights as the primary end of government. In the same letter, however, John recognized the inadequacy of nation-states and the international system to realize the common good and with it the rights of individuals.

"In times past," wrote Pope John, "it seemed that leaders of nations might be in a position to provide for the universal common good, either through normal diplomatic channels, or through top-level meetings, or through conventions or treaties. . ." (133). But "under the present circumstances of human society," John observed, "both the structure and form of governments as well as the power which public authority wields in all the nations of the world must be considered inadequate to promote the universal common good" (135). To meet global problems, the pope argued, a universal public authority is necessary. John did not argue for world government, nor did he specify the kind of "regime" (i.e., set of political arrangements) needed to promote the common good. He did, however, identify "the fundamental objective" of this global authority to be "the recognition, safeguarding and promotion of the rights of human persons."

Pacem in terris offered special praise for the United Nations and U.N. Universal Declaration of Human Rights on the grounds that "in most solemn form, the dignity of the human person is acknowledged to all human beings." Pope John concluded with the earnest hope that the U.N. might "become ever more equal to the magnitude and nobility of its task" to be "an effective safeguard for the rights which derive directly from [our human] dignity as [persons], and which are therefore universal, inviolable and inalienable rights." The pope added that his hope was fired by the expectation that as citizens became more active participants in their own governments they would also become more active world citizens, "consciously aware that they are living members of the whole human family."

John Paul II: Historic Failures

In his inaugural encyclical letter, *Redemptor hominis*, Pope John Paul II reaffirmed the teaching of Pope John and the Council on human rights as central to the church's mission to human unity (RM 17). But after the passage of sixteen years from the publication of *Pacem in terris*, John Paul was less sanguine about the ability of political institutions to meet the standards of the Universal Declaration on Human Rights. He questioned whether governments' official profession of adherence to international instruments constituted an effective commitment to the rights of persons throughout the world. The failures of nations to defend the rights of their citizens, and even more the violations of those very rights by governments' own agents demands, the pope urged, "continual revision of programmes, systems and regimes" in the interest of advancing the human rights enjoyed by all peoples. (17)

In the 1980 encyclical *Dives in misericordia*, John Paul again noted that in the years that have past since the Council dangers only latent in the 1960s during the pontificate of Pope John and the years of the Council have become more evident. He especially noted the danger of " 'peaceful' subjugation of individuals, of environments, of entire societies and of nations. . . ." (DM 11) In particular, the pope cites "the continued existence of torture, systematically used by authority as a means of domination and political oppression and practiced by subordinates with impunity" (11). In short, as John Paul reads the signs of the times, contemporary political institutions, and particularly the nation-state, are at best hypocritical defenders of human rights; at worst, they are the gravest source of systematic violations of those rights. Recent history, concludes the Holy Father, therefore bears out the classical maxim "Summum ius, summa iniuria." (Colloquially translated, this axiom of Roman law means "The highest authority [i.e., the nation-state] is capable of the gravest injustice.") For that reason, the pope argues genuine care for human rights can only come from spiritual sources, especially merciful Christian love.

Thus, the theological ethics of official Catholic social teaching questions the adequacy of the nation-state to realize human rights for all. For Pope John, the problem was one of the inadequacy of the international system to meet global needs. For Pope John Paul, however, the difficulties are more profound. The state system is all too often an instrument not of human rights, but of "oppression, intimidation, violence and terrorism" (RM 17). Like the totalitarian regimes of mid-century, today's governments restrict the rights of their citizens for the sake of the supposed higher good of the state. While in theory governments are constituted to assure the rights of their citizens, in fact they have proven a primary cause of their oppression.

Practical Guidelines

From this succession of reading of the signs of the times, we may draw two practical directives for Catholic involvement in immigration questions:

(1) Based on John XXIII's *principle of the global common good*, we may conclude that when we participate as citizens of our own nation, we are required to think and act as citizens of the world.
(2) Following the teaching of John Paul II, we ought to examine the laws and policies of our own nation and work for their revision with the goal of increasing their effectiveness for enhancing universal human rights. This might be called, using the pope's own words, *the principle of continual revision.*

In no area have nations generally restricted the rights of their own and other peoples for the sake of national interest as in the field of migration. We turn now to consider the other side of the problem: the sovereign rights of nations to control their borders, and so the movement of peoples.

The "New Serfdom" and Rights of Movement

In his recent book *Closed Borders*, Professor Alan Dowty has argued that after the right to life, the single most important human right is freedom of movement. Following a 1963 United Nations study, he contends that the right to leave a country and return is nothing less than "a right to personal self-determination." "Personal self-determination," he explains, "connotes the right to accept or reject the political jurisdiction in which one happens to live—in other words, the right to remain party to one's current social contract or to seek another."[4] This ranking is due freedom of movement, Dowty claims, because denial of the right "eliminates the means to escape all other forms of persecution and injustice."[5] It is especially important in our times because never before have governments had both such great potential for total control over the lives of their citizens and extensive command of their borders. For this reason, the right to emigrate is the "final lifeline for victims of racial, religious, and political persecution." "Freedom of movement," concludes Dowty, "is thus the ultimum refugium libertatis—the last refuge of liberty."[6]

Nations, however, have not seen it that way. In the name of national security, national interest, and social good, governments have limited or denied the right to emigrate to some groups, forced others into unwanted exile, exploited guest-workers, denied admission to refugees in dire need, and ruled refugees of their own making to be economic refugees ineligible for asylum. The result is what Dowty calls a "new serfdom" in which, on the one hand, a multiplicity of legal devices and government rulings effectively reduce persons to disposable objects of state policy, and, on the other hand, the opportunities for refuge have been narrowed or effectively closed. The symbols of this new development are stateless persons, such as Palestinians, who have been denationalized but who can acquire no new nationality. For such peoples, the world—as Chaim Weizman wrote of Jewish exiles of the 1930s—"is divided into places where they cannot live and places where they cannot enter."[7]

The Problem of Sovereignty

Rights of movement are affirmed but not upheld, because nation-states are sovereign powers against whom there is no effective appeal.[8] Pope John Paul's exasperation with a state-of-affairs where human rights are everywhere affirmed in principle, but in practice nearly everywhere denied, is a reflection of the fact that there is no higher authority to which to appeal. Compliance with international agreements, like the Universal Declaration and its associated covenants, is dependent on self-enforcement by the signatory countries. Conservative pressures have long prevented the United States from ratifying the U.N. human rights protocols on the grounds that such agreements on behalf of universal standards would infringe on American sovereignty. The result is that U.S. immigration and refugee policy has been a matter of "calculated kindness," determined not by the rights of persons, but by the interests of the nation.[9]

Part II
Ethical Issues: Within and Beyond Borders

The 1969 *Instruction on the Care of People Who Migrate* views the contemporary movements of peoples as a positive contribution to the integration of the human family. "Migrations . . . give witness to and promote the unity of the human family," the Instruction reads. These movements, it adds, "confirm that communion of brotherhood among peoples 'in which each party is at the same time a giver and receiver' " (IPC 2). Following the idea that migrations contribute to the unity of humanity rather than tensions between peoples of different nationalities, the Congregation of Bishops asserts the rights of individuals, families, and ethnic groups to a homeland. The right to homeland, it contends, entails both the right to emigrate and the right to immigrate.[10] Poverty, population pressures, and government repression, according to the Congregation, are warrants not only for migration from one's country of origin but also for justifiable claims to incorporation in a new land.[11]

The Right to Immigrate

It is frequently asserted that while there is a right to emigrate, there is no right to immigrate. The Westphalian state-system and liberal political philosophy give a certain plausibility to such a distinction. History has proved it to be a pernicious discrimination. A right to emigrate is vacuous if there is no corresponding right to immigrate. Official catholic social teaching is unambiguous on this issue. The reasons that justify emigration equally justify immigration, and only "grave requirements of the common good, considered objectively" permit making exceptions to this rule.[13] As John XXIII taught in *Pacem in terris*, a person has a right "to enter a political community where he hopes he can more fittingly provide a future for himself and his dependents." According to the late pope, moreover, the common good requires that the host country fulfill its duty "to accept such immigrants and to help to integrate them into itself as new members" (PT 106).

On the right of immigration, then, Catholic social teaching is more rational and humane than either international law or the practice of nations. For example, although Article 15 of the Universal Declaration declares, "No one shall be arbitrarily deprived of his nationality nor denied the right to change his nationality," international agreements define rights of asylum and immigration less generously than Catholic social teaching.[14] Also, such agreements as have been ratified have met with less than universal adoption. The United States, for example, has not ratified the International Covenant on Civil and Political Rights.

Where rights to emigration and to change of nationality have been accepted in principle, they have often been denied in practice. As Alan Dowty has pointed out, the twentieth century has seen growing restriction of rights of movement both by sending and receiving countries. Wherever nations fail as a matter of course to honor these rights, and make their recognition only a matter of stipulated exception, they are in effect making persons subservient to state interests. This is the "new serfdom" of which Dowty writes.[15] Such a result is antithetical to any notion of human rights and inconsistent with the legitimate function of government to defend and promote human rights.[16] Nations whose restrictive immigration controls hamper the right to choose a new homeland are complicit in sustaining the new serfdom. From Catholic perspective on universal human rights, they are as much at fault as nations that restrict emigration.

Open Borders: Weighing States' Rights to Control Movement

Sometimes state control of movement, whether of immigration or of emigration, is justified on the grounds that states have the right to regulate their borders and determine the terms of citizenship. Accordingly, it is often asserted in political theory and practice that personal rights to emigration and especially immigration need to be weighed against the rights of sovereign states. This proposition is repeated, for example, in the Texas bishops' October 1985 statement, "The Pastoral Care of Hispanic Immigrants." "On the legal and moral plane, the rights of suffering members of the human family . . . must be balanced with the right of a nation to regulate the movement of peoples across its border in order to maintain its well-being."[17] As a matter of legal practice and a question of constitutional and statutory law, state control of borders cannot be denied. However, the bishops' admission, while politically prudent, is misleading. For since the time of Pius XII magisterial social theology has so thoroughly contested the right of sovereign powers of states to unqualified control of their borders that any assertion of sovereign rights in this area must be judged, from the point of view of Catholic social ethics, a secondary or residual right, not one of primary importance. The older presumption in favor of state authority holds only in exceptionally grave circumstances.[18]

As noted in the National Conference of Catholic Bishops' 1976 *Resolution on the Pastoral Concern of the Church for People on the Move:* "In his 1952 Christmas Address, Pius XII deplored the fact that 'the natural right of the individual to be unhampered in immigration or emigration is not recognized or, in practice, is nullified under the pretext of a common good which is falsely understood or falsely applied, but sanctioned and made mandatory by legislative or administrative measures' " (NCCB 10). Since that time, the consistent official teaching on this matter, repeated most recently by Pope John Paul II in Laborem Exercens (23), is that as a general rule individuals' and families' rights to movement have priority over the rights of nations to prevent their free movement.[19]

Catholic social teaching has asserted the prima facie priority of the personal right to movement over the right of state control on the twin premises of the common good and human rights. The state exists to effect the common good of its citizens. When the common good is unrealized, particularly when a population does not enjoy basic human rights, people are free to make a new home elsewhere. Under the principle of the universal common good (and solidarity), recipient countries are obligated to accept immigrants under the general rule that all governments are expected to uphold human rights of all peoples, particularly those who seek refuge in their territory.

The end of all political authority is "the recognition, respect, safeguarding, and promotion of the rights of the human person."[20] When one nation or another fails to honor those rights, it falls to those nations to which the victims flee or appeal, according to the teaching of John XXIII, to vindicate those rights.[21] Historically, then, the principle of the universal common good is in part a recognition of the failure of governments to realize the common good and to honor human rights. It is a moral remedy, if you will, a principle of redress, to correct the omissions, failures, and violations of nation-states against their own people. In Catholic teaching, therefore, the right of states to exclude immigration, though not necessarily to regulate it, is limited to special, exceptional circumstances. It ought not be a matter of general practice.

Alan Dowty, in, argues that while "not completely achievable" a universal right to free movement is "a basic right" because it is "the last line of defense in the realization of other rights." "The right to change one's nationality may be . . . 'fundamental to the structure of human opportunity.' "[22] In addition, he writes, "freedom of movement is . . . also a means to achieve such other widely espoused goals as greater economic justice, a better distribution of resources, and the spread of shared values."[23]

As a practical matter, however, Dowty (despite his attachment to open borders) acquiesces to the current compromise of a modest increase in legal immigration in return for greater controls on illegal entry. The NCCB has accepted the same compromise with maximal reservations to protect existing resident aliens and the American poor.[24] In the long run, however, the Catholic affirmation of the right to immigrate requires lobbying on behalf of still more open borders as well as for foreign policies that contribute to reducing the occasions for mass migrations.

General Duties to Immigrant Peoples

From the universal right to immigrate, as articulated in Catholic social teaching, two general consequences seem to follow. First, Catholic citizens are required to work to see that as far as possible the laws of their countries adhere to the universal norm, viz., the recognition of the right to a homeland. Though limited by the terms of the legislative debate, the NCCB's 1985 resolution that then pending immigration reform include "legalization opportunities for the maximum number of undocumented" and that there be "no administrative arbitrariness in determining who shall be excluded" represents, within the limits of the current American political consensus, the intention of Catholic social teaching that immigration be regarded as a universal right.[25] The practical import of Catholic teaching, of course, goes further, namely, that the United States and other nations ought to permit virtually open borders for all those who have serious reason to abandon their ancestral homeland and seek a new life elsewhere.

Secondly, where laws do not respect this right, Catholics and others are under obligation to give aid to those in need who cannot legally receive asylum or acquire new nationality. This is again an obligation of redress for times and situations where laws and policies in the real world fall short of the demands of rational morality. Both the sanctuary movement and ecclesiastically sanctioned work with migrants, such as that advocated by Los Angeles's Archbishop Mahony last April for those who do not apply for naturalization under Simpson-Rodino-Mazzoli, follow this principle of redress. To ignore those illegal residents who do not qualify for amnesty under current law, Mahony wrote, "would be to disregard the rich heritage of Catholic social teaching regarding workers, immigrants and those for whom the church has made a 'preferential option': the poorest of the poor." "The new law tells us that these people are outside the framework of our concern as a society," the Archbishop concludes, but "our Christian tradition tells us the opposite. The Gospel itself and the teachings of our church call us to be most concerned for these most needful and neglected members of our community."[26]

Migration for Economic Reasons

One further distinction between U.S. law and Catholic social teaching is worth noting: Catholic social teaching honors the right to change nationality for economic reasons. John XXIII affirmed the notion that seeking humane conditions of life warrants claims to new nationality.[27] Citing Vatican II's teaching on "The Common Purpose of Created Things," the 1969 Instruction also asserted that "where a state which suffers from poverty combined with great population cannot supply such use of goods to its inhabitants . . . people possess a right to emigrate, to select a new home in foreign lands and to seek conditions of life worthy of man [*sic*]" (IPC 7, n.14). The logic of this passage is clear. The goods of the earth belong to everyone. When one country cannot provide for the material well-being of its people, then those nations which have excess resources have a duty to admit immigrants who come in search of a better life. The economic warrant does not justify an unlimited right to freedom of opportunity. It does not, for example, warrant exodus of educated groups in a so-called "brain drain" or of propertied classes in "capital flight" from poor countries.[28] It basically addresses the needs of people who suffer severe economic deprivation. Degrading poverty and economic entrapment, not relative deprivation and increased opportunity, lie behind the assertion of the right to immigrate for economic reasons.

The pejorative designation of "economic refugees" in current U.S. practice is repugnant to the spirit of Catholic social teaching. Even in contemporary liberal political theory, economic deprivation, exploitation, and oppression are recognized to be grounds for rights claims equal in weight to political persecution or repression.[29] The preservation of a distinction in American immigration policy between political and economic refugees denies the enormous, prolonged, and unrelieved suffering of people in impoverished lands like Haiti or from the poorer regions of Mexico. In Catholic social ethics, degrading poverty is as much a denial of human dignity as subjection to political tyranny. From the recognition of the right to economic migration, a number of conclusions follow:

(1) Economic immigrants ought to be legitimate claimants to integration as citizens and legal residents in the United States.
(2) The poor ought to have priority over other economic migrants in admission to the United States and in eligibility for U.S. citizenship. To effect such a new priority for the poor, privileges for men and women with certain employable skills or professional qualifications need to be strictly limited. (There is little, if any, empirical evidence that an option for the poor places an economic burden on the host country.)[30]
(3) People who have suffered extreme economic deprivation ought to be given the same priority for admission as political refugees from more repressive regimes. The current privileged status of political refugees, especially those fleeing communist regimes, no longer makes moral sense. They still deserve special consideration, but alongside refugees from right-wing authoritarian regimes and economic migrants from the poorest countries.

Finally, the reality of economic migration points to still another obligation: to help prevent economic migration, where possible, through international cooperation and development assistance.[31] This obligation is all the more weighty where political, military, or economic intervention has either contributed to economic deprivation or prevented its correction. At the present time, this principle would seem to apply in a special way to U.S. involvement in Central America.[32]

So much for the general principles of the right to movement. With no further specification by the Theology Project of the ethical questions I am to address, I have chosen to present a taxonomy of the moral problems in the pastoral care of migrants and refugees. As I see it, the ethics of pastoral care falls into four broad areas: (1) ethical questions that relate to the church's direct religious ministry to migrant and refugee peoples, (2) those questions affecting the integration into U.S. society of people already resident in the United States; (3) issues related to the transformation of U.S. law and public policy to realize universal rights of movement; and (4) methods of meeting the urgent needs of displaced persons for whom

U.S. law or administrative practice makes no allowances. For convenience sake, I label these the ethics of religious ministry, the ethics of social integration, the ethics of societal transformation, and the ethics of refuge.

Ethics of Religious Ministry

"It is urgently necessary for people to go beyond a narrowly nationalistic attitude in their [emigrants'] regard," wrote Paul VI in *A Call to Action*, "and to give them a charter which will assure the right to emigrate, favor their integration, facilitate their professional advancement and give them access to decent housing . . . ." So did Paul identify the specific obligations of the citizens of host countries to aid immigrants. He added, "It is everyone's duty, but especially that of Christians, to work with energy for the establishment of universal brotherhood, the indispensible basis for authentic justice and the condition for enduring peace" (OA 17).

The duty to work toward the recognition that we are one human family is the most fundamental of pastoral duties in the church's ministry to people on the move. Religious ministry to migrants, which culminates in the celebration of the Eucharist, the living symbol of the one Body of Christ, takes its orientation, according to numerous church documents, from this unity of the human family under God.

Two Basic Obligations

From the obligation to contribute to building up the one human family, we identify two basic duties for pastoral ministry to migrants. The first is the obligation to show hospitality; the second is the obverse, namely, the duty to fight discrimination.[33] Neither obligation is without its costs. Hospitality always means extending oneself, and hospitality to many needy people may sorely tax the resources of a diocese, parish, or local community. Even more, the fights against discrimination, especially when it involves members of one's own community, even disadvantaged members, can be very demanding for pastoral leaders who are ordinarily conciliators. But to build a more inclusive community, pastors, bishops, educatiors, social workers, and political leaders need to face the prejudice in their communities and to confront discrimination in whatever form it takes.

Pluralism and Integration

One special problem in the domain of hospitality is the question of cultural pluralism. Both the universal church and church in the United States have affirmed the need to honor cultural diversity as part of the strategy of pastoral care of migrant peoples.[34] At the same time, they assert the right of migrant peoples to integration into their host communities. In principle, these two ideals ought to be compatible; in practice, they are often enough concurrent processes. But as a matter of politics and public policy, the two approaches may often be opposed. Think of the controversies over bilingualism and affirmative action.

In the area of respect for immigrant cultures, the church has a special role to play. The first is to preserve the conditions of political civility and Christian charity in the midst of debates over policy. Since both goals are estimable, the work of politics is to find a practical balance between the two. Differences on policy ought not, therefore, be a source of acrimonious division.

Secondly, the church itself can play a dual role at once, as a home to immigrant culture and, in the public arena, as an agency defending against discrimination and promoting social integration. We still have something to learn in this matter from the history of the church in the United States. The old national parishes served as a shelter for cultural cohesion at the same time they provided assistance in making a home in America. While we have a heightened respect for cultural pluralism, there is no denying the long-term trend is toward assimilation. We could do far worse than to update the model of the immigrant American church, because it successfully effected both cultural pluralism and societal integration.

One other model, however, is worth thinking about. In many cities parishes are faced with a variety of immigrant groups in the same geographic area. Cultural segmentation, because of the paucity of religious leaders, is not feasible. An alternate model has sometimes been tried which deserves greater attention. That is the establishment of culturally-centered base communities within one parish. The worship of such parishes takes place in two ways: on a regular basis and for special feasts in the base communities, and on Sundays in the whole parish community in which the diverse base communities are joined. Such a parish makes the church as the sacrament of human unity present in an exceptionally visible way.

I turn now from the church to society, to consider what church teaching requires in the way of incorporation of new peoples into a host country.

The Ethics of Social Integration

Catholic social teaching is quite explicit about the specific rights of resident aliens in host countries. We have already seen how Paul VI urged the integration of migrants in their new countries, "their professional advancement" and "access to decent housing" (OA 17). The 1969 Vatican Instruction on Pastoral Care explains that "the right to seek conditions of life worthy" of a person entails "family housing, education of children, [humane] working conditions, social insurance, and taxes [sic]" (7). A 1978 Letter to Episcopal Conferences from the Pontifical Commission for the Pastoral Care of Migrant and Itinerant Peoples, in a summary of church teaching, adds still other claims: "the right of man to preserve and develop his own ethnic, cultural and linguistic patrimony, to profess his own religion publicly, and to be recognized in accordance with his dignity as a person under all circumstances" (PCM 3).

In essence the rights of people on the move are the universal rights of persons, embracing, as the the Letter says, "the full extent of the whole family of peoples [and] above any class-based or nationalistic egoism" (PCM 3). In plain words, unless there is a grave reason to the contrary, immigrants are entitled to the whole range of human rights including eligibility for citizenship.

Undocumented Aliens

There are two groups whose status frequently puts their rights in jeopardy: undocumented aliens and temporary guest workers. In the United States at present, undocumented residents who do not qualify for amnesty under Simpson-Rodino present a case of special concern. Numerous statements on this question by official church bodies and individual bishops make clear the church's commitment to the undocumented. Archbishop Mahony's statement on amnesty, in particular, makes clear that the legal and political settlement is unsatisfactory from a moral point of view. The church's option for the poor lays on it an obligation to support large groups of people, especially from Central America, who emigrated to the United States after 1982. They are caught in a tragic bind between severe political and economic pressures in their countries of origin, on the one side, and the compromise restriction in U.S. law, on the other. Catholic social teaching makes it incumbent on Catholics at all levels to work for legal recognition, not just of those who do not qualify for the current amnesty because of their late arrival, but for the rights of immigration of all those who seek to stay in this county as a result of economic deprivation or political repression in their homelands.

Guest Workers

Church teaching extends to temporary workers the same protections as long-term immigrants. For example, Paul VI in 1973 endorsed a statute for guest workers which would guarantee them "respect of their personality, security of work, vocational training, family life, schooling for their children . . . social insurance and freedom of speech and association" (NCCB 1976, 12). Such conditions are far from a reality in most industrial democracies. For the most part, migrant workers are subject to the ups-and-downs of demands in the labor market. The interests of employers rather than the rights of workers largely shape national regulation of the flow of workers. This is a situation of which Pope John Paul II has beem sharply critical.

In *Laborem exercens*, John Paul addressed the issue of the potential financial or social exploitation of temporary laborers. He advanced the case of migrant workers both with respect to domestic labor and to capital in the host country. Between migrant and domestic laborers, he argued, there should equality of conditions. "[T]he same criteria should be applied to immigrant workers as to all other workers in the socity concerned," he wrote. "The value of work should be measured by the same standard and not according to the difference in nationality, religion or race." Turning to business, the pope finds it illicit for employers to make any greater profits by employing foreign laborers than they would were they to employ natives. "The situation of constraint in which the emigrant may find himself," the pope admonished, "should not be exploited." He concluded, "Once more the fundamental principle must be repeated . . . capital should be at the service of labor and not labor at the service of capital" (23).

Temporary workers pose one of the more difficult questions of international justice: Is it preferable to hold domestic standards of employment high, and thereby decrease the demand for foreign workers? Or is it more just to admit foreign laborers with some protections as a form of relief to them, their families, and their countries?

Responding to the debate over the 1985 Simpson-Mazzoli bill, the NCCB, in the interest of providing greater justice for the present pool of U.S. workers, argued for (1) a preference for legal immigration over temporary worker status, and (2) maximal legalization of current resident aliens.[35] Professor Dowty, on balance, also supports the priority of increased permanent immigration over temporary work authorization on the grounds that it provides more secure and humane conditions both for immigrants and the domestic population. But once the Simpson-Rodino legislation has time to take hold and the trauma of the 1980 refugee influx has become part of history, there may be reason once again to consider a differentiated immigration program with provision for temporary guest workers.

Elsa Chaney makes a number of arguments on behalf of migrant workers appealing to the principle of solidarity, historic inequities between nations, and the growth of economic interdependence.[36] She contends that precedents exist to guarantee a greater measure of human rights protection for migrant workers, especially in agreements between North African and Middle Eastern countries and receiving nations in Western Europe. In the case of temporary workers in the United States, such an agreement could be worked out between Mexico, Central American countries, and the United States.[37] In the medium term, perhaps what is needed is a staged policy with liberalized amnesty provisions in a revised Simpson-Rodino package as soon as possible, five-to-seven years of adherence to the priority for long-term immigrants, and then, at the end of the interim period, the evolution of international arrangements for guest workers from south of the border.

International Justice and U.S. Foreign Policy

It is generally acknowledged that stemming large immigration flows requires much more than regularization of immigration policies alone. The international community in collaboration with sending and receiving countries needs to address the causes of population movements, particularly endemic poverty. Elsa Chaney proposes increases in development assistance from the United States and promotion of trade with neighboring LDC's. Let the commerce between nations, she argues, be "trade instead of migration."[38] "Any effort to control illegal immigration without addressing the source," says Alan Dowty, "will be futile." Measures that may diminish pressures for migration include "creating new jobs, increasing the purchase of Mexican goods, and instituting training programs for Mexican returnees (much as the French have done for Algerians ready to return home)."[39] These suggestions either are parallel with proposals in Catholic social teaching or consistent with the main lines of Catholic social thought on international economic justice and solidarity among nations.[40]

Under the principle of solidarity, Catholic social teaching holds that affluent nations have the obligation to make sacrifices to close the gap with poor lands.[41] Short of sacrifice, the

United States could still do a great deal for the poor in Mexico, Central America, and the Caribbean. Conscientious nonintervention on the part of the United States might give several countries the opportunity to develop by their own lights or through regional cooperation free of Yankee interference. In the case of Mexico and one or two grave cases like Haiti, more in the way of deliberate assistance and collaboration will probably be necessary. Much careful analysis needs to go into economic development, including reflection and self-criticism about how North American practices have aggravated the suffering in the Caribbean basin.[42] With the waning of American "re-assertionism" in the post-Reagan period, U.S. businesses, universities, professional groups, and government agencies need to evaluate how they can contribute to stable and equitable economic growth in the North American community.

The Ethics of Societal Transformation

Throughout this paper I have noted not only how Catholic social teaching sets an ethical standard for the rights of migrants considerably beyond American policy and practice. I have also argued, at a number of points, that Catholic social teaching entails working for changes in U.S. law, and I have pointed out where Catholic authorities have argued for needed changes and even committed the local church to working at the edges of the law for migrants who are just claimants on our sense of solidarity. At this point, I would like to make a case, if all too briefly, for working to change U.S. law.

Everyone is interested in seeing that the institutions or communities to which he or she is committed are moral, not only in their public professions but even more in their structures and policies. Universal human rights is a developing phenomenon in which our understanding of the scope of rights and their range of applications is continually expanding. Catholic rights theory is among the most expansive to be found anywhere.[43] Its expansiveness is a result of the church's world-wide experience with men and women of every condition. From the perspective of official Catholic theology, human rights are a sign of reverence for the sacredness of the human person made in the image and likeness of God. The 1971 Synod of Bishops made an extraordinary move, which unfortunately the Holy See has not taken as a precedent, to apply universal human rights to ecclesial structures and practices.[44] Human rights served as the basis of the bishops' own examination of conscience.[45] The Synod's move suggests how seriously it regarded the universality of human rights, the observance of which would be a mark of the holiness or sinfulness of the church's own life. In an inchoate way, at least, the Fathers of the Synod worked for the integrity of the church— that is, the purification of its life to adhere to a more comprehensive and humanly adequate standard of morality than had theretofore been the case.[46] Similarly, the NCCB, in committing itself to seeing that church institutions realize the economic rights it proposed for American society in *Economic Justice for All*, set a new standard of ecclesial integrity for the American church.[47]

In the same way, even though the American political tradition has been strong on the assertion of national sovereignty and weak in commitment to international obligations, when American citizens work for immigration reform they are working for the integrity of

American society and our political system. By working to move the country to observe universal human rights by extending those rights to peoples-in-movement, they are enriching the moral quality of our nation. At least in part then, our obligation to transform American immigration policies comes from our moral interest in seeing the political institutions from which we receive so much of our moral sense and through which we effect so much value realize more comprehensive moral aims. When they fall short of growth to a more generous ethic, their moral authority grows more and more flawed.

The Ethics of Refuge

Finally, what must Catholics do, even as they work for legal and political change, for migrant peoples they find at their doorstep? What is our responsibility for illegal, undocumented aliens? What are our duties toward unexpected and unwanted refugees? Are there duties to care for people who come to our shores in the hope of making a new life, even if American law forbids them safe haven? Do Christian ethics and common humanity require that we work even at the edge of the law to protect those the law ought to protect but does not?

To begin with, it should already be clear that not every immigrant has the same claim on the American conscience. Men and women who do not suffer from persecution and are able to lead a modestly comfortable life in their native lands have no special claim, morally speaking, for entry into the United States, but only a claim to normal, legal immigration. In practice, they may currently possess legal priority as defectors from Communist or left-wing regimes or as workers with some desirable skill. From the point of view of Catholic social teaching and common morality, neither qualification is sufficient to support a demand for asylum or to require that citizens of the United States or another country of refuge accept the risk of working outside the law to protect them. Claims to refuge are justified only by sore distress, whether political or economic, and potential champions of the oppressed would be permitted to go outside the law only as a last resort. For the common good requires that all persons uphold the law and, where the law is lacking, work within legal bounds to change it. Giving sanctuary, therefore, is an exceptional act justified by moral necessity. In other words, a community or individual may be asked to provide refuge in defiance of the law because the alternative (e.g., political murder, genocide, famine, prolonged exploitation) would be disastrous.

The duty to give refuge is one form of the basic humanitarian duty to aid those deprived of their basic rights. Henry Shue lays out the logic of acts of refuge in his book Basic Rights. Basic rights, Shue explains, entail three kinds of corresponding obligations on the part of others, i.e., duties:

(1) To avoid depriving,
(2) To protect from deprivation,
(3) To aid the deprived.[48]

97

The duty to give sanctuary is of the third kind. People are obligated to aid those who, either through the failure of political and social institutions to protect them, through direct violation of their rights by those very authorities responsible for their safety, or through natural disaster, have been deprived of their basic rights. The obligation to aid, of course, is all the more serious when one's country or an organization of which one has been a part is complicit either in causing or in perpetuating the deprivation of rights. In the matter of Central American refugees, there is a strong, *prima facie* case that the obligation is more one of reparation than the simpler humanitarian duty to aid to people-in-necessity. The humanitarian duty is itself a very compelling one. But, if a person of good will or a community of conscience discerns that their own government or fellow citizens are involved in violations which have led to the refugee's flight from their homeland, then the obligation to offer sanctuary is all the more grave. So, along with duties to change laws to provide for refugees in a non-selective way and to implement a foreign policy that avoids depriving poor people of their rights, there is also a serious obligation to provide asylum, not just because of an emergency situation, but because one's government and fellow citizens have been involved in bringing about the pressures that have led to the exodus in the first place. Finally, as an act of solidarity, sanctuary demonstrates that spirit of universal community that Paul VI referred to in *A Call to Action* as "the indispensable basis for authentic justice and the condition of enduring peace" (OA 17).

Part III
Discernment in Communities of Faith

The argument I have been making is that there is a significant difference between Catholic teaching on the universal human rights of migrant peoples and the political realities of the nation-state system. Earlier I noted not only the difference in theoretical perspectives between Catholic social teaching and the nation-state system, but also the growing criticism of the magisterium for the failures of states to honor the rights of their nationals and of alien peoples. At the same time, in the case of the Holy Father's San Antonio homily, I also remarked on the generality of the criticism and the deliberate lack of specificity with respect to controversial actions like sanctuary. Finally, in the last section I have cited certain rights and duties which Catholic social teaching has defined with respect to migrant peoples (or which seem to be clearly entailed by the pastoral strategies undertaken by the church). Together these patterns may appear to project some degree of confusion on just what Catholic teaching requires.

People have reason, I think, to plead they are confused. There are discrepancies between church teaching and national political structures, between universal rights and the sovereignty of nations, between general church teaching and responses by religious activists like those in the Sanctuary Movement, between magisterial criticism and the definition of rights and duties which can be the basis of public policy. There would appear to be grounds for people to claim, therefore, that they can't be expected to act when their moral teachers can't agree on what they are to do. For some, perhaps, ambivalence on the part of the teaching church even provides an excuse to tune-out issues that seem too complex for ordinary people to act on.

Common Assumptions

What are conscientious Catholics to do? Is there any way for them to settle on exactly what their responsibilities are to migrants and refugees? How does the local church—bishop, diocesan officials, pastors, and lay people—determine its obligations?

In fact, there is a great deal more clarity about how to proceed than people may imagine. The basic problem is not church teaching. Rather, it is the misplaced hope that there will be a single Catholic formula for social action on any given issue. Official social teaching, however, has insisted in a variety of ways that no one approach will meet the needs of our complex world, and so approves of pluralism in social strategy. Catholic unity is assured not by uniformity in social strategy but, above all, by the exercise of charity toward Christians following different social programs.

At the same time, there are some assumptions found in Catholic social teaching that all Catholics ought to be able share.

(1) Contemporary Catholic social teaching holds that even in national affairs *we must act as world citizens*. As Vatican II declared, "In our times a special obligation binds us to make ourselves the neighbor to absolutely every person, and of actively helping him [*sic*] . . ." (GS 27).

The same passage identifies foreign laborers and refugees as primary examples of those to whom we must act as neighbors. What is novel here and a challenge to both liberal (American) moral and political philosophy and common sense morality is the assertion that our obligations in justice extend beyond borders to people of every nation.

(2) Acting as world citizens in national affairs is a principal way of effecting the church's identity as the sacrament of the unity of humankind. The catholicity of the church is itself a symbol of that unity. But for the church to be an efficacious symbol of human solidarity, *Catholic Christians must take responsibility to overcome forces which divide humanity*, including restrictive and prejudicial understandings of nationhood.

(3) The *defense and promotion of universal human rights is the outstanding way in which the church upholds the common dignity of the human family*. For Catholics, human rights is not a cause of some fanatical fringe. It lies at the very heart of papal and conciliar social teaching. It has been the overriding theme of Pope John Paul II's pastoral ministry. Episcopal conferences in every part of the world have made human rights the mainstay of their social programs. Finally, grassroots action by Catholic lay people, clergy, and religious from Africa to Latin America and East Asia have made human rights advocacy a primary witness to the gospel of liberation.

(4) To be universal protections, human rights must not be contingent on national interest or market advantage. Accordingly, *a general aim of Catholic social action should be to as-*

sure that both law and public policy implement universal rights standards and that they limit discretionary judgments based on national, ideological or business interests (except in very exceptional circumstances). It is the migrant or refugee's status as a person which grounds her rights, not the convenience of the recipient country.

(5) Advancing the human rights of migrants and refugees demands restricting the autonomy of the market as well as of nations. Promoting a humane existence for migrants involves addressing both foreign and domestic economic policies: the economic conditions that drive people to move from their homelands, the mobility of capital that accelerates migration, and the exploitation by host countries of displaced peoples as pools of cheap, manipulable labor. Correctives for what economists call market imperfections and others see as unjust exploitation are envisioned by the U.S. bishops in what *Economic Justice for All* calls "a new American experiment" in economic rights. In addition, there is a grave need to correct the ways in which U.S. foreign policy and (the lack of) development assistance programs have accelerated the displacement of impoverished peoples and contributed to making them victims of political oppression as well.

Models of Engagement

Local involvement in migrant affairs may be impeded by confusion about the church's strategy for social action. That confusion was captured by the controversy over the Holy Father's praise in San Antonio for those who have worked for migrants from south of the U.S.-Mexico border. In the thirties, forties, and fifties, a style of Catholic action held sway which seemingly provided a direct line from magisterial teaching to social action. The hierarchy, especially the Roman magisterium, provided the teaching, which was reiterated by local bishops and then implemented by laypeople. While traces of that approach remain and some try to return it to a place of dominance, beginning with the Council a whole series of developments has succeeded in diversifying Catholic social action, placing the locus of responsibility for social strategy on the local church and communities of concern.

The first change of significance was the Council's affirmation of the collegiality of bishops, i.e., that the college of bishops as a unit bears the responsibility to pastor and teach. The most significant practical expression of collegiality is the organization of national and regional bishops' conferences to facilitate bishops in adapting the preaching of the gospel to their own countries and regions of the globe. The practical importance of bishops' conferences, whether in Brazil, the Philippines, or the United States, to an effective social strategy cannot be underestimated.

The activism of episcopal conferences has given risen to a second church world-strategy. The U.S. bishops' pastorals on nuclear war and economic justice exemplify this second model. The pastoral letters present both principles of morality, to which they lend their full authority as the church's teachers, and recommendations for public policy, to which less moral certainty is attached. At the level of policy, the bishops' readers are entitled to draw different conclusions of their own. So, while the bishops offer moral guidance through social teaching, they also permit pluralism at the level of action.[51]

Along with the emergence of episcopal conferences, the internationalization of the church (i.e., the maturation of churches in the Third World and the accompanying inculturation of the gospel) also resulted in a greater diversity in the goals and strategies of different churches than at anytime since the Counter-Reformation. This process of differentiation was ratified and advanced by Pope Paul VI in his Apostolic Exhortation *Octagesima adveniens*.

A Call to Action, as it is known in English, put the burden on the local church to determine strategies for social action. Paul wrote:

> In the face of widely varying situations it is difficult for us to utter a unified message and to put forward a solution which has universal validity. Such is not our ambition, nor is it our mission. It is up to the Christian communities to analyze with objectivity the situation which is proper to their own country, to shed on it the light of the Gospel, and to draw principles of reflection, norms of judgment and directives for action from the social teaching of the Church (4).

Seldom has a modern pope uttered such a self-denying maxim. For Paul, it is not the papal mission to utter a unified message with universal validity. Social strategy properly belongs to the local Christian community. In addition, *A Call to Action* limited the guiding role of both Catholic social teaching and the episcopacy in the social strategy of the church. Social teaching is reduced to the status of a guide in the process of discerning how to apply the gospel to a community's own situation. Similarly, the role of the hierarchy is not directive, but consensual. Paul urged Christians groups to act "in communion" with their bishops and "in dialogue with other Christian brethren [*sic*] and men [*sic*] of goodwill." His emphasis lay on sustaining practical bonds of conversation and collaboration in a spirit of charity.

The upshot is that Pope Paul clearly placed the responsibility for strategy as well as action on communities of Christians. "It is up to these communities," he wrote, "to discern the options and commitments which are urgently called for in order to bring about social, political and economic changes seen in many cases to be urgently needed" (4). I take it that the term "communities" applies not only to small ad-hoc groups of conscientious Christians and to larger national and transnational associations such as Pax Christi, but also to local parishes, dioceses, and episcopal conferences. In short, the faithful need not be confused by mixed, or at least diplomatically nuanced, signals from the hierarchy, because the responsibility for social action lies with the whole church in all its parts and especially with those communities naturally suited to shared discernment.

What makes a community suited for discernment? I would propose there are three ways to be a community that reads the signs of the times together. They are:

(1) To be a people, like those living on the U.S.-Mexican border, who find themselves confronted directly by the urgent needs of others;

(2) To be an agency or group with a special capacity to meet those needs, for example, a unit of Catholic Social Services or the United States Catholic Conference; and

(3) To be a gathering of Christians who have heard the call to action and convene express-ly to discern how they might answer the call.

You will note that official church structures—dioceses, diocesan offices, parishes, parish councils, justice and peace committees, and so on—may function as communities of discernment under any one or a combination of titles. All things considered, it would be better if official church structures would also be communities of discernment. But *A Call to Action* is a charter of authentic responsibility for all communities of faith, so that responsive faith communities do not need to wait for official church organs to give unambiguous signals before taking action.

Some Suggestions for the Use of Social Teaching in Group Discernment

Finally, I would like to offer some thoughts on the use of official social teaching in com-munities of discernment. What I offer is, in a loose sense, a set of hermeneutical principles, or rules, for studying the social teaching while discerning strategies for social action in con-troversial areas like care of migrants and refugees. I begin with the notion that the social teaching itself is a kind of hermeneutic for applying the gospel to our times.

Rule No. l. The primary source for exploring Christian social responsibility is the gospel. Social teaching, according to Paul VI, is itself only an aid to discerning how to respond to the gospel. "The Gospel," Paul wrote, "is not out-of-date . . . Its inspiration . . . remains ever new for converting men [*sic*] and for advancing the life of society" (OA 4). It is in the con-text of responding to the gospel that Catholic Christians ought to utilize the social teaching of the church as a source of "principles of reflection, norms of judgment and directives for action" (OA 4). The social teaching serves as a kind of ready-to-hand hermeneutic for dis-cerning what to do in response to the signs of the times.

Because the gospel has priority over magisterial statements, the first thing to consider, then, in reading the social teaching is its use of New Testament themes; for example, the unity of love of God and love of neighbor as found in accounts of the (Two) Great Com-mandment(s). With reference to justice for migrant workers, Pope Paul called for Christians to work for "universal brotherhood [sic]," which he called "the indispensable basis of peace and justice and the condition for enduring peace." (OA 17) He founded his own plea on the First Letter of John (4:8): "Whoever fails to love, does not know God, because God is love." Identifying such New Testament connections is helpful, because it tells the community how the magisterium itself has heard the gospel message in our day, while at the same time points directly to the gospel as the primary source of Christian inspiration and invites the com-munity to make its own response.

Rule No. 2. Test to see whether there is a congruence between the principles articulated in the social teaching and reading of the signs of the times. Congruence between the two in-creases the weight of obligation to take action. Reading the signs of the times is an impor-tant innovation in Catholic social teaching, but reading the signs of the times need not conflict with the general principles of natural law. John XXIII saw certain signs of the times as establishing moral imperatives for the self-determination of states, for the recognition of human rights, for the emancipation of women, for nuclear disarmament. In an official commentary, Maurice Cardinal Roy, indicated that signs of the times have the effect of natural law prescriptions when they have become the base for a moral consensus.[52]

But the signs of the times differ from natural law obligations in three significant ways: (1) They proceed from an examination of the sufferings and aspirations of people by the light of gospel ideals. Accordingly, they may give rise to a greater sense of urgency, as they have in the teaching of both Paul VI and John Paul II, than just a set of universal moral principles.[53] (2) Signs of the times is a more dynamic method of doing social ethics than natural law. It seeks to articulate an emerging sense of morality, and so it can give rise to new norms or to new priorities among norms. (3) Because the signs of the times method evaluates historical developments by light of messianic ideals, it will appear to many to give rise to a more radical, idealistic ethic. This idealism, however, has a realistic check in that it is a response to human suffering and collective aspiration and aims to bring humanity closer to the divine intentions for history. From the point of view of post-conciliar social theology, adherence to the divine plan is the greatest form of social and political realism.[54]

While John Paul II has a more pessimistic view of signs of the times than the Council or Paul VI did, he continues to evaluate our moral obligations, not according to a realistic estimate of human sinfulness, understood in a Niebuhrian or liberal sense, but in accord with the divine plan.[55] Catholic moral realism takes the divine will for human unity to be a deeper, more realistic current in human affairs than the popular prejudices or national interests which divide people from one another.

The coincidence of reading the signs of the times with general principles, such as human-rights precepts, however, points to a very strong presumption in favor of a particular line of action. Such, for example, would be the congruence between the increase in refugee movements in recent decades and the demand for universal rights to a homeland and so to a right of immigration. A convergence on this point makes barriers to asylum and the integration of refugees in host societies a top priority for social action.

But what happens when there is divergence between the two methods? What are we to do, for example, when the rights of individuals and the rights of states conflict, especially, say, when the church's international relations specialists add the weight of realism to the interest of states?

Rule No. 3. When there is a conflict between reading the signs of the times and certain practical conclusions or general norms, following the schema of Octagesima adveniens, the community of discernment, after considering the directions of the magisterium, has the freedom to follow its own discernment of strategies for action.

The checks on the community's independent course of action would include: compatibility with the general orientation of the church's social teaching and the reading of signs of the times; rootedness in the gospel and the great overarching themes of the Catholic tradition: human dignity, the unity of the human family, the option for the poor, the priority of labor, and so on; continuity with norms commonly held by Christians and people of good-will, such as universal human rights. Diligent application of such checks assures the community that it is "thinking" and acting "with the church," despite departure from some particular precedent or the policy of some church agency or prelate.

Rule No. 4. As far as possible, social action ought to be undertaken in communion with bishops and in conversation with other Christians and men and women of goodwill. The Spirit is active both in the church and in the secular world.[55] Bishops are facilitators and coordinators of the charisms given to the community. People ought to be able to look to them for encouragement, support, and guidance. But, given the multiplicity of demands ordinaries face, the total good of the church for which they are responsible, and the limited resources at their disposal, the bishop may not always be a ready collaborator in every field of social action. In addition, not every action which needs to be taken needs to be done by the bishop or official church agency. For these reasons, some activist groups may find that support for their engagement on behalf of migrants and refugees may come instead from the community of conscience, both Christian and secular. The teaching of the Council and recent popes encourages an orthopraxy in which conscientious Catholics collaborate with Christians of other denominations and socially responsible men and women of goodwill.[56] Where social strategy is informed by the Catholic tradition and the bonds of communion in charity with the hierarchy are preserved, grassroots communities and associations of Catholics ought to have no inhibitions about drawing support from the communities of conscience where the Spirit of God is manifestly active.

Rule No. 5. Within and without the church, there is ample latitude for a legitimate plurality of options.[57] In the body of Christ, there is one Spirit, but many members with different functions. Within the one church, there will be many gifts; within one movement, there may be several approaches to the same problem. Committed Christians ought not only acknowledge the legitimacy of alternative positions, but they should also hold charity toward one another of greater importance than any plan of action. While solidarity in action is desirable, solidarity need not, and ought not, lead to either uniformity or sectarianism around strategies or issues.

Thus, lack of public support by a church leader or agency for a particular action or differences over policies like bilingualism or temporary admission of guest workers ought not be an occasion for deep divisions or resentment. "From Christians who at first sight seem to be in opposition," wrote Paul VI, "[the church] asks an effort at mutual understanding of the other's positions and motives" and "an attitude of more profound charity which, while recognizing the differences, believes nonetheless in the possibility of convergence and unity. 'The bonds which unite the faithful are mightier than anything which divides them' " (OA 50).

Conclusion

The church is the sacrament of unity. The unity-in-diversity it exhibits in itself symbolizes the unity God intends for humankind. It is a unity-in-diversity which, however imperfectly realized, has been an ideal for the United States as well: "E Pluribus Unum" (From Many, One People). In our own day, that unity is still far from realized. Consequently, as the sacrament of unity, the Catholic Church is to the American people at once "a sign of contradiction" and "a light unto the nations." For it both offers a prophetic criticism of Americans' self-satisfied indifference to poverty and oppression in other lands and serves as an image of the fullness of life and eschatological unity which God intends for all the peoples of the earth.

Sign of Contradiction

Insofar as its prophetic mission places the church ahead of what the world of nation-states is now capable, in its division, its self-centered nationalism, and its ethnic and racial prejudices, the church becomes "a sign of contradiction." The gospel of human unity it proclaims is a scandal to those whose trust lies in the inter-state system.

"One form of contradiction" between the Church and the contemporary world repeatedly identified by Pope John Paul is the increase of poverty in a world of great affluence. "The great poverty of many peoples," wrote Cardinal Wojtyla in his 1978 retreat for Pope Paul VI, "first and foremost the peoples of the Third World, hunger, economic exploitation, colonialism . . . is a form of opposition to Christ on the part of the powerful . . . ."[58] In *Dives in misericordia*, John Paul likened the current world situation to "a gigantic" development of "the parable in the Bible of the rich banqueter and the poor man Lazarus" (11). Such social indifference represents a kind of practical atheism that frequently wears a veneer of Christian culture and even zealous orthodoxy. "This form of contradiction of Christ," as Cardinal Wojtyla said in his 1978 papal retreat, "often goes hand in hand with a partial acceptance of religion, of Christianity and the Church. . . ."[59] This tacit, practical atheism manifests itself in insensitivity to the suffering of the poor and in a failure of political will to break the cycles of impoverishment.

On several occasions, most recently last September in San Antonio in his address to Catholic Charities U.S.A. and again in Detroit, the Holy Father has drawn the attention of American Catholics to the story of the Rich Man and Lazarus, as a parable for our times and our country.[60] In his Hart Plaza Address in Detroit, he wondered whether Americans had failed to take heed that the message of the parable applies to us. He recalled that at Yankee stadium eight years before he had raised the challenge of the parable for his American listeners. Then he added, "I now ask you today: What have you done with that parable? . . . Have you put it aside thinking that it is no longer relevant to you or to the situation in your country?"[61]

The pope's teaching is a sign of contradiction to our national self-assurance that what is best for America is best for the world. Though he often speaks in the abstract generalities of a trained philosopher, the Holy Father has elaborated a clear critique of the relations of rich to poor, both within and across nations. That the critique is addressed even-handedly, to democratic and totalitarian regimes, to capitalist and Marxist economies, to liberal and socialist societies, should not prevent us in the United States from hearing the criticisms. Even more than our major adversary, the United States is the contemporary archetype of the affluent power center. Among the pope's criticisms are:

- the ever faster growth of the gap between rich and poor;
- the hardening of indifference to the poor on the part of the affluent along with a sense of impotence about being able to help the disadvantaged;
- the spread of domination, totalitarianism, neocolonialism and imperialism;
- an immensely destructive arms-trade that serves no just cause and deprives the poor of resources that should go to their development.

Speaking in Monterey, the Holy Father reflected on the self-satisfied hardness-of-heart that infects economically and technologically advanced societies like our own.

> In these closing years of the 20th century, on the eve of third millenia of the Christian era, a part of the human family—the most economically and technically developed part is being specially tempted, perhaps as never before, to imitate the ancient model of all sin—the original rebellion that expressed itself saying "I will not serve."[62]

In short, the pontiff pointed an accusing finger at American chauvinism. The challenge he offered was for Americans to act not just as citizens of this country but as citizens of the world.

Light of the Nations

While a sign of contradiction the church is also a light to the nations. It gives hope that the world can be transformed. The church as sacrament not only realizes by its own catholicity the unity God intends for all humanity, but it also helps realize that eschatological unity by its work in the world. "While the church's unity is not her own achievement but a precious gift of the Lord," said the Pope in Los Angeles last September, "it is nonetheless her serious responsibility to be an instrument for guarding and restoring unity in the human family. . . . She does this by efforts to break down prejudice and ignorance as she fosters new understanding and trust. . . ."[63]

Its work on behalf of refugees and migrants at all levels makes the church a light unto the nations. The legislative testimony of the USCC and regional bishops' conferences, the services of Catholic Charities, the acceptance of cultural diversity in parish liturgy, the hospitality of Christian families, the political action of communities of faith, all are efficacious signs of the unity to which God calls all peoples. To American civil society, these deeds of love show that possibilities of greater community than we ordinarily imagine are feasible, both within and across borders. The action of the faith community in the world contributes directly to the latter's transformation. Next year, and a generation from now, men, women, and children should be better able to live as a single human family because of the church's active commitment in politics today.

As a sacrament, however, the church symbolizes much more than can ever be realized by human wisdom and labor alone. The sacrament is a thick symbol. It projects a graced reality that is far, far richer than anything either church or society will ever realize. Today's labors on behalf of justice and human rights for refugees and migrants prepare the way for the age to come when people will come from east and west to share at the one banquet table in the Kingdom of God.

Bibliography

**Official Catholic Social Teaching:
Primary Documents (with Abbreviations)**

Pope John XXIII, *Pacem in Terris (Peace on Earth)*, in O'Brien and Shannon, eds., *Renewing the Earth: Catholic Documents on Peace, Justice and Liberation* (Garden City: Doubleday/Image, 1977) (PT).

Pope John Paul II, *Laborem exercens*, in Gregory Baum, *The Priority of Labor* (New York/Ramsey: Paulist, 1982), Appendix, 93-152 (LE).

_____, *Redeemer of Man: Redemptor Hominis* (Washington: USCC, 1983) (RM).

_____, *Rich in Mercy: Dives in Misericordia* (Washington: USCC, 1981) (DM).

Paul VI, *A Call to Action (Octogesima Adveniens)*, in *Renewing the Earth*, 347-383 (OA).

Vatican Council II, *Dogmatic Constitution on the Church* (Lumen Gentium), in Walter M. Abbott, General Editor, *The Documents of Vatican II* (New York: Herder and Herder, 1966), 14-101 (LG).

_____, *Pastoral Constitution on the Church in the Modern World* (Gaudium et Spes), in *The Documents of Vatican II*, 199-308 (GS).

Statements on Care of Migrant Peoples

Bishop Anthony Bevilacqua, "Ministry to the World's Uprooted People," *Origins* 14:31 (Jan. 17, 1985) 517-522.

Bishops of Texas, "The Pastoral Care of Hispanic Migrants," *Origins* 15:25 (Jan. 16, 1986) 520.

Committee on Social Development and World Peace, USCC, *Cultural Pluralism in the United States* (Washington: USCC, 1980) (CP).

National Conference of Catholic Bishops, "Resolution on Immigration," *Origins* 14:31 (Dec. 5, 1985) 424.

_____ , *Together A New People: Pastoral Statement on Migrants and Refugees* (Washington: USCC, 1986).

_____ , *Resolution on the Pastoral Concern of the Church for People on the Move* (Washington: USCC, 1976).

_____ , *The Hispanic Presence: Challenge and Commitment* (Washington: USCC, 1983).

Archbishop Roger Mahony, "Welcoming the New Immigrants," *Origins* 15:31 (Jan. 16, 1986) 518-19.

_____ ,"What About Those Who Do Not Qualify for Amnesty?," *Origins* 16:47 (May 7, 1986) 826-28.

Pontificia Commissione per la Patorale delle Migrazioni e del Turismo, *Chiesa e Mobilita Umana: Documenti della Santa Sede dal 1883 al 1983* (Roma: Centro Studi Emigrazione, 1985).

Pontifical Commission for the Pastoral Care of Migrant and Itinerant Peoples, *Letter to Episcopal Conferences on the Church and People on the Move* (Washington: USCC, 1969).

Sacred Congregation for Bishops, *Instruction on the Pastoral Care of People Who Migrate* (Washington: USCC, 1969) (IPC).

Related Statements

Pope John Paul II, "Agriculture and the Church's View of Work," *Origins* 17:18 (Oct. 15, 1987) 310-11.

_____ , "Ethnic Universality of the Church," *Origins* 17:18 (Oct. 15, 1987) 305ff.

_____ , "The Hart Plaza Address: Human Solidarity," *Origins* 17:18 (Oct. 15, 1987) 329-33.

Books

Boundaries: National Autonomy and its Limits, ed. Peter G. Brown and Henry Shue. Maryland Studies in Public Philosophy (Totowa, N.J.: Rowman and Littlefield, 1981).

Charles R. Beitz, *Political Theory and International Relations* (Princeton: Princeton University Press, 1979).

Ted Conover, *Coyotes: A Journey Through the Secret World of America's Illegal Aliens* (New York: Vintage, 1987).

Development Strategies Reconsidered, ed. John P. Lewis and Valleriana Kallab (Washington: Overseas Development Council, 1986).

Alan Dowty, *Closed Borders: The Contemporary Assault on Freedom of Movement* (New Haven: Yale University Press, 1987).

Avery Dulles, *Models of the Church* (Garden City, N.Y.: Doubleday, 1974).

_____, *The Catholicity of the Church* (Oxford: Clarendon Press, 1985).

Gil Loescher and John A. Scanlan, *Calculated Kindness: Refugees and America's Half-Open Door, 1945-Present* (New York: Free Press, 1986).

William Shawcross, *The Quality of Mercy: Cambodia, Holocaust and Modern Conscience* (New York: Simon and Schuster, 1985).

The Social Teachings of John Paul II, Social Thought 13:2/3 (Spring/Summer 1987).

Fawaz Turki, *The Disinherited: Journal of a Palestinian Exile,* with Epilogue (New York: Modern Reader, 1974).

Henry Shue, *Basic Rights: Subsistence, Affluence and U.S. Foreign Policy* (Princeton: Princeton University Press, 1980).

George Hunston Williams, *The Mind of John Paul II: Origins of His Thought and Action* (New York: Seabury, 1981).

Karol Wojtyla (Pope John Paul II), *Sign of Contradiction* (New York: Seabury, 1979).

Notes

1. See "The Call to the Church of Thousands of Voices," *Origins* 17:17 (Oct. 8, 1987) 281-284, esp. 283, no. 8.

2. Pope's Address to Catholic Charities, Origins 17:17, 287.

3. On the central place of human rights in the pastoral ministry of the Church, see *Resolution on the Pastoral Concern of the Church for People on the Move*, NCCB, November 11, 1976 (Washington: USCC, 1976), pp. 10-13; see also *Pastoral Constitution on the Church in the Modern World*, in *Renewing the Earth: Catholic Documents on Peace, Justice and Liberation*, ed. David J. O'Brien and Thomas Shannon (Garden City, N.Y.: Doubleday/Image, 1977), no. 41.

4. Alan Dowty, *Closed Borders: The Contemporary Assault on Freedom of Movement*, A Twentieth Century Fund Report (New Haven, Ct.: Yale, 1987), p. 4.

5. Ibid., p. 17.

6. Ibid.

7. Ibid., p. 91.

8. On the traditional status and changing status of the nation-state system, see *Boundaries: National Autonomy and Its Limits*, ed. Peter G. Brown and Henry Shue (Totowa, N.J.: Rowman and Littlefield, 1981), especially chs. 1-3, pp. 1-106, with essays by Michael Walzer, Elsa Chaney, and Judy Lichtenberg, and a response by Walzer.

9. For a history of changing U.S. attitudes toward refugees in the post-World War II period, see Gil Loescher and John A. Scanlan, *Calculated Kindness: Refugees and America's Half-Open Door, 1945-Present* (New York: Free Press, 1986).

10. Sacred Congregation of Bishops, *Instruction on Pastoral Care of People Who Migrate* (Washington: USCC, 1969), no. 10.

11. Ibid., nos. 6-7.

12. On the Westphalian system of sovereign nation-states, see Richard Falk, *A Study of Future Worlds* (New York: Free Press, 1976). Falk, like the Roman magisterium, sees the international system is inadequate to meet the moral challenges of the late twentieth century. Also, see the NCCB's *Challenge of Peace: God's Promise and Our Response* (Washington: USCC, 1983), nos. 237-244.

13. *Instruction on Pastoral Care*, no. 10.

14. Dowty, *Closed Borders*, p. 106.

15. Ibid., p. 106.

16. See *Peace on Earth (Pacem in terris)*, nos. 60-66, in *Renewing the Earth*, pp. 139-141.

17. *Origins* 15:31 (Jan. 18, 1986), 520.

18. The *Instruction on Pastoral Care* uses the strongest possible language about the exclusion of refugees and migrants:

> Public authorities unjustly deny the rights of human persons if they block or impede emigration or immigration, except where grave requirements of the common good, considered objectively, demand it (no. 7).

Pius XII in *Exsul Familia* had already noted that "in practice," rights of movement are "nullified under the pretext of the common good which is falsely understood or falsely applied, but sanctioned" by law. Cited in the NCCB's *Resolution on The Pastoral Concern of the Church for People on the Move* (Washington: USCC, 1976), p. 10. 1976.

19. The texts which assert the primacy of the personal right to movement over state interests include: *Exsul Familia, Peace on Earth, A Call to Action*, the Vatican *Instruction on Pastoral Care of People Who Migrate*, and the NCCB *Resolution on the Pastoral Concern of the Church for People on the Move.*

20. *Peace on Earth*, no. 139.

21. Ibid., nos. 98-99, 103-108.

22. Dowty, *Closed Borders*, p. 19. Dowty's assertion that the right to self-detemination in choice of nationality is a paramount right parallels Henry Shue's concept of a basic right. According to Shue, a basic right is one which is necessary for the enjoyment of other rights. Thus, rights to personal security and to subsistence are basic rights because they make possible the exercise of other rights. See Shue, *Basic Rights: Subsistence, Affluence and U.S. Foreign Policy* (Princeton: Princeton University Press, 1980), pp. 18-20. By analogy the right of movement would be a basic right because it represents a fundamental means to vindicate one's other rights.

23. Dowty, *Closed Borders*, p. 19. On the costs and benefits of an open border policy, see pp. 239-250.

24. "Resolution on Immigration," *Origins* 15:25 (Dec. 5, 1985) 424.

25. Ibid.

26. "What About Those Who Do Not Qualify for Amnesty?," *Origins* 16:47 (May 7, 1987) 826-828.

27. *Peace on Earth*, no. 106.

28. See especially *Instruction on Pastoral Care*, no. 8.

29. Anglo-American political philosophy has increasingly come to recognize the need to include economic deprivation alongside political oppression as a fundamental evil from which people have a right to be protected or rescued; see, for example, Shue, *Basic Rights*, pp. 1-34. The most important contribution in this direction comes from Ronald Dworkin (*Taking Rights Seriously*), who argues that justice consists in an equal right to concern and respect, concern consisting in others' duties to avoid or relieve deprivation and suffering and respect having to do with freedom and non-interference.

For application to policy, see *Food Policy: The Responsibility of the United States in Life and Death Choices*, ed. Peter G. Brown and Henry Shue, (New York: Free Press, 1978), especially articles by Singer, Nagel, Brown, Ferkiss, and Shue.

30. See n. 23(b) above.

31. See especially *Development of Peoples*, in *Renewing the Earth*, nos. 43-55.

32. Special obligations to assist in economic development of Central American countries to overcome past injustices would derive from what Shue designates a combination of the three duties correlative to basic rights: to avoid depriving others, to establish institutions that prevent deprivations in basic needs, and to relieve people who have been deprived. See *Basic Rights*, pp. 35-64 (and pp. 155-174).

33. See *Resolution on Pastoral Concern*, p. 18., no. 10; USCC, Committee on Social Development and World Peace, *Cultural Pluralism in the United States* (Washington: USCC, 1980), pp. 4-7.

34. See, for example, *Cultural Pluralism in the United States* and Pope John Paul II's Los Angeles Address, "Ethnic Universality of the Church," *Origins* 17:17 (Oct. 8, 1987) 305ff.

35. "*Resolution on Immigration.*"

36. Chaney, "Migrant Workers and National Boundaries: The Basis of Rights and Protections," in *Boundaries*, pp. 37-72.

37. Dowty, *Closed Borders*, p. 245; see also Jorge A. Bustamente, "Undocumented Immigration: Policy Options for Mexico," paper prepared for the Bilateral Commission on the Future of United States-Mexican Relations, San Diego, August 28-29, 1987; Bustamente et al., "A New Policy Perspective on Immigration," a paper presented at the 13th Annual National Association of Chicano Studies, Sacramento, CA, March 21-23, 1985.

38. Chaney, "Migrant Workers," p. 53.

39. Dowty, *Closed Borders*, p. 245.

40. *Pastoral Constitution on the Church in the Modern World (Gaudium et spes)*, in *Renewing the Earth*, nos. 85-86; *Development of Peoples*, nos. 43-79; *Justice in the World*, ch. 1.

41. Chaney, "Migrant Workers," pp. 51-58.

42. See *Development Strategies Reconsidered*, ed. John P. Lewis and Valerian Kallab, (Washington: ODC/Transaction Books, 1986).

43. The charter of human rights thinking for contemporary Catholicism is "Peace on Earth." Also, see David Hollenbach, *Claims in Conflict: Retrieving and Renewing the Catholic Human Rights Tradition* (New York: Paulist, 1979).

44. *Justice in the World*, in *Renewing the Earth*, ch. 3, pp. 399-401.

45. For an evaluation of performance on human rights within the church, see Leonardo Boff, *Church: Charism and Power*, chs. 2 and 3.

46. On societal integrity, see Gibson Winter, *Elements for a Social Ethic* (New York: Macmillan, 1972).

47. *Economic Justice for All* (Washington: USCC, 1986), nos. 347-358.

48. Shue, *Basic Rights*, p. 60.

49. On the charity and the pluralism of options, see Paul VI's *A Call to Action (Octogesima adveniens)*, in *Renewing the Earth*, nos. 48-52.

50. *Economic Justice for All*, nos. 85-95.

51. See "Pastoral Message," which prefaces *Economic Justice for All*, nos. 19-22, esp. 20.

52. On the relation of the signs of the times to natural law, see Maurice Cardinal Roy, "Letter on the Tenth Anniversary of 'Pacem in terris'," in *The Gospel of Peace and Justice*, ed. Joseph Gremillion (Maryknoll: Orbis, 1978).

53. The classic statement of urgency in response to the signs of the times came from Paul VI in *A Call to Action*:

> A renewed consciousness of the demands of the Gospel makes it the Chruch's duty to put herself at the service of all, to help them grasp their serious problem in all its dimensions, and to convince them that *solidarity in action at this turning point in human history is a matter of urgency* (OA 5). [Emphasis added.]

Many other expressions of such holy impatience can be found in other documents of Paul's pontificate, including statements of the Council and Synods. See *Justice in the World*, the statement of the 1971 Synod of Bishops. See my "On Relative Equality: Catholic Egalitarianism since Vatican II," *Theological Studies* 45:4, 651-675, for an extensive survey of this trend.

While John Paul II remains characteristically less sanguine about the possibilities for social change, his call for responsibility toward the poor have also acquired a sense of urgency, especially during his 1987 United States pilgimage.

54. While John Paul II, in many respects, may be described as a political as well as a theological realist, he shares with Paul VI the convictions that "the divine plan" is ultimately the most realistic way to conceive of human relations. Paul VI, however, was more alelrt to the possibilities for good in human institutions. *A Call to Action*, for example, called for a rebirth of utopian thinking (no. 37), arguing that the Spirit opens up new social and political possibilities (nos. 37, 48). John Paul's reading of the signs of the times, however, is that humanity has repeatedly failed to realize those possibilities. See my "Social Justice and Consumerism in the Thought of Pope John Paul II," *Social Thought* 13:2/3 (Spring/Summer 1987) 60-73, especially 65-70.

55. On the activity of the Spirit effecting the diving plan in both church and world, see *The Pastoral Constitution on the Church in the Modern World*, no. 22-32, 38-39, 44-45.

56. Ibid., pp. 44-45; *A Call to Action*, no. 4.

57. Ibid., p. 50.

58. Karol Wojtyla (Pope John Paul II), *Sign of Contradiction* (New York: Seabury/Crossroads, 1979), pp. 198-199.

59. Ibid., p. 199.

60. See "Pope's Address to Catholic Charities," *Origins* 17:17 (Oct. 8, 1987) 286-288, and "Hart Plaza Address: Human Solidarity," *Origins* 17:18 (Oct. 15, 1987) 329-333.

61. Ibid., 330-331.

62. See "Agriculture and the Church's View of Work," *Origins* 17:18 (Oct. 15, 1987), 310.

63. See "The Ethnic Universality of the Church," *Origins* 17:18 (Oct. 15, 1987), 305ff.

The Pastoral Care of Newcomers Today: Practices and Models of the Catholic Church in the United States

Silvano M. Tomasi, cs
Provincial Superior
Missionaries of St. Charles Scalabrinians
New York Province

I. Introduction

The Church was born as a multicultural community. The book of the Acts of the Apostles (2:1-13) records the amazement of this experience. The large crowd, gathered at the "one place" where the believers were meeting and had received the Holy Spirit, "were all excited, because each one of them heard the believers talking in his own language." The native languages spoken at this first Pentecost represented practically all the countries bordering on the Mediterranean and some others in Asia. Confronted with this experience of unity and diversity, "amazed and confused, they kept asking each other, "What does this mean?" Then, as a result of Peter's preaching, "about three thousand people were added" to the initial nucleus of disciples. Immediately they started the process of creating community and the dynamics of their interaction are described in this way: "They spent their time in learning from the apostles [catechesis], taking part in the fellowship [communion], and sharing in the fellowship meals and the prayers [social concern and liturgy]" (Acts 2, 42). In Jerusalem, the Church began its task of becoming from multicultural, intercultural.

In the course of history, the Church came face to face with the issue of cultural diversity on many occasions. It had to ask time and again the question: "What does this mean?" Its response to that question determined some of the most dramatic moments of its secular journey, such as in the cases of the implantation of the faith among Slavic peoples, among the Chinese, among the Indian cultures of the New World.

The charismatic moment of the first Pentecost, however, remained unique. More tentative approaches had to be developed in order to respond to the questions of the meaning of diversity in unity and of how to build a community of faith that could embody this vision. Thus, we find that already John Chrisostom in the 4th century forms a community of Goths just outside Constantinople by ordaining deacons, priests, and a bishop of their language and by following them closely (Theodoretus, V, 30). In 1215 the Fourth Lateran Council (12th ecumenical) declared: "We find in most countries, within the same cities and dioceses living together people of diverse languages who, though bound by one Faith, have varied rites and customs. Therefore, we strictly enjoin that the Bishops of these cities or dioceses provide the proper men, who will celebrate the Liturgical Functions according to their rites and languages. They will administer the sacraments of the Church and instruct their people both by word and by deed" (Pius XII, 1952). At the doctrinal level, the teaching of the Church on the practice of hospitality, on the respect of different rites, on the right of individuals to catechesis, and on the reception of sacraments in their own language has been constant. In the last one hundred years, an extensive official documentation has clarified and developed further this teaching (cf. Pontifical Commission for the Pastoral Care of Migrants, 1985).

In the growth of the Catholic community in the United States, a pragmatic approach was adopted with regard to the pastoral care of arriving immigrants and refugees: offer of Christian sympathy, acknowledgement of their numerical contribution to the increase of Catholic population, social and educational assistance. The general pastoral policy of the Church hierarchy could perhaps be summed up in the words of the *Pastoral Letter to the Laity* issued by the First Provincial Council of Baltimore on October 17, 1829:

> From the East and the West, strangers have come to sit down at our table.... The vast tide of emigration which has rolled across the Atlantic during the half century just elapsed ... has swelled our population to an extraordinary extent.... As our congregations have in great measure been hitherto an emigrant population, so has our ministry been to a considerable extent composed of adopted citizens. But the children of the former, and the successors of the latter have for some time past assumed more of our native character, and must necessarily become chiefly, if not altogether national, henceforth (*Pastoral Letters U.S. Bishops*).

The fundamental choice of the particular Church in the United States, then, has been that of inculturating the faith in line with the national character of the country. This formidable task was complicated by the parallel historical process of incorporating into the Church the varied ethnic groups arriving and making here their permanent home. The pastoral strategies used to achieve this second goal have only recently received some attention on the part of Church historians and sociologists and they show remarkable regional creativity and diversity (Dolan, 1987). The findings begin to reveal what the addition of disciples of different native languages meant to the local building of "fellowship".

II. Today's Concern

The age-old question of diversity in the Church has become again a challenge to pastoral planners. The languages in which the Sunday liturgy is celebrated in the country's metropolitan areas range from Vietnamese to Polish, from Arabic to Spanish, from Tagalog to Haitian Creole. The statistics of current immigration are familiar and impressive. In a literal sense, for most of the country it can be repeated what the Holy Father John Paul II said in Los Angeles in his recent pastoral visit:

California has become a haven for immigrants, a new home for refugees and migrants, a place where people from every continent have come together to fashion a society of the most varied ethnic diversity.... As a result, the Church ... is truly Catholic in the fullest sense, embracing peoples and cultures of the widest and richest variety.

The Pope moves on to say:

The Church's concrete methods of evangelization and her efforts to promote peace and justice are shaped to a large extent by the fact that the Church is one and yet diverse. The good news of Jesus must be proclaimed in the language that particular people understand, in artistic symbols that give meaning to their experience, in ways that correspond as far as possible to their own aspirations and needs, their manner of looking at life and the way in which they speak to God. At the same time there must be no betrayal of the essential truth while the Gospel is being translated and the Church's teaching is passed down.

Evangelization is closely aligned with social action on behalf of migrants. Then, an apparently contradictory expression is used: "The ethnic universality of the Church demands a keen sensitivity to authentic cultures and a real sense of what is required by the process of inculturation." By its definition, ethnicity is particular and, therefore, the implication here must be that the Church is universal but living in specific cultures, which in turn affect the "concrete methods of evangelization" (John Paul II, 1987). An analysis of the concrete methods now utilized is an exploratory exercise. The available data is scattered and soft and, as in the past, the immediate local social reality dictates pragmatic forms of accommodation. The reasons for this situation could be the following:

1. The official and collegial articulation of public policy concerns regarding immigration on the part of the Church has dealt mostly with entry policy: fairness in admission of immigrants and refugees; generous numbers; family reunion; economic and social assistance for the immediate resettlement period; emergency rescue. Very recently, in 1983, with the pastoral letter *The Hispanic Presence: Challenge and Commitment*, and in 1986 with the pastoral statement on migrants and refugees, *Together, A New People*, a direct discussion of evangelization has been added with reference to the ecclesial consequences of the presence of new and large cultural groups.

2. There is a changed public perception of the Catholic Church in the 1980s. From the immigrant stage begun in the 1830s the Church is now a more educated, middle class and professional community. Its institutional presence in the country is part and parcel of what we are and its moral statements can serve as a national critical conscience (J. Hennessey, 1981: 307-31). Catholicism, however, still has the majority of all newcomers as its constituents. The Notre Dame Study of Catholic Parish Life concludes: "How the contemporary situation is resolved in terms of meeting the cultural needs of the new immigrants is a criti-

cal question that today's Catholic leadership must face" (Notre Dame Study of Catholic Parish Life, 1985).

3. Perhaps even more significant than the cultural variable, the class and race factors play a dominant role. The poor tend to be less visible, though a stated priority option, even in pastoral action. They have intrinsic difficulties, because of their unequal bargaining power, in creating one community from both middle class and marginal, poor people in the same parish and diocese.

4. The long-range impact of current immigrations in terms of demographic change and international relations doesn't seem widely perceived. For example, the fact that the percentage increase in the civilian population from 1980 to 1987 has been 30 percent for Hispanics and 6 percent for non-Hispanics has a direct bearing on the future of the Catholic community. The projected Asian-American population of almost 10 million by the year 2000, will surely affect cultural, economic, and political relations with Asia (cf. L. Bouvier and R.W. Gardner, 1986).

5. The lack of knowledge of conciliar and canonical directives and of the structures they allow and propose for implementation on the local level of the pastoral teaching on "unity in diversity" (cf. V. DePaolis, 1986) adds to the hesitancy on introducing practical and flexible pastoral models.

On the other hand, American immigration and religious history show that the interaction between immigrants and Church officials, "beyond the tragic and sometimes colorful fights, an accommodation took place that allowed inclusion and participation in one multicultural ecclesial community" (S.M. Tomasi, 1987). Is the same success story unfolding now? Are old pastoral practices still applicable and viable?

III. The Persistent Dilemma of Identity and Communion

From the establishment of the American Hierarchy to the Second Vatican Council, Catholic fraternal societies, the Catholic school, the personal parish or mission, and ethnic sisters and priests served as main vehicles for the integration of newcomers into the Church. The pace of integration and the ways of representation were sources of debate and conflict, but the ultimate goal of denominational cohesiveness and assimilation was to be achieved as the Bishops' decision demanded. The prevailing ecclesiology of the time, stressing the institutional dimension or model of Church, facilitated the implementation of such a policy. The post-conciliar theology provides three important new insights to support the organization of pastoral care among immigrants. First, there is a clearer emphasis on culture and cultural rights as human rights so that the maintenance of its cultural identity on the part of an immigrant group is not only a functional aspect in the process of integration but, in principle, a possible option for the perpetuation of the group. "The immigrant members of the Church, while freely exercising their rights and duties and being in full communion in the particular churches . . . must be able to remain completely themselves as far as language, culture, liturgy and spirituality, and particular traditions are concerned, in order to reach that ecclesial integration which enriches the Church of God" (John Paul II, 1985).

Second, conciliar ecclesiology rediscovers the Church as a mystery of communion. The universal Church exists in the particular church and all the particular churches make up the universal Church, as Lumen Gentium states, in quibus et exquibus (LG 23,1). Immigrants in a particular church are a call to create a more universal communion, where culture and faith must interact, without becoming identified, and where diversity enriches unity (cf. E. Corecco, 1987). In the transition from theology to pastoral organization, the effort to take both into account in providing service models came often to reflect the dynamics of interaction between diocesan officials and immigrants. Diocesan officials tend to keep immigrants within the established diocesan structures to avoid proselytizing and the emergence of independent churches while the immigrants tend to assert their cultural rights. Thus, the commonly subscribed objective of preserving the faith assumes different meaning as it is seen from the receiving diocese and from the arriving immigrants.

Thirdly, the parish is redefined in light of the theology of Church highlighted by the Council. The parish is seen as a group of faithful, as a community, a portion of the People of God, where the territory is not essential, but an instrument to specify a concrete community of persons within a diocese (Coccopalmerio, 1987). In this way, the parish is the community of those faithful who can participate in the Eucharist normally in the same place either because they live together in a certain common locality (territorial parish) or because they belong to the same community (personal parish). The diocese, therefore, is the particular church that through faith, the Eucharist and the person of the bishop, creates unity without destroying diversity. There is an analogy between the universal church and the particular church. The respect of culture, language, customs on the part of the universal church for the particular churches is paralleled by the same respect on the part of the particular church for the communities of faithful by which and from which it is formed (Canon 368). In this context, the presence of immigrant and cultural groups make the particular church truly universal. A combination of historical experience and theological insight seems to be still operative today in formulating prudential judgments and decisions concerning how to articulate a pastoral policy and practice in dealing with newcomers. The challenge will be the development of an ecclesial community that expresses the rediscovered sense of communion at a higher level of unity where particular Church and immigrant groups are both at home.

IV. Models of Immigrants' Pastoral Care

The current pastoral landscape reveals a surprisingly rich variety of practices in answering the spiritual needs of the newest immigrants and refugees. The resulting image can be compared to the glassine overlays provided in some atlases so that viewers can study complications in typography or changes affected through history. With any transparent layer imposed on the spiritual landscape, the map of the pastoral care of migrants is better understood in pluralist America, even though some of the layers stress cultural diversity and some unity and communion. Of course, there is as yet no exhaustive answer to the question raised in Jerusalem: "What does this mean?" In Miami, for example, a diocese that is becoming the crossroads of the American hemisphere, the dilemma of encouraging Cubans and Nicaraguans, Anglos and Haitians to attend church together in the neighborhoods where they live, as the diocesan policy demands, contrasts with the public statements of pastoral agents there who believe that language parishes could help ease ethnic tensions within the Church and ease the exiles' transition into American life (*The Miami News*, August 6, 1987, 1A). A priest remarked: "When you have a Mass in Spanish at 9:00 a.m. and a Mass in English at 11:00 a.m., you don't get a bilingual community. What you get are two separate communities using the same church at different times. Unfortunately, sometimes you have turf battles, and those are anti-gospel and anti-productive." The dilemmas of past history continue.

Local Parish

It seems quite understandable that the parish community be seen as the critical structure. "Whether one views the Congregation as carrier of a people's traditions and values, as an embodiment of religious truth and value, or as an agent of social change, its place in the self-understanding of the major religious traditions is undeniable" (D.A. Roozen, 1984, 26). Today the pastoral debate at the grass root level focuses on the immediate functioning and on the canonical status of the immigrant congregation. Such debate can still turn explosive, as the Vietnamese case in San Jose, California, indicates (*USA Today*, May 18, 1987, 3A). Throughout the country, diocesan officials have adopted one or more of three dominant models.

1. *The cultural group parish or mission* is established by the diocesan bishop on the basis of pastoral criteria other than strictly territorial ones, e.g., specialized groupings of persons with such particular pastoral needs as languaqe, culture, or rite (cf. A. Coriden, 1985: 418-19). Recent research on the process of incorporation of immigrants in the United States has brought to light the simultaneous use of different models, even though the emphasis was placed on the personal or national cultural groups parish—as it is variously called in Chicago and New York—and on the integrated parish in California (S. Tomasi, 1975; J. Dolan, 1987, vol. II; J. Parot, 1981). Regional differences in pastoral practices were due to the local bishop's view of the role of the Church in the American context and his policy on assimilation; to the degree of concentration of the immigrants in a neighborhood; and to the availability of clergy of a given nationality and language (cf., for the case of Connecticut, Liptak, 1987). There is a commonly agreed conclusion on the historical effectiveness of the

personal or national parish as the first stage of Americanization and the development of the Roman Catholic melting pot. Olson writes:

> For millions of Roman Catholic immigrants, the nationality parish played a key role in easing the adjustment to urban society in the United States. Instead of finding themselves in an alien world full of strange nationality groups and a church dominated by the ascetic rationalism of the Irish, these immigrants were able to create a familiar world of traditional holidays, ceremonies, and saints in their churches; preserve the language and traditional values in their parochial schools; control social life in their parish societies; and confront God and mortality with the assistance of a priest who spoke their language and shared their past. For all the stress and misgivings the nationality parish imposed on the Church in the late 1800s and early 1900s, it became a mainstay of Roman Catholic survival in the United States, the single most important institution in deflecting the proselytizing campaigns of evangelical Protestants and containing the centrifugal forces of nationalism and language. In the nationality parishes, despite their cultural diversity, the Church maintained its Catholicity in the United States (J. Olson, 1987, 125).

The same role is played now by the personal or ethnic parish, where it is used either as a formal, canonical or de facto model. Personal parishes, for example, were established recently for Vietnamese in Falls Church (1979) and Richmond (1983), Virginia, and in Houston and New Orleans; for Poles in Washington, D.C., and Dallas; for Spanish-speaking also in Washington, D.C. (1986). Since the Vietnamese parish Mary, Queen of Vietnam, was established in New Orleans in 1983, it has given 15 seminarians (four ordained for New Orleans already), it has the largest CCD program in the nation with 2,200 youngsters taught by 65 lay volunteers, and it tries to ensure that as the younger Vietnamese assimilate into American parishes they don't get cut off from the Vietnamese community (Julie Sly, 1985).

The shortcomings of this model are its transitional nature and the need of clergy familiar with the language and culture of the ethnic group. Pastoral planners, however, can keep in mind the experience of the Archdiocese of Hartford where a parish organized in the 1890s by German immigrants who felt uncomfortable in the then predominantly Irish and Italian churches, became the center of a black community in the 1940s with a few black Catholic and commuting German-Americans attending it, and then with another demographic change in the 1950s it was designated in 1956 a national Hispanic parish now carrying out the exact same function it did for the Germans (Roozen, 1984, 160-76).

This Hispanic parish has a charismatic group, a parish council and social service program run by Spanish language immigrants, who even plan public prophets, Masses are warm and celebrative and families sit together and no one is bothered when toddlers run about during the service. The singing has gusto, the familiar flavor of Puerto Rico with the accompaniment of guitars, drums, and a cuatro (double-string guitar). Sermons are informal, dealing with domestic issues, personal morality, justice, and Christian responsibility in the neighborhood and factory. The exchange of the sign of peace is an event. A lay person commented: "I have come here for seven years because I feel at home. I like the feeling of the Mass and, afterwards, I like to talk to my friends and socialize." A middle class parish is often concerned with larger social issues, is more formal and individualistic in its style, and given the higher degree of education of the congregation, it tends to be more intellectual in its faith expressions. Sociologists have developed the concept of "ethlass" to express the interplay of ethnicity and social class. Today's adoption of the cultural group parish model seems to remain a valuable pragmatic answer, especially when class and culture are combined in an immigrant group to the point of making immediate integration too much of an uneven partnership. The desire for a sense of community as refuge and a base of personal identity as well as a spring-board for social mobility and healthy integration becomes evident in the attempts of the immigrants to bend Church policy in order to obtain their qoal. In South Florida the sudden, massive arrival of Hispanics visibly impacted parish life.

In the space of a few years, parishes that were Anglo-American became thoroughly Hispanic. It was decided by Bishop (later Archbishop) Coleman F. Carroll that national parishes or schools would not be established as had been the case with German or Polish immigrants in the past. Instead, newcomers (both priests and people) were integrated into existing and new parishes. Nonetheless, certain Miami parishes did turn out to be, in effect, Cuban national parishes, though not specifically designated as such. . . . By 1980, in the Archdiocese of Miami, where Hispanic populations are the highest in the Southeast, thirty-three parishes (25.4%) were predominantly Hispanic (M. McNally, 1987).

Another interesting conclusion derived from the study of national parishes in Pittsburgh deals with the question of ethnic religious personnel: "This [Pittsburgh Slovak parishes] analysis suggests that the nationality of church leaders was less important than their position regarding the religious practices of immigrant groups" (J. Alexander, 1987).

A system of religious practices brought here from the Caribbean Islands or Central America or Asia englobes the whole immigrant person. This system of beliefs and rites will inevitably evolve. On the other hand, U.S. society, some believe, is not conducive to spirituality in isolation from a religious community (D. Roozen, 1984, 164). If the immigrant is plucked out of his religious system, will he remain a practicing Catholic? The personal parish model is presently used with Vietnamese, Poles, Koreans and some other smaller groups in a limited way and probably also in response to the availability of clergy from these ethnic communities and from their churches of origin. Dioceses, however, continue their pragmatic tradition. For example, there are about 14,000 Catholic Vietnamese in Houston. They are centered in 15 communities served by Vietnamese priests. Two of them have been created Vietnamese parishes with a Vietnamese priest as administrator. The other communities form a part of an American parish. The priests in charge of such communities are living at the rectory, except for the Dominican Fathers who have a house placed at their disposal by the diocese together with other American diocesan priests (Rev. Philippe Le-Xuan-Thuong, 1986). A combination of official Church policies, urban demographic change, and availability of immigrant clergy may transform a parish into either an ethnic or national parish or into a multi-ethnic institution.

2. *The multi-ethnic or integrated parish* is the parish that ministers to immigrants from a variety of cultures in one worshipping community. This parish model has been the official policy of the archdiocese of New York since the 1950s as "a practical answer to the pressing problem of large numbers of Puerto Ricans suddenly appearing in the area of an existing parish" (J. Fitzpatrick, 1987). One or more Spanish-speaking priests would help the Puerto Ricans in their pastoral and liturgical needs through special separate services. The parish staff is the key in fostering convergence of ethnic communities through education, the shared use of human services, single liturgies on special occasions, and the celebration of popular religious events of ethnic groups. Experience has shown that separate groups are necessary for worship and separate committees are needed for pastoral projects in each language group. From an administrative point of view, the advantages of a multi-ethnic parish are obvious: no duplication of buildings; more centralized management; the clergy in place, with some language training, can respond to at least emergency needs. The immigrants attending these parishes are encouraged to adapt more quickly to the customs of the local church (cf. Bardek, 1955). From a pastoral point of view, there seems to be missing the sense of being fully at home in an institution "owned" by the group and the persistence of conflict. A study of a new multi-ethnic parish in Brooklyn concludes: ". . . the staff and leadership of St. Ignatius has always felt the strain of coping with the pluralism of the parish." (Trebold, 1982).

The California dioceses have moved in the direction of a planned policy for integrated parishes. The Archbishop of San Francisco sees the avoidance of conflict in the acceptance of new linguistic, cultural, and ethnic groups as "another great and precious gift of God." Dioceses and parishes must "give positive outreach to all these groups to integrate them into parish families, so that they feel welcome and wanted and truly part of our parishes and never marginalized" (J. Quinn, 1981). From the experience of San Francisco's parishes that have undergone a greater mixture of ethnic groups, Fr. McGuire proposes an incarnational spirituality for intercultural ministry: "Self-emptying . . . adjusting to the difficult proposition that the way we do thinqs around here may not be the only way to do them" (A. McGuire, 1985).

The viability of the integrated parish model rests on education to welcome, to understand and accept the immigrants popular religiosity and often their poverty and to respect their natural desire for ethnic community. Small Christian Communities could coexist in the parish with their cultural differences and celebrate the same faith. The formation and intercultural cooperation of ethnic leaders, the ability to share faith stories, and effective leadership by the parish pastoral team are critical variables for success (A. McGuire, 1985; J. Duggan, 1987).

From the idea of fellowship in the Acts of the Apostles to that of communion in the documents of Vatican II the underlying assumption remains that unity is ultimately a gift of the Spirit and, like community, is always an ideal on the horizon. The end result of this pastoral model is ideally contained in the words of John Paul II: "Just as it is necessary to avoid the possibility of migrants living totally alongside other people, forming a world apart, neither must they let themselves be "assimilated," absorbed to the point of being dissolved into the surrounding society, renouncing their original riches, their identity. Everything must be done so that they may participate, with their own heritage, in the common cultural, spiritual and human good of the national community which they have joined" (John Paul II, 1985-2). Thus, in this model, the pastoral challenge is building a faith community without the benefit of a homogeneous culture and shared experiences and perceptions. But many parishes are not prepared to minister cross-culturally to the foreign born.

3. *The parish of parallel ethnic congregations* is the experience of having two or more communities using the same buildings independently without much interaction. This third parish model involves two or more congregations, one American and one immigrant, operating independently but with varying degrees of partnership that ranges from just co-location in the same building to joint planning of financial resources, volunteers, and programs. This model is not infrequent with some Protestant denominations (A. Hill, 1984). In Orange County, California, where 20,000 Vietnamese Catholics are spread out in 27 cities, pastoral care has been organized in this way.

The Vietnamese Center is not a parish or a mission, as we do not have a church or school facilities of our own. Through the arrangement of the chancery office, we have been allowed to use the church and classroom of nine parishes of the Diocese for religious services and catechism for children on weekend basis. We may keep the collection at Masses to support the priests and five Vietnamese nuns who run the catechetical program. Local pastors and parishes and pastors have been very generous to us, but oftentimes we came across the trouble of time limitations and schedules of local churches (Rev. Th. Do Thauh Ha, 1986).

The success of the approach with the help also of several religious associations is measured by the fact that "none of our people has deserted the Catholic Church," many conversions have taken place, mental stability has been brought about. "Of course, our people wish to get into the mainstream of American life, but they do not want to lose their Vietnamese identity and culture which has some solid values such as family closeness, respect for the law and superior, hard work and love for learning." The existing difficulties, however, make desirable a mission or personal parish. The multi-congregational model has been hailed by some Christian missiologists as an "outstanding promise for applying the sociological, theological, biblical, and ethical principles of pluralism to the typical inner-city situation in America" (C.P. Wagner, 1979).

The parish is the battleground where the future participation and inclusion of the newest immigrants is decided, but the form and type of parish is not uniform and a variety of modifications of the three models briefly sketched is found throughout the United States.

In discussing successful parishes, Thomas Sweetser, Director of the Chicago-based Parish Evaluation Project notes that ethnic parishes are still developing even among Hispanics and reports the response to a survey question on whether the parish should make an effort to welcome all races and classes into the parish:

The response varied with the location of the parish. The predominantly Black and Hispanic parishes showed a high favorable reaction to accepting all races and classes. So did suburban parishes that are not experiencing an immediate threat of an ethnic or racial turnover. The parishes that showed a low positive response to welcoming all races and classes are the ones who are experiencing an ethnic or racial change in membership. Even in parishes where people are willing to open the doors to different ethnic and social groups, many parishioners are reluctant to welcome these groups into the neighborhood or into the local school" (T. Sweetser, 1983). The lesson of coping with unity in diversity has to be learned constantly anew.

Diocesan, Regional, and National Efforts

At the diocesan, regional, and national levels organizational steps have been taken with the progressive centralization of ecclesiastical administration and the development of national episcopal conferences.

1. The *Directory of Pastoral Care of Migrants* shows that ethnic ministry coordination at the *diocesan level* is also a pragmatic response to local needs. Thus, in Brooklyn there is an Episcopal Vicar for Migrants with office, staff, and services. The diocese of Oakland, California, has a Coordinator of Directors of Ethnic Groups, who are convened regularly and are salaried from the diocesan budget. A second diocesan model is that of independent offices or coordinators for specific language groups. For example, Cleveland and Honolulu have an office of Filipino Ministry and most dioceses have Hispanic Pastoral Offices. (Directory, 1987) As it spells out types of structures and methods for pastoral care at all levels, the 1969 *Instruction on the Pastoral Care of People Who Migrate* calls for diocesan coordination: "If it seems necessary, let there be a particular Office for Immigrants constituted at the episcopal curia in the dioceses to which immigration takes place." The effectiveness and support of such diocesan offices is not uniform, even though their usefulness and even necessity in articulating the immigrants' agenda in the planning and decision-making process of a diocese is clear as it is evidenced, for example, by the 1986-1988 preparation for the Archdiocesan Synod of the Church of Boston.

2. A rather recent development are *regional pastoral activities* for newcomers. There are eight regional offices for Hispanic Apostolate; there are the Northeast Italian Apostolate Conference, the East Coast Hmong Apostolate, and the Alta-Baja California Bishops' Conference. A cluster of dioceses may cooperate in providing catechetical resources and personnel for a concentration of immigrants of a particular language, as in the case of Hmong and Laotians in California from the Fresno Center.

3. At the *national level*, the concern with newcomers' social and spiritual needs is responded to by the NCCB Bishops' Committee on Migration and the Committee on Hispanic Affairs and the offices that implement the Committees' agendas, including National Migration Week and national Encuentros. At this level of policy formation, the legitimization of pastoral practices and the encouragement of local action are principal functions together with teaching and advocacy.

V. Conclusion

1. In historical perspective the dominant role of the parish, in whatever form--territorial, ethnically mixed, one cultural group parish, a mission with the care of souls--appears as the stable and critical structure for the incorporation of newcomers.

2. The link of faith and language, considered by German and all other European immigrants an indispensable element for the preservation of faith in the United States has been proven necessary for the first generation, but not in the long run: a new language and culture can be adopted without losing the faith. Experience suggests that pastoral structures should be directed toward building community on the foundation of faith while respecting cultural traits as the concrete specification of faith as long as such a culture is able to motivate action in an ethnic group. Indications are that the American-born generation of the newest immigrants is moving toward the same evolution.

3. Less structured strategies for faith preservation and evangelization used with recent immigrants are missions in their language, ethnic media, associations, and renewal groups. These still play a major role and sometimes are the mainstay effort in parishes not equipped to minister to newcomers.

4. The role of Catholic schools, base communities, and religious movements are presently at the center of renewed debate. The school system of the Church was started for the education of immigrant children. Now the economic difficulties of the new immigrants in meeting tuition costs, the decrease of religious personnel, and the controversy over bilingual education, a multicultural curriculum, as well as the development of a policy with regard to non-Catholic and non-Christian immigrants in Catholic schools and the relationship of the school to evangelization, are all issues that challenge their effectiveness with newcomers.

5. Looking at the future, a critical question seems to be this: Can base communities, Cursillo movements, encuentros, and occasional liturgical and church-related celebrations play the same role that institutionalized structures like the personal parish played in keeping the Hispanics within the Catholic tradition, especially since they subscribe to a holistic experience of faith and community? How can lay leadership function effectively in these movements, events, and small communities in the middle class culture of the particular Church in the United States?

6. While there is general theoretical agreement that evangelization and Americanization must be kept separate, there seems to be a limited reflection on Americanization as a process of secularization for immigrants coming from still rural societies.

7. Finally, pastoral creativity can flourish in terms of new strategies and models if the pluralism and "ethnic universality" of the Church is seen at the level of the diocese as the particular Church of the Vatican II theology. The variety of pastoral practices and structures becomes possible and enriching because the unity is guaranteed around the Eucharist

and the bishop. The issue of separateness would be resolved and perhaps the experience of communion, not possible without justice and respect of cultures, will be felt as the answer to the initial question of what this diversity means.

References

June G. Alexander, 1987, *The Immigrant Church and Community: Pittsburgh's Slovak Catholics and Lutherans*, 1880-1915 (Pittsburgh: University of Pittsburgh Press).

Philip Bardek, 1955, "Problems of Religious Practice Among Puerto Ricans on the Mainland," in William Ferree et al., eds., *Report on the First Conference on the Spiritual Care of Puerto Rican Migrants* (New York: Archdiocese of New York), 50-55.

Leon F. Bouvier and R.W. Gardiner, 1986, "Immigration to the U.S.: The Unfinished Story," *Population Bulletin*, 41(4), November 1986.

F. Coccopalmerio, 1987, "Il concetto di parrocchia nel Vaticano II," in A. Longhinato et al., *La parocchia e le sue strutture* (Bologna: Edizioni Delioniane), 58-68.

E. Corecco, 1987, "La presenza dei migranti nella Chiesa particolare," *Orizzonti pastorali oggi* (Padova: Ed. Messaggero), 39-58.

J.A. Coriden et al., 1985, *The Code of Canon Law: A Text and Commentary* (New York: Paulist Press).

Th. Do Thanh Ha, Rev., 1986, Personal Correspondence.

V. de Paolis, 1986, *Integration of Immigrants into the Church as the Exercising of a Right to Freedom Within the Canonical Legislation of the Church* (Washington, D.C.: USCC/PCMR).

Jay P. Dolan, ed., 1987, *The American Catholic Parish: A History from 1850 to the Present* (New York: Paulist Press), Vols. I and II.

John F. Duggan, 1987, "Religious Experience and the Multicultural Church Community" (Ph.D. Dissertation, University of Toronto).

Joseph F. Fitzpatrick, 1987, *Puerto Rican Americans: The Meaning of Migration to the Mainland* (Englewood Cliffs, N.J.: Prentice Hall).

James Hennessey, 1981, *American Catholics: A History of the Roman Catholic Community in the United States* (New York: Oxford University Press).

Alec Hill, 1984, "Ministry Among Newcomers," in W.D. Balda, ed., *Heirs of the Same Promise* (Arcadia, Ca.: National Convocation on Evangelizing Ethnic America), 79-88.

John Paul II, 1985-2, "Church Promotes Integration of Migrants," Address to Participants in the Second World Congress on the Pastoral of Emigration, *L'Osservatore Romano* (English ed.), October 28, 1985.

_____, 1985, "World Migrants' Day Message," *L'Osservatore Romano* (English ed.), September 12, 1985.

_____, 1987, "The Ethnic Universality of the Church," *Origins*, 17(18): 305-309, October, 1987.

Phiippe Le-Xuan-Thuong, Rev., 1986, Personal Correspondence.

Dolores A. Liptak, 1987, *European Immigrants and the Catholic Church in Connecticut, 1870-1920* (New York: Center for Migration Studies).

Anthony McGuire, 1985, *Light of Nations: A Resource Directory for Ministry to Ethnic Groups* (San Francisco: Archdiocese of San Francisco).

Michael J. McNally, 1987, "A Peculiar Institution: A History of Catholic Parish Life in the Southeast (1850-1980)," in Dolan, *The American Catholic Parish*, Vol. I, 112-14.

National Conference of Catholic Bishops, 1983, *The Hispanic Presence: Challenge and Commitment* (Washington, D.C.: USCC).

_____, 1984, *Pastoral Letters of the United States Catholic Bishops: Vol. I, 1792-1940* (Washington, D.C.: USCC), 36-37.

_____, 1986, *Together, A New People: Pastoral Statement on Migrants and Refugees* (Washington, D.C.: USCC).

_____, 1987, *Directory of Pastoral Care of Migrants, Refugees, and People on the Move* (Washington, D.C.: Bishops' Committee on Migration).

Notre Dame Study of Catholic Parish Life, 1985, "American Catholic Parishes in Profile," *Origins*, 14(41): 670-76, March, 1985.

James S. Olson, 1987, *Catholic Immigrants in America* (Chicago, Nelson Hall).

Joseph J. Parot, 1981, *Polish Catholics in Chicago, 1850-1920: A Religious History* (De-Kalb, Ill.: Northern Illinois University Press).

Pius XII, 1952, *Exsul Familia*, AAS XXXXIV, 13 (September 30, 1952), 649-704, in G. Tessarolo, ed., *Exsul Familia: The Church's Magna Charta for Migrants* (Staten Island, N.Y.: Center for Migration Studies).

Pontifical Commission of Pastoral Care of Migrants and People on the Move, 1985, *Chiesa e Mobilita Umana, Documenti della Santa Sede dal 1883 at 1983* (Rome: Centro Studi Emigrazione).

John R. Quinn, 1985, "A New Archdiocese," Address of Archbishop Quinn to Priests of the Archdiocese of San Francisco, May 5, 1985.

D.A. Roozen et al., 1984, *Varieties of Religious Presence: Mission in Public Life* (New York: The Pilgrim Press).

Julie Sly, 1985, "America's Vietnamese Catholics: Preserving Their Heritage in the Land," *St. Anthony's Messenger*, February, 1985, 30-34.

Thomas Sweetser, 1983, *Successful Parishes: How They Meet the Challenge of Change* (Minneapolis: Winston Press).

Theodoretus, *Historia ecclesiastica,* 82, 1257.

Silvano M. Tomasi, 1975, *Piety and Power: The Role of the Italian Parishes in the New York Metropolitan Area, 1880-1930* (New York: Center for Migration Studies).

_____, 1987, "A Lesson from History: The Integration of Immigrants in the Pastoral Practice of the Church in the United States," *People on the Move*, XVIII (48): 33-50.

Robert Trabold, 1982, "Building an Immigrant Community: St. Ignatius Parish, 1971-1981" (M.S. Thesis, Long Island University).

C. Peter Wagner, 1979, *Our Kind of People: The Ethical Dimensions of Church Growth in America* (Atlanta: John Knox Press).

I Was a Stranger and You Welcomed Me

Rev. William A. Logar
Parish Community of Saint Linus
Stockton, California

Immigration is common to our history in the United States. This continent has been populated by immigrants. It began with those who, probably following the caribou, crossed the Bering Sea ice mass some 12,000 years before the birth of Christ.[1] Immigration continued with those who came with the Western European discovery of the continent in the 15th century. Today's immigrants are those who enter through the contemporary version of Ellis Island, the southwestern frontier and the western U.S. ports, particularly Los Angeles and San Francisco.

Immigrants to this country came, and come, from a variety of cultures and religions. Roman Catholics began to arrive with the Spanish/Portuguese explorations and have continued uninterrupted since then. Throughout our history there have been successive waves of immigrants[2] to our land, and as each new group of immigrants arrive, there has been a certain inevitable tension between the newcomer and the groups that came earlier. This tension is based upon a variety of factors: the newcomer vs. the established dweller; the coming together of cultures hitherto unknown to each other; and the known confronting the unknown.

The coming together of these diverse groups in an ecclesial context has been a preoccupation of Church leaders for many years. A variety of solutions have been tried to answer the spiritual needs of both the immigrant/stranger and the already established Catholics. The solutions proposed by the various ecclesial authorities will be the subject of this article.

The documents that will concern us are those documents published by both the Holy See and the National Conference of Catholic Bishops. I plan three divisions in this presentation:

1) A synopsis of the legislation of both the Holy See and the National Conference of Catholic Bishops;
2) An analysis of the various canonical solutions;
3) Prospects for the future.

The majority of texts used in the research of this paper were published by the particular church authority prior to the promulgation of the Code of Canon Law in 1983. However, those texts (laws, decrees, instructions, etc.) do not necessarily lose their force. If they are not expressly abrogated by the code, they may retain their force.[3] Thus a review of this legislation permits us to see what the church expects of us in our pastoral practice, and how we should look at one another.

The person who is on the move is the first point of concern to us. He or she (or they) are many times

> doubly marginal: they are forced to migrate because of inadequate resources and unequal distribution of goods; then, in their countries of adoption, they are sometimes ignored or subject to new injustices. Perhaps it is because of such compounded injustice that Jesus specifically promises His Kingdom to those who recognize Him in the immigrant.[4]

The church has been concerned that the migrants receive proper pastoral care as well as that they engage themselves in the life of the new country. Pius XII, in 1952, addressed these needs in the Apostolic Constitution *Exsul Familia*. In the introduction, he states:

> The Holy Mother Church, impelled by her ardent love of souls has striven to fulfill the duties inherent in her mandate of salvation for all mankind, a mandate entrusted to her by Christ. She has been especially careful to provide all possible spiritual care for pilgrims, aliens, exiles and migrants of every kind. This work has been carried out chiefly by priests who, in administering the Sacraments and preaching the word of God, have labored zealously to strengthen the Faith of the Christians in the bond of charity.[5]

This document, promulgated prior to the code, still retains importance. The Pontifical Commission for the Pastoral Concern of Migrant and Itinerant Peoples stated in 1978: "That document, which embraces all aspects of itinerancy, is still valid today. New shoots grow from old tree trunks."[6]

Over the years, some of the concerns of the authorities have been:

1) the provision of proper pastoral care;

2) the need at times for special chaplains for different classes of persons;

3) the giving of special faculties for these chaplains;

4) the sending church's responsibilities to the people leaving;

5) the receiving church's responsibilities to the people arriving;

6) the distribution of clergy and its effects on people;

7) the need for collaboration and solidarity;

8) that no one should be on the fringe.[7]

In the instruction that follows Paul VI's *motu proprio*, the Sacred Congregation of Bishops examined these general principles:

1) New forms of migration

2) Unity of the Human Family

3) Problems inherent to migration

4) The influence on religious life

5) Respect for the fundamental rights of the human person

6) The right of having a homeland

7) The right of emigrating

8) Service to the Common Good

9) The duty of public authority to prepare job opportunities

10) Duties towards the host community

11) The right of keeping one's native tongue and spiritual heritage

12) The manner of religious care

13) "Pluralism" in a new world

14) The mission of the whole people of God

15) A pastoral notion of people who migrate[8]

The document *Chiesa e mobilità umana* explains the concern of the church for the migrants with a quote from *Christus Dominus*:

> Special interest is felt for those who, owing to their way of life, cannot benefit from the ordinary ministry of parish priests, or who are totally deprived of any form of assistance: a great many emigrants, exiles, refugees, seafarers, airline staff, nomads and others like them, all fall in to this category. Proper forms of spiritual assistance must also be made available for tourists.[9]

The concern of the church for the proper care of migrants has produced a variety of legislative activity. The sum total of all that activity has been the use and promotion of a variety of models for each individual situation. Flexibility and adaptation are evident in the variety of possibilities offered.

Pius XII, in *Exsul Familia*, wanted the Consistorial Congregation[10] to care for the needs of emigrants of the Latin rite. Thus, among other things, the flow of priests to the most developed nations was moderated, so that if emigrants went to less well developed nations, the priests should follow them there (not to where the monetary advantages were greatest). The concern was that the emigrants have the pastoral care necessary for their spiritual needs. The scope of this legislation was supra-diocesan, yet the concerns of the local diocese were not forgotten, and cooperation with the local bishop was stressed. The director of emigrants was to see what was happening in the world, and advise the bishop *ad quem* of the expected movement,[11] so that the receiving church would be able to prepare itself for the coming of the immigrants and not just react to the presence of these immigrants once they arrived.

Paul VI's concern in the 1960s and 1970s, those first post-Vatican II years, is seen in these quotes from his *Motu proprio:*

> It [Vatican II] recommended special solicitude for the faithful who, because of their condition of life, cannot sufficiently make use of the common, ordinary pastoral care or are completely cut off from it as are very many migrants, exiles and refugees. It [Vatican II] earnestly exhorted the episcopal conference, particularly the national ones, to study carefully the more pressing problems confronting those mentioned above and, through common agreement and united efforts, to look to and to promote the spiritual care of those people by *suitable means and institutions* [emphasis added]. Moreover, the same Council addressed these additional exhortations to bishops: they should show themselves solicitous towards all, no matter what their age, condition or nationality, whether they be natives or strangers or foreigners.
>
> It is easy to understand that this . . . care cannot be effectively exercised without . . . evaluation of . . . heritage as well as mental outlook of emigrants . . . yet, as is evident, caution must be exercised lest differences of this kind and adaptations to the groups from various countries, even though legitimate, become detrimental to that unity to which, according to St. Paul's counsels, all in the Church are called : "For in one Spirit we were all baptized into one body, whether Jews or Gentiles, whether slaves or free, for you are all one in Christ."[12]

His concerns were the springboard for the instruction that followed his *Motu proprio.* Because of changes of circumstances and necessities, the instruction advises changing the pastoral *modus operandi* and church structures to meet the need. Yet the solicitude for the person, and the appropriate structure to meet his or her need, continues. The law teaches us that the concern of the immigrant (the person) is going to dictate the law (law, sabbath, sacraments are for people and not vice versa). The church teaches that the *prima lex* is the *salus animarum.*

Pope Paul VI responded, personally and through the Congregation of Bishops, with the 1969 instruction. Paul not only looked at the person (the emigrant/immigrant) but attempted to put other points in perspective (basic human rights, enjoying one's homeland, responsibilities of various people vis-a-vis people on the move, right to preserve one's native language, responsibility to the receiving community, etc).

The various levels of who should concern themselves with these needs were mentioned: from the Congregation of Bishops, through the national conferences, local ordinaries, chaplains and missionaries, religious men and women, to the members of the individual parishes in the dioceses where the migrants come.

With this short synopsis we conclude this brief reflection on the legislation prior to the Code. The *jus vigens* generally replaces previous law, but not necessarily all of it. If the previous legislation is not contrary to the present code, it very well may continue to contain its force, as laws not expressly abrogated by the code may retain their force.[13]

The response of the church to the needs of the migrant/traveler has been varied, creative, and flexible through the years. In the United States it has taken the form of national parishes, special chaplains, vicars episcopal, and creative parish structures. Another canonical structure that has been attempted to fill a need in recent times has been the personal prelature.

In the code we find a variety of models--vehicles--that can be used to respond to the needs of people who come into an already established community and yet may not receive or find proper pastoral care. These are the following:

1) Personal Prelatures

2) Vicars Episcopal

3) National/Personal Parishes

4) Chaplains

5) Pastorally sensitive parish teams

I will now turn my attention to a canonical analysis of these models and suggest where we might go in the 1980s and 1990s in the U.S.

Personal Prelatures

Canons 294-297 of the Code pertain to personal prelatures. This is "a prelature, consisting of presbyters and deacons of the secular clergy, erected by the Holy See, after consulting the Conference of bishops involved, to promote an appropriate distribution of presbyters or to perform a particular pastoral or missionary work in various regions or for different social groups."[14] This phenomenon is not new, as there are different models of prelatures and other associations of the faithful in the code and in the history of the church.[15] There has been some reflection on this type of prelature to date.[16] The legislation regarding personal prelatures speaks specifically of the pastoral necessities of promoting an adequate distribution of priests and of performing particular works in different areas or for different groups.[17]

There are appealing points to the notion of a personal prelature. It would allow the grouping of apostolic ministers (mainly priests and deacons, but others would be able to work with them) to address the needs of specific regions or groups. Thus, as Fransiscus contends,[18] migrant workers could be the object of a prelature in a particular region. It would allow for specialized training and competent staff, and, if done in careful harmony with the local dioceses/parishes, it could prove invaluable in answering the needs of those on the move.

The negatives are similar in nature to those that will be discussed in relation to the personal parish: Once established, realities such as parishes and prelatures are very difficult to disestablish, when the need for which they were founded has been fulfilled.[19] Secondly, it would be critical to avoid divisiveness in the working of the prelature. This is not easily done, as such prelatures may fall victim to the temptation, among others, of exclusiveness and superiority, qualities inimical to the unity in the Eucharist that is the church. That does not have to be, but I feel that it would take a lot of work, prayer, and help of the Holy Spirit to avoid. Thirdly, a lack of coordination with the local church can always result. This has always been seen by the authorities as something to be avoided.[20]

Episcopal Vicars

Episcopal vicars[21] were mentioned in *Christus Dominus* and urged when the exigencies of the diocese required their implementation. The code merely incorporated the conciliar imperatives and the legislation of *Ecclesiae sanctae*. By this time in our history their place is relatively well known. One must remember that they are not entirely new. Some canonists refer to the figure of the archdeacon as having germinally present the idea of the episcopal vicar.[22] Their authority can be territorial, personal, or over a certain type of affair.

The possibility of episcopal vicars as an answer to the needs of migrants is one of the more flexible and interesting possibilities in the code. The positive aspects are the following:

They are flexible. They respond to the need of the individual diocese. They enjoy ordinary power as defined by the diocesan bishop, and they give the members of the faithful the feeling that their concerns and needs are of importance in the life of the diocese, and are not being neglected. They are usually known by all the priests in the diocese, and usually work in conjunction with all the priests, thus preserving and working for the ecclesial diocese.

The scope of their jurisdiction and competence are to be determined by the diocesan bishop. This allows the bishop to decide, with the presbyterate, the pastoral council, and the faithful, exactly what the concerns of the diocese are in regards to the particular group in question and to respond to these needs with the appropriate appointment of a vicar. Canon 477,1 determines that the appointment of the episcopal vicar is to be for a determinate time. This builds into the very existence of the vicar a note of flexibility. So often in life something begins and then it is either impossible to terminate it or people are unwilling to do so. Thus bureaucracies are begun and then the Lord Himself is unable to terminate them. The genius of the law in this regard is that it builds into the very figure of the episcopal vicar this flexibility and terminability. When the express need of the vicar is met, then the church is able to conclude that, bring it to closure, and continue on.

The episcopal vicar enjoys executive power in the diocese, i.e., he has the power to act administratively, as the diocesan bishop acts,[23] with the exception of those things that the diocesan bishop has reserved to himself. This gives the episcopal vicar a great scope of action within the diocese. When it concerns a determinate group of newcomers, this would allow the vicar the latitude to provide pastoral care for these newcomers, without falling into the inflexible cul-de-sac that I feel is inherent in the personal parish. The importance of the group is emphasized by the appointment of this figure in the diocese, yet with the time limit it forces both the diocese and the group of newcomers to come to terms with the question of unity in Eucharist and life that sometimes is lost sight of with other options.

The negatives are the following. Sometimes, because of his self-understanding as "episcopal" vicar, the vicar may be tempted not to consult with the local pastors in his pastoral work. This endangers unity, and may well cause ill-feeling in the diocese. Another possible negative would be a lack of sensitivity to parochial boundaries and programs, thus maybe ignoring something that is already in place and working for the group in a certain parish. Concomitant with the above is the temptation to exclusivity in operation and thought, again ignoring the local clergy and what they might very well be doing to meet the needs of the target group.

Whatever answer is taken to address the question of the newcomers, we are always led to the necessity to see in the eucharistic table the locus where all ecclesial life begins and ends.

> As a community of faith it [the church] calls all peoples to be the People of God. This call to unity, however, must take into account the different points of departure of the various immigrant communities whose cultural heritage has shaped religious traditions and life styles. For this reason, catechesis and liturgy must adapt to cultural diversity and different languages for an effective communication of the Gospel message. . . . While the immigrants have the duty to work for one local Christian community, they have the right to meet their special needs through special institutions, in a process leading to unity, not divisiveness, as the historical development of American Catholicism indicated and theological reflection supports.[24]

Thus we cannot allow nor have the divisions that at times society makes and keeps. Thus we are not allowed to have the segregation that so often is a fact of life of our social, political, and unfortunately religious existence. The episcopal vicar is the figure that combines importance, flexibility and creativeness in the response to a pastoral need, and looks to closure in the fact that the appointment can only be made for a time (unlike that of the vicar general, which is usually *ad nutum episcopi*).[25]

Personal Parishes

The personal parish has been one form of response that has been used in this country to attempt to address the need of the migrant. Canonically it is the equivalent of a territorial parish, but one that instead of using territory to define the limits of its canonical authority, uses language, ethnic origin, or some similar criteria (such as rite) to establish who in fact is a member of the parish.[26] Much has been written about the effectiveness of the non-territorial parish and its influence in the lives of newly arrived peoples to these shores.[27] What can and should be said about the national parish from a canonical perspective?

Positively, the personal parish has been influential in the preservation of the culture of the arriving peoples, their gradual adjustment to the reality of life in the United States and their coming to terms with life in a multicultural ambience. It has provided a familiar locus so that the newly arrived can find something familiar in an otherwise, at times, bewildering cultural ambience. The scope of the possibilities is limited only by the scope of the parish itself. The people have their own pastor, the parish is familiar, feast days are celebrated as at home, the culture and language are preserved, especially in the local customs of the people, and in general the relation to church is good.

The caveats are the following. The establishment of a parish is an important juridic act of the diocese. It requires consultation with the presbyteral council of the diocese.[28] Here it is of note that the council is consulted, not the college of consultors. Usually the presbyteral council is the larger of the two bodies. It is the more public of the bodies, and represents a greater base in the diocese. Thus the importance of the parish is seen in light of the whole diocese. A decision against establishment is an equally important juridic act. Thus to suppress (or otherwise change substantially) a parish is not an easy thing, juridically, politically, or emotionally. To establish a parish is to enter into a relatively inflexible mode of operation. Thus the national parish is not as flexible an answer to this particular question. The response of the Church to this question over the years has been a flexible answer, especially in the solutions offered.

There is another aspect to non-territorial parishes that disturbs me. In our society there is, and has been to date, a tendency to ghettoize different groups according to a variety of categories. Thus we have segregated blacks in one section of town, we have had our white suburban neighborhoods, our barrios, our this and that neighborhood. In my opinion, non-territorial parishes continue this tendency. This type of parish in effect establishes a special group, with special pastor, special church, special, special, etc. Its tendency is to cut the groups off from the rest of the church in the diocese, so that the reality of what Paul states, "we are neither Jew nor Greek, slave nor free person . . ."[29] is frustrated, and all you have in one church is Jew or Greek, slave or free person. In my opinion, this is even more important than inflexibility as a negative aspect of the non-territorial parish.

In effect, many parishes are segregated by nationality/ethnic origin/language group already. I am pastor of a small parish on the southeast corner of the city of Stockton. The parish itself is 80 percent Hispanic, with the remaining 20 percent divided between Filipino-Americans, folks from Belize, Guam, Portugal, Italy, several generations living in the U.S., a French Canadian couple whose native language is French, etc. With the exception of the 20 percent, I am pastor of a "national" parish, especially as some of the other parishes in the city, for one reason or another, may not celebrate functions that are typically Hispanic. We have, in our country, managed to establish these types of parishes just from the demographics of our cities. The need now is to find ways to bring these differing peoples together in that one body of Christ, around the Eucharistic table, without adding more divisions. As our bishops said to us:

> As a sign of the human family without barriers, immigrants expect from the Christian community and from society an immediate implementation of old and new experiments of social ministry which free them from cultural and social mar-

ginality. A nation and a Church built by immigrants can properly celebrate only by continuing the work for "liberty and justice for all."[30]

The following, concluding remarks to this section are based upon my participation in the conference. I had prepared this paper guided by negative attitudes—personal, pastoral, and canonical—against personal parishes. At the conference, several people spoke of the effectiveness of personal parishes in the life of the church in this country: how they have helped in the retention of both the culture and the cultural values of the particular group for which they were formed; how the ability to use their own language in worship and to have contact with clergy who know (and knew) the cultural setting of the sending church enabled them to grow in faith and to adjust to the new environment. These were factors in the growth and adjustment of the people as they set roots here in the United States. There were several references to the level and preservation of faith and cultural values in these parishes, the increase of vocations to both priesthood and religious life, the growth of children in the life of the parish and the community, and in general a definitely positive aspect to these parishes.

It should be noted that our bishops, in 1988, are not enamored of personal parishes. Often a diocese is burdened with the question of what to do with the plant of a parish when the complexion of the neighborhood of the parish changes.[31] In response to this negative attitude of the bishops, someone at the conference stated, "but there is so much good that can come from personal parishes at this moment, why not use the model and face the problem, if and when it arrives." I think said observation is excellent and merits considerable thought.

One more personal caveat would be that if in personal parishes we are indeed going to provide high quality clergy, fine. It has been known to happen (though I am assured that this is the exception, not the rule) that the clergy who arrive are not the high quality clergy we are looking for, but rather those who cannot and/or will not function effectively in their native diocese, or anywhere else for that matter. Realistically, in this day and age, with the serious problem of the shrinking number of priests, how many "sending churches" can afford to, and in fact will, send their quality priests to minister to the people who have left; also, how many of those priests want to follow their faithful who have left? Will Bishop X of Diocese Y be willing to send one or two or more of his best priests to another State (if within the U.S.) or another country to care for emigrants who came from his diocese/state/country? This make the questions of personal parishes somewhat more problematic than those at the conference might have thought. It was and is my impression that there seems to be a groundswell of enthusiasm in favor of personal parishes. Yet will we be able to staff them effectively? And have we thought out the ramifications?

Allow me finally a short *excursus* on the subject of *tutor* or *tutela* or, as we would say, the institution of a guardian. In Roman Law and in Common Law there is the concept of *tutela* or guardianship, which means that those who need protection under the law are given it.[32] This concept refers to those who need the protection of some institution so that they will be able to exercise their rights and develop in life without undue interference until such time as they can exercise their complete majority. In our modern society in the United States, this concept, coupled with the law of negligence, is making a disaster of the concept of personal responsibility. Everything has the tendency of becoming the fault of someone else. I get into an accident on the freeway; obviously the accident was caused by the negligent and faulty design of the freeway by the State and the negligence of the other driver. I smoke cigarettes, but when I get cancer it is not my fault, but the fault of the vendor of the cigarettes. When do I have to assume the risk, and the responsibility of my own actions? When I go to another country I know, in a general sense, where I am going. I cannot depend, like a little child, upon those whom I encounter there to take care of my each and every need. Certainly in a parish the people should be sensitive to the needs of all who are present in the parish. But that is a two way street, and those who are in the parish need to be sensitive to the needs and the presence of others there too. I cannot expect to always have the *tutela legis* taking care of me without, at a certain point, assuming the risk and the responsibility of life where I am, and where I choose and chose to be.

Chaplains

Special chaplains (missionaries, etc.) are another response that has been suggested by Rome and various other bodies as a response to the needs of migrants and travelers. These chaplains are similar to episcopal vicars, but are not identical.

The special chaplain is nothing more than a priest deputed to care for a certain group of people and given the appropriate faculties necessary for that. Pius XII in Exsul familia noted their importance and existence. When these special chaplains were appointed, they were to be given the same power as pastors, in fact, they were "equivalent in the care of souls to a pastor."[33] Canonically this was an important note, because the law endows the pastor with ordinary power. This power of the chaplain was personal and cumulative.[34] The code modified that, saying rather that the chaplain should be given "all faculties . . . that are necessary."[35] This is of importance in that it shows the church's concern that the people ministered to are given all that is necessary. Thus the law is flexible in its concern for pastoral care.

Throughout the legislation on the question of migrants, travelers, etc., there is the continual call to unity and the reminder that the ultimate norm is the unity that the Eucharist establishes. Canons 564-572 govern the appointment of these chaplains. The code incorporates and refines what was in the previous legislation, allowing for the flexibility of the response to depend upon the needs of the local church situation.

Pastorally Sensitive Parish Staffs

From the beginning of the history of the church, people have gathered around the eucharistic table to make present the church of Jesus Christ. From earliest times this has generally been based upon the territorial model. Distance, even with the advent of the automobile, limits us in what we can and cannot do in a given time frame. For centuries, the church has relied upon territory to define the more normal form of organization within the body of faithful. People gather together in villages and towns, neighborhoods and suburbs. We seem to want to do things locally, whether in the corner store or the corner mall. Thus when we come together on Sunday morning, territory is going to play a similar role in the life of the church.

When the authorities of the church have reflected upon the needs of the migrant and attempted to answer those needs with appropriate legislation, the concept of meeting those needs at the level of the local parish has always been included as crucial to the solution of the newcomer in the land. The reason for this is, or should be, clear. When the local community is challenged with the presence among it of newcomers, it then must put into practice the basic teachings of Jesus, to love God and love our neighbor as ourselves. My neighbor is not just my cultural neighbor. The parish becomes, therefore, the locus for the struggle to make real the gospel. This mix of people, from this determinate place, must attempt to make real the Eucharist.

> This notion takes on clearer motivation when there is some continuity in the transfer from one place to another, which generates a certain stability of persons. The factors that determine, in any case, the goals of pastoral care are ethnic, linguistic, and cultural differences. The local church where these people arrive cannot, therefore, escape from the consideration of its special duty, as laid down by Pope Pius XII in the Apostolic Constitution *Exsul familia*, of making provision "ut alienigenis, sive advenis sive peregrinis, spirituales posset praebere adsistentiam necessitatibus haud imparen nec minoram, qua ceteri fideles in sua diocesi perfruuntur."[36]

Paul VI, through the Congregation of Bishops, also reminded the immigrants of their responsibility to the receiving community.

> "Whoever is going to encounter another people, should have great esteem for their heritage and language and customs." Therefore, immigrants should willingly adapt themselves to the community which receives them and they should hasten to learn its language so that if their stay is drawn out for a rather long time or becomes permanent, they will be able more easily to take their place in the new society. On the other hand, all this will eventuate in a healthy and effective way if all form of coercion and hindrance is removed and if it takes place spontaneously and gradually.[37]

The authorities have always stated that the staff of the parish should be equipped—educationally, culturally, and personally—to meet this challenge.[38] To try to be all things to all people is not easy. The canons on the pastor set forth a beautiful ideal, difficult to fulfill. Throughout the history of the church in the United States this has been difficult, from the first days in the colonies with the difficulties between immigrant Germans and the local

English speaking colonists, to the Hmong and the other non-English speaking immigrants to this country today. Yet the church has always urged that one of the premier responses to this is the culturally sensitive parish staff, composed of a variety of persons, who would attempt to make real the unity of the church in Christ at the local level.[39]

This is probably the most difficult of answers that are proposed in this conference and in this paper. It forces those involved to confront the prejudices and petty problems of an ethnic mix in one parish, without the luxury of going off to a different place. It is probably going to be the solution that will require the most rubbing together of the various diamonds. Yet it is the solution that steers clear of the dangers of ghettoizing the various groups, of separating the different peoples into different worshipping communities. It requires much of the ministers, yet that is precisely what the consistent legislation of the church has done. The church, in her solicitude, offers a great variety of options. She wants every effort to be used to reach out to the traveler, to be sure they have the possibility of approaching the table of the Lord (literally and figuratively). Great flexibility is given. Yet those called on to be most flexible are the locals, the receiving church, the parish, the hospitable community gathered in love around the table of the Lord.

Some will say: we want different worshipping communities. In a sense, this will take place, and takes place in a variety of ways now. We have the different types of liturgies in our churches—quiet, singing, folk, solemn, cathedral, simple, as well as ethnic. Yet as the parish continues to come to grips with the different folks within it, they, the folks themselves, will be constantly challenged by the reality of what they profess on Sunday mornings—one Lord, one faith, one baptism, one Holy, Catholic, and Apostolic church—and how that is being incarnated here at the parish community of Sts. Peter and Paul.

In the conference, Fr. Tomasi gave an excellent, detailed description of the actualities of the various models based on the parish that can be found in various places in the U.S. Church. His description of these models is exhaustive and good. I attempt to give a canonical base to my perception of the parish models. Since the parish is normative in the code, it is also the easiest model with which to be creative, as the code endows the parish community with sufficient resources, legal and spiritual, to complete its work without always having to ask permission. As a model it is the most intimately known and the easiest to work with.

Distribution of Clergy

In the legislation we have reviewed, the question of the clergy mobility has been raised with regard to both distribution of clergy as well as the pastoral needs of migrants and other pastoral problems.[40] A cursory look at the statistics available in the 1987 Official Catholic Directory gives the following figures regarding clergy distribution in the United States. The following statistics are the regional ratios of Catholics to priests. It was arrived at by adding the totals of diocesan and religious clergy, minus the totals of retired and teaching clergy, then dividing that into the total Catholics in the region as reported in the directory.[41] The number of Catholics for each priest is in each region is as follows:

New England	1,090
Mid Atlantic	1,219
South Atlantic	881
East North Central	1,175
East South Central	638
West North Central	794
West South Central	1,487
Mountain	1,198
Pacific	1,540

While I recognize the delicacy of the subject (what bishop wants to see priests move in these days) the statistics are here. The concern for the migrant should not forget those who have migrated from the North and Northeast to the Sunbelt and the West.

In this presentation I have attempted to analyze the various pastoral models which can be used to respond to the needs of migrants/immigrants as they arrive in this country. We have seen the continued concern of church authorities, on various levels, for those who are strangers, newcomers to a land and a people. Every effort has been made to provide structures to respond to their needs. At the same time the authorities have stressed the responsibilities of those on the move to adapt themselves to the people and land to which they come. The process has been, is, and will continue to be a challenge to all involved.

It should be obvious from my comments that I favor the parish model and the judicious use of the episcopal vicar/chaplain models in pastoral work. These models best serve, in my opinion, the unity of the church and the reality of the Eucharist. The parish model probably offers the greatest challenge, because it is on that level that there is the greatest meeting of different groups and the greatest possibility of stress. Yet we should be challenged and challenge on precisely this level.

If in fact we choose that model, the choice, to be effective, must be voluntary. Many times we, in fact, use this model, but not voluntarily. We relegate the immigrant group to second class status (unpopular times for masses; use of facilities only after everyone else, and grudgingly; unwillingness to celebrate popular ethnic events, etc.) so that there is not a true unity in the parish. At that point the figure of the vicar can be most useful in the resolution of the difficulties. Properly fulfilled, his is the role to intercede and promote the rights of those in his care, throughout the diocese.

The integration of immigrants as exercising the right of freedom in the church has been the subject of a monograph by Velasio De Paolis.[42] It should not be forgotten that by baptism we are constituted members in the church, and as members we have certain rights. As De Paolis and others contend, commenting on Canons 208-223,[43] the rights and obligations own rite and develop their own spiritual lives.[47] This is basically new legislation, and it will slowly begin to have its effect in our church life. Those in positions of ministry should be conscious of this aspect of our juridic and ecclesial life.

The statistics on clergy distribution are not encouraging. However I maintain that, as a pastor, I am responsible for those in the parish. Thus I am to be continually challenged to respond to all, without prejudice, in as far as that is possible. When this does not happen, so often we are afraid to challenge that pastor, so often because of the shortage of personnel. Can we ask ourselves, why build new structures when sometimes the problem is the present staff in the particular parish. Somehow we should be willing to face that challenge. Allied to that is the question of migrating clergy. Members of diocesan personnel boards are all too familiar with the gyrovague[48] clergy, wandering from continent to continent, diocese to diocese, university to university. If we are to accept immigrant clergy for work in our dioceses, then they should be trained in the life of this country also[49] so as to aid in the realization of their responsibilities to the receiving church, the people of God gathered around the table of the Lord.

The foregoing is a reflection upon some of the issues I maintain are important to consider in our response to immigrants to our country and to our church. I hope that they will help us in our common task, building up the Body of Christ, the Church.

Notes

1. *Peoples and Places of the Past*, National Geographic Society, 1983, p. 19.

2. Unless otherwise noted, the author refers to Roman Catholic groups of immigrants, as that is the scope of this article.

3. *Code of Canon Law: A Text and Commentary*, ed. Coriden et al., (New York: Paulist Press, 1984), c. 6, pp. 28-29; *Codigo de Derecho Canonico, Edicion bilingue comentada*, ed. Lamberto de Echeverria (Madrid: Biblioteca de Autores Cristianos, 1983), c. 6, pp. 15-16; other commentaries.

4. National Conference of Catholic Bishops, *Pastoral Concern of the Church for People on the Move*, November 11, 1976

5. Pius XII, *Exsul familia*, Introduction.

6. *Chiesa e mobilità umana*, no. 28.

7. This list is illustrative, not exhaustive.

8. Sacred Congregation for Bishops, *Instruction on the Pastoral Care of People Who Migrate*, Vatican City, August 22, 1969, nos. 1-15.

9. *Chiesa e mobilità umana*, no. 18.

10. *Exsul familia*, tit. II, no. 1, 1.

11. Ibid., tit. II, no. 14.

12. Paul VI, *Motu Proprio, Pastoralis Migratorum.*

13. Canons 3-6 and appropriate commentaries.

14. Canon 294.

15. Cf. cc. 298-329.

16. Michael O'Reilly, O.M.I., "Personal Prelatures and Ecclesial Communion," *Studia canonica*, 18:2 (1984) 439-456; Thomas J. Fransiscus, C.SS.R., "The Personal Prelature: An Apostolic Possibility for Migrant Farmworkers in the United States." Diss., Catholic University of America, 1981.

17. The Society of St. James, Boston, is certainly a model of this, though it is not a personal prelature.

18. Fransiscus, "The Personal Prelature," pp. 102-104.

19. Personal prelatures are founded by Apostolic authority. Thus the competent body for suppression would be the same Holy See.

20. *Exsul familia*, nos. 20 and 24; *Chiesa e mobilità umana*, nos. 19 and 26; National Conference of Catholic Bishops, *Together, A New People: Pastoral Statement on Migrants and Refugees*, November 8, 1986, 5.A.

21. Canons 475-481.

22. *Commento al Codice di Diritto Canonico*, ed. Pio Vito Pinto (Rome: Urbaniana University Press, 1985), pp. 277-78.

23. Canon 479.

24. National Conference of Catholic Bishops, *The Church and the Immigrant Today* (1976), VI.

25. Canon 477. The vicar general or episcopal vicar who is a bishop is governed by special legislation, i.e., c. 406.

26. Canon 518.

27. Joseph E. Ciesluk, J.C.L. "National Parishes in the United States," Diss., Catholic University of America, 1944; Joseph P. Fitzpatrick, S.J., *One Church Many Cultures* (Kansas City, Mo., Sheed & Ward), pp. 103-04; Dolores Liptak, in *Catholic Historical Review*, 71 (January, 1985) 52-64; Sheryl Chen, "Ethnic Parishes Aren't Catholic," *U.S. Catholic*, 48 (February, 1983) 12-13; Austin Lindsay, "Challenge of the Ethnic Parish," *Today's Parish*, 14 (October, 1982) 23.

28. Canon 515, 2.

29. 1 Cor. 12:13; Gal. 3:28.

30. National Conference of Catholic Bishops, *The Church and the Immigrant Today*, VII, Conclusion.

31. So often the parish has begun in one section of town where the ethnic/language/personal group is found at one particular time in history. Later, when the city changes its shape, the group moves to another location, integrates into the parish in the location ad quem and leaves the old building in the hands of the new people in that particular section of town. Dioceses have been left with maintaining a buildings that no one uses, or are very under used, a situation all too familiar in the eastern cities of our country.

32. For example, a child under the age of puberty, the furiosi or mentally unstable, the spendthrift, and women. In Roman Law the second and third category received curators, while the infant and women received the tutor.

33. *Exsul familia*, no. 35.

34. It was personal in that it was only with the persons entrusted to his care; it was cumulative because it was on even terms with that of the pastor of the place, even if exercised in a chapel or other oratory entrusted to the chaplain.

35. Canon 566, 1.

36. *Exsul familia*, no. 23.

37. Sacred Congregation for Bishops, *Instruction on the Pastoral Care of People Who Migrate*, no. 10.

38. Ibid. nos. 12 and 30.3; cc. 519, 521, 528-30.

39. Cf. cc. 528-530; Paul VI, *Motu proprio, Pastoralis migratorum*.

40. *Exsul familia*; *Ecclesiae sanctae* I.4; *Instruction on the Pastoral Care of People Who Migrate* 23.2; *Chiesa e mobilità umana*, 20; *The Church and the Immigrant Today*, VI.

41. *The Official Catholic Directory* (Willmette, IL: P.J. Kenedy & Sons, 1987).

42. Velasio de Paolis, C.S., *The Integration of Immigrants into the Church as the Exercising of a Right to Freedom within the Canonical Legislation of the Church* (Washington: NCCB, Bishops' Committee on the Pastoral Care of Migrants and Refugees, 1985).

43. Canons 208-223, "The Obligations and Rights of All Christian Faithful"; cc. 224-231, "The Obligations and Rights of Lay Christian Faithful."

44. Canon 212,1.

45. Canon 212,2.

46. Canon 213.

47. Canon 214.

48. An old monastic word referring to monks who were always moving from one monastery to another, never settling down. *Rule of Benedict*, ch. 1.

49. The dioceses of California have attempted to meet this challenge with regard to Hispanic clergy coming from Latin America. A program has been established in Guadalajara, Mexico, to enable clergy to adapt themselves to U.S. life. If the program is being used by the dioceses is unknown to this author. Its effectiveness will be seen in time, if it is utilized.